INSTITUTE OF GEOLOGICAL SCIENCES

Natural Environment Research Council

Report 82/9

Type, figured and cited Jurassic Cephalopoda in the collection of the Institute of Geological Sciences

R. D. Clark

ISBN 0 11 884234 X

London Her Majesty's Stationery Office 1982

CONTENTS

Bibliographical reference
CLARK, R. D. 1982. Type, figured and cited Jurassic Cephalopoda in the collection of the Institute of Geological Sciences. *Rep. Inst. Geol. Sci.*, No. 82/9

Author
R. D. Clark, BSc, *formerly of:*
Palaeontology Unit,
Institute of Geological Sciences,
Exhibition Road, London SW7 2DE

Type, figured and cited Jurassic Cephalopoda in the collection of the Institute of Geological Sciences

R. D. Clark

INTRODUCTION

All the specimens catalogued here are housed in the Type and Stratigraphical Collection of the Palaeontology Unit of the Institute of Geological Sciences (IGS), at present in Exhibition Road, London and Murchison House, Edinburgh.

The entries are arranged, where sufficient information is available, in ascending stratigraphical order by Stage, Zone and Subzone according to the scheme outlined in Tables 1–3, and conform to the following format:

1. taxonomic designation as originally quoted, and type status.
2. publication details: author, date, figure and page.
3. stratigraphy, revised where known.
4. locality, including changes in local government boundaries.
5. collector, and the means and date of acquisition.
6. registered number within the IGS collections.

Specimens in the collections of IGS are registered under a variety of alphabetic symbols which may require some explanation. The general symbol for specimens in the Type and Stratigraphical Collection in London is GSM, the letters deriving from the former Geological Survey and Museum, which was sometimes referred to in older publications as the Museum of Practical Geology or more simply MPG (it was also known as the Jermyn Street Museum prior to its removal to South Kensington in 1934). Current policy in Edinburgh is to register or re-register all figured and cited material under the symbol GSE. A second element is known as the Survey Collection and comprises those fossils collected in the field by officers of the Geological Survey and the Palaeontology Unit in the course of mapping, the specimens being registered under symbols issued to the individual collectors, e.g. JR 636 is a fossil collected in 1885 by John Rhodes. Material collected in the examination of borehole cores have been registered under another series of symbols (B, Ba-Bz, BDA-BDZ, BLA-BLZ) e.g. Bj 4189 was collected from the Stowell Park Borehole in Gloucestershire. A further major constituent of the Type and Stratigraphical Collection is the British part of the collection of the Geological Society of London which retains the registration system it had before it was presented, mainly in 1911, and is prefixed 'Geol Soc Coll'.

Specimens from the Survey, boreholes and Geological Society Collections, where considered to be of importance or interest, have been incorporated into the Type and Stratigraphical Collection, normally without losing their original registered numbers (except in Edinburgh where the practice is to re-register).

Reference to IGS specimens should be made in the following form:

IGS GSM 26509
IGS Geol. Soc. Coll. 1419
IGS VW 804

Two plates are included here illustrating the previously unfigured holotypes of some species of the Callovian genus *Proplanulites* and of the Toarcian ammonites *Simplicidactylites simplicicosta* and *Leptodactylites leptus*. These fossils were described by S. S. Buckman in his 'Type Ammonites' (1909-1930) but after his death in 1929 the plates were not published.

Acknowledgement is made to the assistance given by P. J. Brand of IGS Edinburgh who supplied information on the specimens held in Scotland. The Institute would welcome notification of corrections and omissions, as well as of any future reference to specimens in its care.

R. D. C.
Easter 1978.

Table 1 Zones and subzones of the Lower Jurassic (after Dean, Donovan and Howarth, 1961, modified by Howarth 1973, 1978)

Stage	Zone	Subzone
Toarcian	*Dumortieria levesquei*	*Pleydellia aalensis* *Dumortieria moorei* *Dumortieria levesquei* *Phlyseogrammoceras dispansum*
	Grammoceras thouarsense	*Pseudogrammoceras fallaciosum* *Grammoceras striatulum*
	Haugia variabilis	
	Hildoceras bifrons	*Catacoeloceras crassum* *Peronoceras fibulatum* *Dactylioceras commune*
	Harpoceras falciferum	*Harpoceras falciferum* *Harpoceras exaratum*
	Dactylioceras (Orthodactylites) tenuicostatum	*Dactylioceras (Orthodactylites) semicelatum* *Dactylioceras (Orthodactylites) tenuicostatum* *Dactylioceras (Orthodactylites)clevelandicum* *Protogrammoceras paltum*
Pliensbachian	*Pleuroceras spinatum*	*Pleuroceras hawskerense* *Pleuroceras apyrenum*
	Amaltheus margaritatus	*Amaltheus gibbosus* *Amaltheus subnodosus* *Amaltheus stokesi*
	Prodactylioceras davoei	*Aegoceras (Oistoceras) figulinum* *Aegoceras (Aegoceras) capricornus* *Aegoceras (Aegoceras) maculatum*
	Tragophylloceras ibex	*Aegoceras (Beaniceras) luridum* *Acanthopleuroceras valdani* *Tropidoceras masseanum*
	Uptonia jamesoni	*Uptonia jamesoni* *Platypleuroceras brevispina* *Polymorphites polymorphus* *Phricodoceras taylori*
Sinemurian	*Echioceras raricostatum*	*Paltechioceras aplanatum* *Leptechioceras macdonnelli* *Echioceras raricostatoides* *Crucilobiceras densinodulum*
	Oxynoticeras oxynotum	*Oxynoticeras oxynotum* *Oxynoticeras simpsoni*
	Asteroceras obtusum	*Eparietites denotatus* *Asteroceras stellare* *Asteroceras obtusum*
	Caenisites turneri	*Microderoceras birchi* *Caenisites brooki*
	Arnioceras semicostatum	*Euagassiceras sauzeanum* *Agassiceras scipionianum* *Coroniceras (Coroniceras) reynesi*
	Coroniceras (Arietites) bucklandi	*Coroniceras (Arietites) bucklandi* *Coroniceras (Coroniceras) rotiforme* *Coroniceras (Vermiceras) conybeari*
Hettangian	*Schlotheimia angulata*	*Schlotheimia complanata* *Schlotheimia extranodosa*
	Alsatites liasicus	*Laqueoceras laqueus* *Waehneroceras portlocki*
	Psiloceras (Psiloceras) planorbis	*Psiloceras (Caloceras) johnstoni* *Psiloceras (Psiloceras) planorbis*

HETTANGIAN STAGE

Psiloceras (Psiloceras) cf. **plicatulum** (Quenstedt)
Donovan 1952, p. 635.
Lower Lias, *planorbis* Zone.
Watchet, Somerset.
Geological Society Collection (ex H. Ball), presented 1911.
Geol. Soc. Coll. GSd 4379 [misprinted as d 4379]

Psiloceras (Caloceras) johnstoni (J. de C. Sowerby)
Donovan 1952, plate 22, fig. 3, p. 638.
Lower Lias, *planorbis* Zone, *johnstoni* Subzone.
Harris' Quarry, near Marksbury, Avon [Somerset].
D. T. Donovan Collection, presented 1952.
GSM 85015

Psiloceras (Psiloceras) plicatulum (Quenstedt) **bristoviense** Donovan HOLOTYPE of ssp.
Donovan 1952, plate 22, fig. 1, p. 636.
Lower Lias, **planorbis** Zone.
Nover's Hill Quarry, Bristol, Avon.
D. T. Donovan Collection, presented 1952.
GSM 85014

Psiloceras (Psiloceras) plicatulum (Quenstedt) **bristoviense** Donovan PARATYPE of ssp.
Donovan 1952, plate 22, fig. 2, p. 636.
Lower Lias, *planorbis* Zone.
Nover's Hill Quarry, Bristol, Avon.
D. T. Donovan Collection, presented 1952.
GSM 85013

Psiloceras (Psiloceras) plicatulum (Quenstedt)
Donovan 1952, p. 635.
Lower Lias, *planorbis* Zone.
Watchet, Somerset.
Museum Collection.
GSM 29310

Ammonites planorbis J. de C. Sowerby
J. Buckman 1844, p. 49.
Lower Lias, *planorbis* Zone.
Strensham, near Tewkesbury, Gloucestershire.
S. S. Buckman Collection (ex J. Buckman), purchased 1912.
GSM 27591

Schlotheimia (Waehneroceras) portlocki (Wright)
Donovan 1952, plate 22, fig. 5, p. 646.
Headley Park, Bristol, Avon.
Lower Lias, *liasicus* Zone, *portlocki* Subzone.
D. T. Donovan Collection, presented 1952.
GSM 85019

Psiloceras (Caloceras) bloomfieldense Donovan HOLOTYPE
Donovan 1952, plate 22, fig. 4, p. 640.
Lower Lias, *liasicus* Zone, *?laqueus* Subzone.
Bloomfield Quarry, Farmborough, Avon [Somerset].
D. T. Donovan Collection, presented 1952.
GSM 85017

Alsatites sp.
Donovan 1952, p. 644.
Lower Lias, *liasicus* Zone.
Field Quarry, Corston,Avon [Somerset].
G. A. Kellaway Collection, presented 1937.
GSM 60142

Aegoceras longipontinum Oppel
Tate & Blake 1876, plate 5, fig. 4, p. 273.
Lower Lias, *liasicus* Zone, *laqueus* Subzone.
Redcar, Cleveland [Yorkshire].
R. Tate Collection, purchased 1875.
GSM 23861

Indeterminate bisulcate ammonite
Donovan 1952, plate 29, fig. 2, text-fig. 2.
Lower Lias, *angulata* Zone.
Field Quarry, Corston, Avon [Somerset].
D. T. Donovan Collection, presented 1952.
GSM 85035

Schlotheimia similis Spath
Donovan 1952, plate 23, fig. 1, p. 650.
Lower Lias, *angulata* Zone.
Keeling's Quarry, Keynsham, Avon [Somerset].
D. T. Donovan Collection, presented 1952.
GSM 85018

Schlotheimia similis Spath
Donovan 1952, plate 23, fig. 2.
Lower Lias, *angulata* Zone.
Keeling's Quarry, Keynsham, Avon [Somerset].
D. T. Donovan Collection, presented 1952.
GSM 85016

Schlotheimia (Schlotheimia) lymense (Spath)
Donovan 1952, plate 23, fig. 3, p. 651.
Lower Lias, *angulata* Zone.
Keynsham, Avon [Somerset].
L. F. Spath Collection, purchased 1946.
GSM 73497

SINEMURIAN STAGE

Schlotheimia charmassei (d'Orbigny)
S. S. Buckman 1906, plate 10, figs. 19-20, p. 239.
Lower Lias, *bucklandi* Zone.
Redcar, Cleveland [Yorkshire].
R. Tate Collection, purchased 1875.
GSM 14034

Coroniceras (Primarietites) hyatti Donovan
Donovan 1952, plate 28, fig. 2, p. 736.
Lower Lias, *bucklandi* Zone, *rotiforme* Subzone.
Stowey Hill Quarry, Stowey, Avon [Somerset].
D. T. Donovan Collection, presented 1952.
GSM 85026

Coroniceras (Primarietites) caprotinum (d'Orbigny)
Donovan 1952, p. 733.
Lower Lias, *bucklandi* Zone, *rotiforme* Subzone.
Keeling's Quarry, Keynsham, Avon [Somerset].
D. T. Donovan Collection, presented 1952.
GSM 85028

Coroniceras (Primarietites) caprotinum (d'Orbigny)
Donovan 1952, p. 733.
Lower Lias, *bucklandi* Zone, *rotiforme* Subzone.
St. George's Road, Keynsham, Avon [Somerset].
D. T. Donovan Collection, presented 1952.
GSM 85027

Vermiceras scylla (Reynès)
Donovan 1952, p. 725.
Lower Lias, *bucklandi* Zone, *rotiforme* Subzone.
Somerdale, Keynsham, Avon [Somerset].
D. T. Donovan Collection, presented 1952.
GSM 85023

Vermiceras scylla (Reynès) **stoweyense** Donovan
HOLOTYPE of ssp.
Donovan 1952, plate 29, fig. 3, text-fig. 8c, p. 725.
Lower Lias, *bucklandi* Zone, *rotiforme* Subzone.
Stowey Hill Quarry, Stowey, Avon [Somerset].
D. T. Donovan Collection, presented 1952.
GSM 85022

Arietites bucklandi (J. Sowerby)
Tate & Blake 1876, plate 5, fig. 2, p. 283.
Lower Lias, *bucklandi* Zone.
Redcar, Cleveland [Yorkshire].
R. Tate Collection, purchased 1875.
GSM 22586

Schlotheimia ventricosa (J. de C. Sowerby)
S. S. Buckman 1906, p. 240.
Lower Lias, *bucklandi* Zone.
Redcar, Cleveland [Yorkshire].
R. Tate Collection, purchased 1875.
GSM 14035

Schlotheimia compta (J. de C. Sowerby)
S. S. Buckman 1906, p. 241.
Lower Lias, *bucklandi* Zone.
Redcar, Cleveland [Yorkshire].
R. Tate Collection, purchased 1875.
GSM 23547

Arietites conybeari (J. Sowerby)
Tate & Blake 1876, plate 6, fig. 1, pp. 284-285.
Lower Lias, *bucklandi* Zone.
Redcar, Cleveland [Yorkshire].
R. Tate Collection, purchased 1875.
GSM 22594

Coroniceras (Metophioceras) rougemonti (Reynès)
Donovan 1952, p. 726.
Lower Lias, *bucklandi* Zone, *conybeari* Subzone.
Somerdale railway cutting, Keynsham, Avon [Somerset].
D. T. Donovan Collection, presented 1952.
GSM 85025

Coroniceras (Metophioceras) rougemonti (Reynès)
Donovan 1952, p. 726.
Lower Lias, *bucklandi* Zone, *conybeari* Subzone.
Chewton Road, Keynsham, Avon [Somerset].
D. T. Donovan Collection, presented 1952.
GSM 85024

Coroniceras (Primarietites) hyatti Donovan
PARATYPE
Donovan 1952, p. 736.
Coroniceras hyatti Donovan
Guérin-Franiatte 1966, p. 125.
Lower Lias, *bucklandi* Zone, *rotiforme* Subzone.
Keeling's Quarry, Keynsham, Avon [Somerset].
D. T. Donovan Collection, presented 1952.
GSM 85034

Arietites bucklandi (J. Sowerby)
Donovan 1952, plate 27, fig. 1, p. 719.
Lower Lias, *bucklandi* Zone, *bucklandi* Subzone.
Manor Road Quarry, Keynsham, Avon [Somerset].
D. T. Donovan Collection, presented 1952.
GSM 85020

Arietites quadratus Donovan HOLOTYPE
Donovan 1952, plate 27, fig. 2, p. 720.
Lower Lias, *bucklandi* Zone, *bucklandi* Subzone.
Burnett Road, Keynsham, Avon [Somerset].
D. T. Donovan Collection, presented 1952.
GSM 85021

Epammonites parthenope (Reynès)
Spath 1956, plate 10, fig. 8, p. 157.
Lower Lias, *bucklandi* Zone, middle *bucklandi* Subzone.
Stowell Park borehole, Northleach, Gloucestershire (Depth 1769 feet).
Survey Collection 1950.
Bj 5460

Tmaegoceras sp.
Gebhard and Schlatter 1977, plate 1, fig. 4, pp. 10, 11.
Lower Sinemurian.
Burton Row, Brent Knoll borehole, Somerset.
Survey Collection 1971.
BDE 6341

Trigonellites sp.
Strickland 1845, text-figs. A,B, pp. 232-235.
Lower Lias, *semicostatum* Zone.
Bidford-on-Avon, Warwickshire.
Geological Society Collection (ex H. E. Strickland), presented 1911.
Geological Society Collection 4457

Ammonites vetustus Simpson HOLOTYPE
Simpson 1855, p. 88.
Simpson 1884, p. 125.
Arnioceras vetustum (Simpson) HOLOTYPE
Howarth 1962, plate 15, fig. 2a, b, p. 103.
Lower Lias, *semicostatum* Zone.
Robin Hood's Bay, Yorkshire.
W. B. Clarkson Collection, purchased 1913.
GSM 26404

Arnioceras niger (Blake)
Spath 1919, p. 68.
Lower Lias, *semicostatum* Zone.
Robin Hood's Bay, Yorkshire.
L. F. Spath Collection, purchased 1943.
GSM 72132

Coroniceras (Primarietites) reynesi (Spath)
Donovan 1952, plate 29, fig. 1, p. 738.
Lower Lias, *semicostatum* Zone, *reynesi* Subzone.
St. George's Road, Keynsham, Avon [Somerset].
D. T. Donovan Collection, presented 1952.
GSM 85030

Coroniceras (Primarietites) reynesi (Spath)
Donovan 1952, p. 738.
Lower Lias, *semicostatum* Zone, *reynesi* Subzone.
St. George's Road, Keynsham, Avon [Somerset].
D. T. Donovan Collection, presented 1952.
GSM 85029

Ammonites nodulosus J. Buckman PARATYPE
J. Buckman 1844, p. 90.
Lower Lias, *semicostatum* Zone, *scipionianum* Subzone.
Cheltenham, Gloucestershire.
S. S. Buckman Collection (ex J. Buckman), purchased 1908.
GSM 22927

Metarnioceras pseudokridion (Spath)
Spath 1956, plate 9, fig. 6, p. 154.
Lower Lias, *semicostatum* Zone, *scipionianum* Subzone.
Stowell Park borehole, Northleach, Gloucestershire.
Survey Collection, 1950.
Bj 5169

Agassiceras scipionianum (d'Orbigny)
Donovan 1952, p. 746.
Lower Lias, *semicostatum* Zone, *scipionianum* Subzone.
Keeling's Quarry, Keynsham, Avon [Somerset].
D. T. Donovan Collection, purchased 1952.
GSM 85031

Arnioceras pseudoturneri Spath HOLOTYPE
Spath 1956, plate 10, fig. 5a, b, p. 152.
Lower Lias, *semicostatum* Zone, *sauzeanum* Subzone.
Stowell Park borehole, Northleach, Gloucestershire.
Survey Collection, 1950.
Bj 4787

Arnioceras pseudoturneri Spath
Spath 1956, plate 10, fig. 4, p. 152.
Lower Lias, *semicostatum* Zone, *sauzeanum* Subzone.
Stowell Park borehole, Northleach, Gloucestershire.
Survey Collection, 1950.
Bj 4781

Euagassiceras resupinatum (Simpson)
Donovan 1952, p. 743.
Lower Lias, *semicostatum* Zone, *sauzeanum* Subzone.
Ashley Down station, Bristol.
D. T. Donovan Collection, presented 1952.
GSM 85032

Euagassiceras spinaries (Quenstedt)
Donovan 1952, p. 744.
Lower Lias, *semicostatum* Zone, *sauzeanum* Subzone.
Keeling's Quarry, Keynsham, Avon [Somerset].
D. T. Donovan Collection, presented 1952.
GSM 85033

Ammonites semicostatus (Young & Bird)
Woodward 1893, p. 85.
Arnioceras sp.
Kellaway & Wilson 1941, plate 9, fig. 1, p. 164.
Lower Lias, *semicostatum* Zone or low *obtusum* Zone.
Old brickpit, Hornblotton Mill, near Alford, Castle Cary, Somerset.
Survey Collection, 1885.
GSM 62457

Ammonites turneri J. de C. Sowerby
J. Buckman 1844, p. 91.
Lower Lias, *semicostatum* Zone.
Cheltenham, Gloucestershire.
S. S. Buckman Collection (ex J. Buckman), purchased 1908.
GSM 22915

Anaptychus
S. S. Buckman 1923, plate CDXXIV.
Lower Lias, bed 74f of Lang, *turneri* Zone, ?upper *brooki* Subzone.
Lyme Regis, Dorset.
S. S. Buckman Collection, purchased 1928.
GSM 37288

Microderoceras gigas (Quenstedt)
S. S. Buckman 1928, plate DCCLXII A, B.
Lower Lias, *turneri* Zone, *birchi* Subzone.
Lyme Regis, Dorset.
S. S. Buckman Collection (ex T. Wright), purchased 1929.
GSM 49339

Ammonites tortilis d'Orbigny
J. Buckman 1844, p. 91.
Caenisites caeneus S. S. Buckman HOLOTYPE
S. S. Buckman 1925, plate DLXXII.
Euasteroceras caeneum (S. S. Buckman) HOLOTYPE
Donovan 1953, p. xiii.
Caenisites caeneus S. S. Buckman HOLOTYPE
Donovan et alii 1957, pp. 15-40.
Lower Lias, *turneri* Zone, *birchi* Subzone.
Cleeve brickfield, Bishop's Cleeve, Gloucestershire.
S. S. Buckman Collection (ex J. Buckman, ex Count Albrizzi) purchased 1926.
GSM 47573

Xipheroceras scoresbyi (Simpson) TOPOTYPE
S. S.Buckman 1911, plate XXXIX C.
Lower Lias, *turneri* Zone, ?upper *birchi* Subzone.
Robin Hood's Bay, Yorkshire.
J. Lycett Collection, purchased 1865.
GSM 23616

Arnioceras ('Eparnioceras') semicostatoides (Spath)
Spath 1956, plate 10, fig. 1, p. 151.
Lower Lias, *obtusum* Zone, *obtusum* Subzone.
Stowell Park borehole, Northleach, Gloucestershire.
Survey Collection, 1950.
Bj 4491

Ammonite on wood
Lyell 1865, text-fig. 461, p. 426.
Lower Lias, Black Marl, *obtusum* Zone.
Lyme Regis, Dorset.
Geological Society Collection (H. de la Beche), presented 1911.
Geological Society Collection 4424.

Galaticeras sp.
Howarth & Donovan 1964, p. 289.
Lower Lias, *obtusum* Zone.
Brightling No. 1 borehole, Sussex.
Presented by British Petroleum Ltd., 1957.
GSM 102186

Xipheroceras revertens, S. S. Buckman HOLOTYPE
S. S. Buckman 1928, plate DCCLXXI A, B.
Lower Lias, *obtusum* Zone, *obtusum* Subzone.
Lyme Regis, Dorset.
S. S. Buckman Collection, purchased 1929.
GSM 49345

Xipheroceras binodulatum S. S. Buckman PARATYPE
S. S. Buckman 1927, plate DCCVI B.
Lower Lias, *obtusum* Zone, *obtusum* Subzone.
Lyme Regis, Dorset.
S. S. Buckman Collection, purchased 1928.
GSM 49299

Xipheroceras binodulatum S. S. Buckman HOLOTYPE
Buckman 1927, plate DCCVI A.
Lower Lias, *obtusum* Zone, *obtusum* Subzone.
Lyme Regis, Dorset.
S. S. Buckman Collection, purchased 1928.
GSM 49298

Xipheroceras ziphus (Hehl-Zieten)
S. S. Buckman 1926, plate DCXXXII.
Lower Lias, *obtusum* Zone, *obtusum* Subzone.
Lyme Regis, Dorset.
S. S. Buckman Collection, purchased 1927.
GSM 47832

Ammonites planicosta J. Sowerby
Wright 1875, pp. 335-338, plate 25, figs. 1-3.
Xipheroceras planicosta S. S. Buckman HOLOTYPE
S. S. Buckman 1911, p. iv.
Xipheroceras rasinodum (Quenstedt)
Donovan 1953, p. 34.
Xipheroceras planicosta S. S. Buckman HOLOTYPE
Donovan 1973, p. 9, plate 3.
Lower Lias, *obtusum* Zone, *obtusum* Subzone.
Lyme Regis, Dorset.
Royal School of Mines Collection (ex Earl of Enniskillen).
GSM 25033

Arnioceras (Eparnioceras) flavum S. S. Buckman **(semicostatoides** Spath)
Lehman 1971, plate 61, pp. 338-339.
Lower Lias, *obtusum* Zone.
Yorkshire.
Museum Collection.
GSM 22703

Schlotheimia miscella (Oppel)
S. S. Buckman 1906, p. 241.
Lower Lias, *obtusum* Zone, *stellare* Subzone.
Badgeworth, Gloucestershire.
R. Tate Collection, purchased ?1870.
GSM 14033

Ammonites brooki J. Sowerby
J. Buckman 1844, p. 89.
Lower Lias, *obtusum* Zone, *stellare* Subzone.
Vale of Gloucester, Gloucestershire.
S. S. Buckman Collection (ex J. Buckman), purchased 1912.
GSM 27593

Schlotheimia angustisulcata Geyer
S. S. Buckman 1906, p. 246.
Lower Lias, *obtusum* Zone, *stellare* Subzone.
Robin Hood's Bay, Yorkshire.
R. Tate Collection, purchased ?1870.
GSM 14032

Ammonites retentus Simpson HOLOTYPE
Simpson 1855, p. 84.
Simpson 1884, p. 120.
Retenticeras retentum (Simpson) HOLOTYPE
S. S. Buckman 1920, plate CLXVI.
Arkell 1957, fig. 267, 1a,b, p. L243.
Howarth 1962, p. 105.
Lower Lias, *oxynotum* Zone, *simpsoni* Subzone.
Robin Hood's Bay, Yorkshire.
W. B. Clarkson Collection, purchased 1913.
GSM 26401

Aetomoceras simpsoni (Bean *in* Simpson)
S. S. Buckman 1912, p. 66b.
Lower Lias, *oxynotum* Zone, *simpsoni* Subzone.
Robin Hood's Bay, Yorkshire.
R. Tate Collection, purchased 1875.
GSM 24362

Ammonites lens Simpson HOLOTYPE
Simpson 1855, p. 80.
Simpson 1884, p. 116.
Gleviceras lens (Simpson) HOLOTYPE
Howarth 1962, plate 15, fig. 3a,b, p. 105.
Lower Lias, *oxynotum* Zone, *simpsoni* Subzone.
Robin Hood's Bay, Yorkshire.
W. B. Clarkson Collection, purchased 1913.
GSM 26405

Oxynoticeras oxynotum (Quenstedt)
Donovan 1958, p. 195.
Lower Lias, *oxynotum* Zone.
Cutting near Canard's Grave, Shepton Mallet, Somerset.
Survey Collection, 1885.
2900 HBW

Paracymbites obsoletus Trueman & Williams
Trueman & Williams 1927, p. 247.
Paracymbites dennyi (Simpson)
Donovan 1966, p. 315.
Lower Lias, *?oxynotum* Zone.
Gas Works, Gloucester.
L. Richardson Collection, purchased 1931.
Zd 3072-3074

Hypechioceras sp.juv.aff. **hierlatzicum** (von Hauer)
Spath 1956, plate 9, fig. 10, p. 149.
Lower Lias, *oxynotum* Zone.
Stowell Park borehole, Northleach, Gloucestershire.
Survey Collection, 1950.
Bj 4148

Hypechioceras sp.ind. (Group of **hierlatzicum** von Hauer)
Spath 1956, plate 9, fig. 11, p. 149.
Lower Lias, *oxynotum* Zone.
Stowell Park borehole, Northleach, Gloucestershire.
Survey Collection, 1950.
Bj 4151

Hypechioceras aff. **hierlatzicum** (von Hauer)
Spath 1956, plate 9, fig. 12, p. 149.
Lower Lias, *oxynotum* Zone.
Stowell Park borehole, Northleach, Gloucestershire.
Survey Collection, 1950.
Bj 4123

Hypechioceras pierrei Spath HOLOTYPE
Spath 1956, plate 9, fig. 13a,b, p. 149.
Getty 1973, p. 10, plate 1, fig. 6a,b.
Lower Lias, *oxynotum* Zone.
Stowell Park borehole, Northleach, Gloucestershire.
Survey Collection, 1950.
Bj 4196

Hypechioceras sp.nov.?
Spath 1956, plate 9, fig. 9a,b, p. 149.
Lower Lias, *oxynotum* Zone.
Stowell Park borehole, Northleach, Gloucestershire.
Survey Collection, 1950.
Bj 4189

Parechioceras? sp.ind.cf. **quenstedti** (Schafthäutl *in* Geyer)
Spath 1956, plate 9, fig. 14, p. 149.
Lower Lias, *oxynotum* Zone.
Stowell Park borehole, Northleach, Gloucestershire.
Survey Collection, 1950.
Bj 4127

Bifericeras cf. **quadricosta** (Quenstedt)
Donovan 1958, p. 395.
Lower Lias, *oxynotum* Zone.
Cutting near Canard's Grave, Shepton Mallet, Somerset.
Survey Collection, 1885.
2896 HBW

Oxynoticeras oxynotum (Quenstedt)
Donovan 1958, p. 395.
Lower Lias, *oxynotum* Zone.
Cutting near Canard's Grave, Shepton Mallet, Somerset.
L. Richardson Collection, purchased 1931.
Zd 3148

Bifericeras (nudicosta group)
Spath 1938, plate 21, fig. 6, p. 168.
Lower Lias, *oxynotum* Zone.
Gloucestershire.
L. F. Spath Collection, purchased 1943.
GSM 72235

Bifericeras aff. **nudicosta** (Quenstedt)
Spath 1925, text-fig. 13(2), p. 363
Lower Lias, *oxynotum* Zone, *oxynotum* Subzone.
Gloucestershire.
L. F. Spath Collection, purchased 1943.
GSM 72165

Bifericeras nudicosta (Quenstedt)
S. S. Buckman 1918a, plate CXXVIII.
Donovan 1958, p. 395.
Lower Lias, *oxynotum* Zone.
Canard's Grave, Shepton Mallet, Somerset.
S. S. Buckman Collection, purchased 1924.
GSM 47094

Ammonites birchii J. Sowerby
Woodward 1893, p. 85.
Bifericeras sp.
Kellaway & Wilson 1941, plate 10, fig. 6, p. 164.
Lower Lias, *oxynotum* Zone.
Well, west of Sutton, near Alhampton, Castle Cary, Somerset.
Survey Collection, 1885.
GSM 62461

Microceras parvum (Quenstedt) [author given in error]
Buckman, *in* Richardson 1904, p. 215.
Bifericeras parvum S. S. Buckman HOLOTYPE
S. S. Buckman 1918a, plate CXXVII.
Donovan 1958, p. 395.
Lower Lias, *oxynotum* Zone, *oxynotum* Subzone.
Canard's Grave, Shepton Mallet, Somerset.
S. S. Buckman Collection, purchased 1924.
GSM 47093

Bifericeras biferum (Quenstedt)
S. S. Buckman 1918a, plate CXXIV
Bifericeras bifer (Quenstedt)
Donovan 1958, p. 395.
Lower Lias, *oxynotum* Zone.
Canard's Grave, Shepton Mallet, Somerset.
S. S. Buckman Collection, purchased 1924.
GSM 47091

Ammonites simpsoni (Bean *in* Simpson)
Woodward 1893, p. 85.
Oxynoticeras sp.juv.
Kellaway & Wilson 1941, plate 9, fig. 10, p. 164.
Lower Lias, *oxynotum* Zone.
Well, west of Sutton, near Alhampton, Castle Cary, Somerset.
Survey Collection, 1885.
GSM 23948

Bifericeras wrighti Bovier
Donovan 1958, p. 395.
Lower Lias, *oxynotum* Zone.
Canard's Grave, Shepton Mallet, Somerset.
Survey Collection, 1885.
GSM 23598

Victoriceras victoris (Dumortier)
S. S. Buckman 1918b, p. 293.
S. S. Buckman 1919, plates CXXXVI A-B.
Lower Lias, *raricostatum* Zone.
Kilmersdon Colliery, Radstock Grove, Radstock, Avon [Somerset].
S. S. Buckman Collection, purchased 1922.
GSM 32002

Microceras subplanicosta (Oppel)
Spath 1925, text-fig. 13, 10, p. 363.
Lower Lias, *raricostatum* Zone.
Gloucestershire.
L. F. Spath Collection, purchased 1943.
GSM 72163

Deroceras cf. **miles** (Simpson)
Trueman & Williams 1927, plate 27, fig. 12, p. 240.
Lower Lias, *raricostatum* Zone.
Railway cutting, Toddington, Gloucestershire.
L. Richardson Collection, purchased 1931.
GSM 51468

Microceras reclinatum Trueman & Williams HOLOTYPE
Trueman & Williams 1927, plate 27, fig. 3, text-fig. 1d, pp. 245-246.
Lower Lias, *raricostatum* Zone.
Railway cutting, Bayliss Hill, Honeybourne, Worcestershire.
L. Richardson Collection, purchased 1931.
GSM 51459

Echioceras aff. **aeneum** Trueman & Williams
Spath 1925, text-fig. 14, 1, p. 364.
Lower Lias, *raricostatum* Zone.
Lyme Regis, Dorset.
L. F. Spath Collection, purchased 1943.
GSM 72167-8

Metaderoceras fulvum Trueman & Williams
HOLOTYPE
Trueman & Williams 1927, plate 28, fig. 1, p. 243.
Lower Lias, *raricostatum* Zone.
North end of Hunting Butts tunnel, near Cheltenham, Gloucestershire.
L. Richardson Collection, purchased 1931.
GSM 51470

Leptonotoceras? or gen.nov.? sp.nov.
Spath 1956, plate 9, fig. 8a,b, p. 148.
Lower Lias, *raricostatum* Zone.
Stowell Park borehole, Northleach, Gloucestershire.
Survey Collection, 1950.
Bj 3898

Cymbites sp.
Richardson 1916, plate 2, fig. 31.
Paracymbites cf. **undulatus** Trueman & Williams
Trueman & Williams 1927, p. 248.
Paracymbites dennyi (Simpson)
Donovan 1966, p. 315.
Lower Lias, *raricostatum* Zone.
Railway cutting, Broadway, Worcestershire.
L. Richardson Collection, purchased 1931.
Zd 2954

Paracymbites undulatus Trueman & Williams
HOLOTYPE
Trueman & Williams 1927, p. 248.
Paracymbites dennyi (Simpson)
Donovan 1966, plate 53, figs. 9-10, text-fig. 2b, pp. 315-316.
Lower Lias, *raricostatum* Zone.
Folly Lane brickpit, Cheltenham, Gloucestershire.
L. Richardson Collection, purchased 1931.
Zd 3035

Leptonotoceras sp.nov.
Richardson 1916, plate 2, figs. 29-30, p. 149.
Lower Lias, *raricostatum* Zone.
Railway cutting, Toddington, Gloucestershire.
L. Richardson Collection, purchased 1931.
Zd 2988

Crucilobiceras cf. **subdensinodum** Spath
Trueman & Williams 1927, p. 241.
Lower Lias, *raricostatum* Zone, *densinodulum* Subzone.
Stanton, Gloucestershire.
L. Richardson Collection, purchased 1931.
Zd 3000

Leptonotoceras cf. **leptonotum** Spath
Trueman & Williams 1927, plate 27, fig. 6, p. 246.
Lower Lias, *raricostatum* Zone.
Railway cutting, Toddington, Gloucestershire.
L. Richardson Collection, purchased 1931.
GSM 51462

Leptonotoceras cf. **leptonotum** Spath
Trueman & Williams 1927, plate 27, fig. 7, p. 246.
Lower Lias, *raricostatum* Zone.
Railway cutting, Toddington, Gloucestershire.
L. Richardson Collection, purchased 1931.
GSM 51463

Cymbites globosus (Oppel)
Richardson 1916, p. 151.
Paracymbites obsoletus Trueman & Williams
HOLOTYPE
Trueman & Williams 1927, plate 27, fig. 8a-c, p. 247.
Cymbites (Paracymbites) obsoletus Trueman & Williams HOLOTYPE
Arkell 1957, fig. 266, 6a,b, p. L240.
Paracymbites dennyi (Simpson)
Donovan 1960, plate 53, figs. 5-7, pp.-t314-316.
Lower Lias, *?raricostatum* Zone.
Stanton Fields railway cutting, Stanton, Gloucestershire.
L. Richardson Collection, purchased 1931.
GSM 51464

Deroceras sp.
Trueman & Williams 1927, plate 27, fig. 9, p. 240.
Lower Lias, *raricostatum* Zone.
North end of Hunting Butts tunnel, Cheltenham, Gloucestershire.
L. Richardson Collection, purchased 1931.
GSM 51465

Deroceras sp.
Trueman & Williams 1927, plate 27, fig. 10.
Lower Lias, *raricostatum* Zone.
Railway cutting, Chestnut Farm, Cheltenham, Gloucestershire.
L. Richardson Collection, purchased 1931.
GSM 51466

Deroceras sp.
Trueman & Williams 1927, plate 27, fig. 11.
Lower Lias, *raricostatum* Zone.
North end of Hunting Butts tunnel, Cheltenham, Gloucestershire.
L. Richardson Collection, purchased 1931.
GSM 51467

Eoderoceras? bispinigerum (S. S. Buckman)
Trueman & Williams 1927, plate 27, fig. 13, p. 241.
Lower Lias, raricostatum Zone.
Railway cutting, Broadway, Worcestershire.
L. Richardson Collection, purchased 1931.
GSM 51469

Crucilobiceras ornatum Trueman & Williams
HOLOTYPE
Trueman & Williams 1927, plate 28, fig. 2, p. 242.
Lower Lias, *raricostatum* Zone.
South end of Hunting Butts tunnel, Cheltenham, Gloucestershire.
L. Richardson Collection, purchased 1931.
GSM 51471

Metaderoceras rubidum Trueman & Williams
HOLOTYPE
Trueman & Williams 1927, plate 28, fig. 3, p. 244.
Lower Lias, *raricostatum* Zone.
Railway cutting, Evesham Road, Cheitenham, Gloucestershire.
L. Richardson Collection, purchased 1931.
GSM 51472

Crucilobiceras rugosum Trueman & Williams
HOLOTYPE
Trueman & Williams 1927, plate 28, fig. 4, pp. 242-243.
Lower Lias, *raricostatum* Zone.
Gasworks excavations, Cheltenham, Gloucestershire.
L. Richardson Collection, purchased 1931.
GSM 51473

Crucilobiceras cf. **cheltiense** Spath
Trueman & Williams 1927, plate 28, fig. 5, pp. 241-242.
Lower Lias, *raricostatum* Zone.
South end of Hunting Butts tunnel, Cheltenham, Gloucestershire.
L. Richardson Collection, purchased 1931.
GSM 51474

Crucilobiceras sp.
Trueman & Williams 1927, plate 28, fig. 8.
Lower Lias, *raricostatum* Zone.
Gasworks excavations, Cheltenham, Gloucestershire.
L. Richardson Collection, purchased 1931.
GSM 51477

Protechioceras spirale Trueman & Williams
HOLOTYPE
Trueman & Williams 1927, plate 28, fig. 6, pp. 248-250.
Palaeoechioceras spirale (Trueman & Williams)
HOLOTYPE
Getty 1973, plate 1, fig. 2a,b, p. 9.
Lower Lias, *raricostatum* Zone.
Gasworks excavations, Gloucester.
L. Richardson Collection, purchased 1931.
GSM 51475

Protechioceras spirale Trueman & Williams
TOPOTYPE
Trueman & Williams 1927, plate 28, fig. 7.
Lower Lias, *raricostatum* Zone.
Gasworks excavations, Gloucester.
L. Richardson Collection, purchased 1931.
GSM 51476

Echioceras microdiscus (Quenstedt)
Davies 1913, pp. 311, 321-322.
Derived from Lower Lias, *raricostatum* Zone.
Calvert borehole, Buckinghamshire.
A. M. Davies Collection, presented 1935.
GSM 54478

Echioceras iridescens Trueman & Williams *in* S. S. Buckman HOLOTYPE
S. S. Buckman April 1925, plate DLIV.
Trueman & Williams September 1925, text-fig. 9b, p. 715.
Lower Lias, *raricostatum* Zone, *raricostatum* Subzone.
Radstock Grove, Radstock, Avon [Somerset].
S. S. Buckman Collection, purchased 1926.
GSM 47561

Echioceras ('Plesechioceras') cf. **typus** S. S. Buckman
Kellaway & Wilson 1941, plate 9, fig. 5, pp. 165-166.
Palaeoechioceras
Getty 1973, p. 9.
Lower Lias, *raricostatum* Zone.
Sutton, near Alhampton, Castle Cary, Somerset.
Survey Collection, 1885.
GSM 62458

Echioceras ('Plesechioceras') cf. **typus** S. S. Buckman
Kellway & Wilson 1941, plate 9, fig. 4, pp. 165-166.
Palaeoechioceras
Getty 1973, p. 10.
Lower Lias, *raricostatum* Zone.
Sutton, near Alhampton, Castle Cary, Somerset.
Survey Collection, 1885.
GSM 62459

Echioceras cf. **lepidum** Trueman & Williams
Kellaway & Wilson 1941, plate 9, fig. 3, p. 166.
Palaeoechioceras
Getty 1973, p. 10.
Lower Lias, *raricostatum* Zone.
Sutton, near Alhampton, Castle Cary, Somerset.
Survey Collection, 1885.
GSM 62460

Echioceras aff.**raricostatoides** (Vadasz)
Spath 1925, text-fig. 14,1, p. 364.
Lower Lias, *raricostatum* Zone.
Near Radstock, Avon [Somerset].
L. F. Spath Collection, purchased 1943.
GSM 72166

Microceras sp.juv.
Spath 1925, text-fig. 13, 3-5, p. 363.
Lower Lias, *raricostatum* Zone.
?Cheltenham, Gloucestershire.
L. F. Spath Collection, purchased 1943.
GSM 73563

Microceras cingendum Trueman & Williams
HOLOTYPE
Trueman & Williams, 1927, plate 27, fig. 5, p. 246.
Lower Lias, *raricostatum* Zone.
Railway cutting, Broadway, Worcestershire.
L. Richardson Collection, purchased 1931.
GSM 51461
[This specimen has partially decomposed.]

Microceras regulare Trueman & Williams HOLOTYPE
Trueman & Williams 1927, plate 27, fig. 4, text-fig. 1c, p. 245.
Lower Lias, *raricostatum* Zone.
Railway cutting, Bayliss Hill, Honeybourne, Gloucestershire.
L. Richardson Collection, purchased 1931.
GSM 51460

Microceras serpentinum Trueman & Williams
HOLOTYPE
Trueman & Williams 1927, plate 27, fig. 2, text-fig. 1b, pp. 244-245.
Lower Lias, *raricostatum* Zone.
Railway cutting, St. George's Road, Cheltenham, Gloucestershire.
L. Richardson Collection, purchased 1931.
GSM 51458

Microceras acuticosta Trueman & Williams
HOLOTYPE
Trueman & Williams 1927, plate 27, fig. 1, text-fig. 1a, p. 244.
Lower Lias, *raricostatum* Zone.
South end of Hunting Butts tunnel, Cheltenham, Gloucestershire.
L. Richardson Collection, purchased 1931.
GSM 51457

Echioceras crassicostatum Trueman & Williams *in* S. S. Buckman HOLOTYPE
S. S. Buckman April 1925, plate DLIII.
Trueman & Williams September 1925, p. 712.
Lower Lias, *raricostatum* Zone.
Kilmersdon Colliery Quarry, Radstock, Avon [Somerset].
S. S. Buckman Collection, purchased 1926.
GSM 47560

Echioceras notatum Trueman & Williams *in* S. S. Buckman HOLOTYPE
S. S. Buckman April 1925, plate DLII.
Trueman & Williams September, 1925, p. 713.
Lower Lias, *raricostatum* Zone.
Near Radstock, Avon [Somerset].
S. S. Buckman Collection (ex T. Stock), purchased 1926.
GSM 47559

Ammonites greenhoughii J. Sowerby
J. Buckman 1844, p. 89.
Gleviceras glevense S. S. Buckman PARATYPE
S. S. Buckman 1918b, plate 28, fig. 2, pp. 289-290.
S. S. Buckman 1924, plate DXXVI.
Gleviceras subguibalianum (Pia)
Arkell 1957, fig. 267, 7, p. L242.
Lower Lias shales, *raricostatum* Zone.
Lansdown, Cheltenham, Gloucestershire.
S. S. Buckman Collection (ex J. Buckman) purchased 1926.
GSM 47551

Echioceras regustatum S. S. Buckman HOLOTYPE
S. S. Buckman 1914, p. 96c.
Paltechioceras aureolum (Simpson)
Getty 1973, plate 5, fig. 3, p. 20.
Lower Lias, *raricostatum* Zone.
Robin Hood's Bay, Yorkshire.
W. B. Clarkson Collection, purchased 1913.
GSM 26439

Paracymbites dennyi (Simpson)
Donovan 1966, p. 315.
Lower Lias, *raricostatum* Zone.
Cheltenham, Gloucestershire.
R. Tate Collection, purchased ?1870.
GSM 24629

Paracymbites dennyi (Simpson)
Donovan 1966, p. 315.
Lower Lias, *raricostatum* Zone, *macdonnelli* Subzone.
Apley Barn borehole, Witney, Oxfordshire.
Survey Collection, 1962.
GSM 87552

Neomicroceras commune Donovan
Donovan 1966, p. 313.
Lower Lias, *raricostatum* Zone, *macdonelli* Subzone.
Dundry borehole, Dundry, Avon [Somerset].
Survey Collection, 1962.
GSM 87561-87563

Neomicroceras commune Donovan HOLOTYPE
Donovan 1966, plate 53, figs. 1-2, text-fig. 1c, p. 313.
Lower Lias, *raricostatum* Zone, *macdonelli* Subzone.
Apley Barn borehole, Witney, Oxfordshire.
Survey Collection, 1962.
GSM 87550

Neomicroceras commune Donovan PARATYPES
Donovan 1966, plate 53, fig. 3, text-fig. 1a,b.
Lower Lias, *raricostatum* Zone, *macdonelli* Subzone.
Apley Barn borehole, Witney, Oxfordshire.
Survey Collection, 1962.
GSM 87551, 87553-87560

Ammonites aureolus Simpson HOLOTYPE
Simpson 1855, p. 94,
Simpson 1884, p. 134.
Echioceras aureolum (Simpson) HOLOTYPE
S. S. Buckman 1914, plate XCVI.
Howarth 1962, p. 106.
Lower Lias, *raricostatum* Zone, *aplanatum* Subzone.
Robin Hood's Bay, Yorkshire.
W. B. Clarkson Collection, purchased 1913.
GSM 26402

Polymorphites bronni (Römer)
Richardson 1916, plate 2, figs. 27-28.
Lower Lias, late *raricostatum* Zone or early *jamesoni* Zone.
Culvert for the river Isbourne, Winchcombe, Gloucestershire.
L. Richardson Collection, purchased 1931.
GSM 51484

Bifericeras tubellum (Simpson *in* Blake)
Richardson 1916, plate 2, figs. 29, 30, p. 149.
Lower Lias, upper *raricostatum* Zone.
Railway cutting, north of Toddington, Gloucestershire.
L. Richardson Collection, purchased 1931.
Zd 2988

PLIENSBACHIAN STAGE

Liparoceras (Parinodiceras) parinodum (Quenstedt)
Spath 1956, plate 10, fig. 3, p. 147.
Lower Lias, *jamesoni* Zone, *taylori* Subzone.
Stowell Park borehole, Northleach, Gloucestershire.
Survey Collection, 1950.
Bj 3337

Belemnites elongatus Miller
Huxley 1864, plate 1, figs. 3, 3a, 3b, p. 15.
Phillips 1866, p. 50.
Lower Lias, *jamesoni* Zone.
Lyme Regis, Dorset or south of Paulton, Somerset.
E. C. H. Day Collection, purchased 1862.
GSM 82650

Tropidoceras aff. **lineatum** Spath
Spath 1928, plate 17, fig. 8, text-fig. 4b, pp. 226-227.
Lower Lias, Belemnite Marl, *jamesoni* Zone.
Charmouth, Dorset.
L. F. Spath Collection, purchased 1943.
GSM 72178

Tropidoceras ellipticum (J. Sowerby)
Spath 1928, plate 16, fig. 4, p. 226.
Lower Lias, Belemnite Marl, *jamesoni* Zone.
Charmouth, Dorset.
L. F. Spath Collection, purchased 1943.
GSM 72169

Gemmellaroceras peregrinum (Haug)
Kellaway & Wilson 1941, plate 9, fig. 11, p. 166.
Lower Lias, *jamesoni* Zone.
Chilthorne Hill Lane, Chilthorne Domer, near Yeovil, Somerset.
Survey Collection, 1938.
GSM 62463

Echioceras microdiscus (Quenstedt)
Davies & Pringle 1913, pp. 311, 322.
Lower Lias, *jamesoni* Zone derived from *raricostatum* Zone.
Borehole at Calvert station, Buckinghamshire.
A. M. Davies Collection, presEnted 1935.
GSM 54479

Apoderoceras triornatum S. S. Buckman HOLOTYPE
S. S. Buckman 1928, plates DCCLXXXIII. A,B.
Lower Lias, *jamesoni* Zone, *taylori* Subzone.
Kilmersdon Colliery, Radstock Grove, Radstock, Avon [Somerset].
S. S. Buckman Collection, purchased 1929.
GSM 49353

Parinodiceras reineckii (Quenstedt)
S. S. Buckman 1927, plates DCCXLVIII A,B.
Lower Lias, *jamesoni* Zone.
Branch Huish, Radstock, Avon [Somerset]
S. S. Buckman Collection, purchased 1929.
GSM 49327

Phylloxynites phyllinum S. S. Buckman HOLOTYPE
S. S. Buckman 1924, plate CDLXV.
Lower Lias, *jamesoni* Zone.
Kilmersdon Colliery, Radstock Grove, Radstock, Avon [Somerset].
S. S. Buckman Collection, purchased 1925.
GSM 37313

Phricodoceras lamellosum (d'Orbigny)
Trueman 1918, p. 265.
S. S. Buckman 1920, plates CXCLIX A-C.
Lower Lias, *jamesoni* Zone.
Kilmersdon Colliery, Radstock Grove, Radstock, Avon [Somerset].
S. S. Buckman Collection, purchased 1923.
GSM 32008

Prodactylioceras nodissimum (Quenstedt)
Spath 1936, p. 443.
Lower Lias, *jamesoni* Zone, ?*taylori* Subzone.
Charmouth, Dorset.
H. E. Norris Collection, purchased 1878.
GSM 23557

Ammonites mutatus Simpson HOLOTYPE
Simpson 1855, pp. 63-64.
Simpson 1884, p. 96.
Deroceras mutatum (Simpson) HOLOTYPE
S. S. Buckman 1914, plate CV.
Apoderoceras mutatum (Simpson) HOLOTYPE
Howarth 1962, p. 109.
Lower Lias, *jamesoni* Zone, *taylori* Subzone.
?Near Whitby, Yorkshire.
W. B. Clarkson Collection, purchased 1913.
GSM 26406

Aegoceras armatum (J. Sowerby)
Wright 1878, plate 29, pp. 340-344.
Deroceras pugnax S. S. Buckman HOLOTYPE
S. S. Buckman, 1914, p. 103c.
Eoderoceras (Eoderoceras) pugnax (S. S. Buckman) HOLOTYPE
Donovan 1954, p. 35.
Lower Lias, *jamesoni* Zone.
Lyme Regis, Dorset.
Royal School of Mines Collection (Museum Collection).
GSM 25025

Deroceras, giant
Buckman 1918b, p. 305.
Apoderoceras tardarmatum S. S. Buckman HOLOTYPE
S. S. Buckman 1925, plates DXLII A,B.
Lower Lias, *jamesoni* Zone, *taylori* Subzone.
Kilmersdon Colliery, Radstock Grove, Radstock, Avon [Somerset].
S. S. Buckman Collection, purchased 1910.
GSM 24749

Platypleuroceras aureum (Simpson)
Howarth 1962, p. 111.
Lower Lias, *jamesoni* Zone, *brevispina* Subzone.
Robin Hood's Bay, Yorkshire.
W. B. Clarkson Collection, purchased 1913.
GSM 26490-26491

Jamesonites reticulatus S. S. Buckman HOLOTYPE
S. S. Buckman 1923, plate CDVII.
Uptonia (Jamesonites) reticulata (S. S. Buckman) HOLOTYPE
Arkell 1957, fig. 275, 5, p. L249.
Lower Lias, *jamesoni* Zone, *brevispina* Subzone.
Branch Huish, Radstock, Avon [Somerset].
S. S. Buckman Collection, purchased 1924.
GSM 47194

Orthocera elongata De la Beche HOLOTYPE
De la Beche 1826, plate 4, fig. 4, p. 28.
Xiphoteuthis elongata (De la Beche) HOLOTYPE
Huxley 1864, p. 17, plate 3, fig. 2.
Lower Lias.
Lyme Regis, Dorset.
Presented 1911 (ex H. T. de la Beche)
Geological Society Collection 4463.

Belemnite
Huxley 1864, plate 1, figs. 5, 5a.
Lower Lias.
Lyme Regis, Dorset.
E. C. H. Day Collection, purchased c.1870.
GSM 94541

Xiphoteuthis elongata (De la Beche)
Huxley 1864, plate 3, fig. 4.
Lower Lias, Belemnite Bed, *jamesoni* Zone.
Charmouth, Dorset.
E. C. H. Day Collection, purchased 1866.
GSM 58644

Xiphoteuthis elongata (De la Beche)
Huxley 1864, p. 18, plate 3, fig. 3.
Lower Lias, Belemnite Bed, *jamesoni* Zone.
Charmouth, Dorset.
E. C. H. Day Collection, purchased c.1864.
GSM 94341

Tropidoceras aff. **erythraeum** (Gemmellaro)
Spath 1956, plate 9, fig. 7a,b, p. 146.
Lower Lias, *ibex* Zone, *masseanum* Subzone.
Stowell Park borehole, Northleach, Gloucestershire.
Survey Collection, 1950.
Bj 2956

Metacymbites sp.nov.?
Spath 1956, plate 9, figs. 3-4, p. 146.
Lower Lias, *ibex* Zone, *masseanum* Subzone.
Stowell Park borehole, Northleach, Gloucestershire.
Survey Collection, 1950.
Bj 2935, 2947

Ammonites centaurus d'Orbigny
J. Buckman 1844, p. 89.
Beaniceras centaurus (d'Orbigny)
S. S. Buckman 1919, plate CXLVI.
Lower Lias, *ibex* Zone, *valdani* Subzone.
Hewletts Road, Cheltenham, Gloucestershire.
S. S. Buckman Collection (ex J. Buckman), purchased 1923.
GSM 32006

Ammonites centaurus d'Orbigny
J. Buckman 1844, p. 89.
Beaniceras senile S. S. Buckman HOLOTYPE
S. S. Buckman 1918a, plate CXXVI.
Lower Lias, *ibex* Zone, *valdani* Subzone.
Hewletts Road, Cheltenham, Gloucestershire.
S. S. Buckman Collection (ex J. Buckman), purchased 1924.
GSM 47092

Ammonites centaurus d'Orbigny
J. Buckman 1844, p. 89.
Beaniceras rotundum S. S. Buckman HOLOTYPE
S. S. Buckman 1918a, plate CXXIX.
Lower Lias, *ibex* Zone, *valdani* Subzone.
Hewletts Road, Cheltenham, Gloucestershire.
S. S. Buckman Collection (ex J. Buckman), purchased 1924.
GSM 47095

Ammonites centaurus d'Orbigny
J. Buckman 1844, p. 89.
Beaniceras costatum S. S. Buckman HOLOTYPE
S. S. Buckman 1919, plate CXXIII.
Lower Lias, *ibex* Zone, *valdani* Subzone.
Hewletts Road, Cheltenham, Gloucestershire.
S. S. Buckman Collection (ex J. Buckman), purchased 1924.
GSM 47096

Ammonites planicostatus J. Sowerby
J. Buckman 1844, p. 90.
Beaniceras crassum S. S. Buckman HOLOTYPE
S. S. Buckman 1919, plate CXLVII.
Lower Lias, *ibex* Zone, *valdani* Subzone.
Glenfall, Cheltenham, Gloucestershire.
S. S. Buckman Collection (ex J. Buckman), purchased 1923.
GSM 32007

Tragophylloceras carinatum Howarth & Donovan PARATYPE
Howarth & Donovan 1964, p. 303.
Lower Lias, *ibex* Zone, *valdani* Subzone or *luridum* Subzone.
Wyboston borehole, Cambridgeshire.
Survey Collection, 1955.
GSM 102184

Beaniceras sp.
S. S. Buckman 1917, p. 264.
Lower Lias, *ibex* Zone, *luridum* Subzone.
Stow-on-the-Wold, Gloucestershire.
S. S. Buckman Collection, purchased 1924.
GSM 47099

Ammonites taylori J. de C. Sowerby
J. Buckman 1844, p. 43.
Aegoceras taylori (J. de C. Sowerby)
Wright 1882, p. 350.
Lower Lias, *?ibex* Zone derived from *jamesoni* Zone.
Coltham Field Brickfields, Hewletts Road, Cheltenham, Gloucestershire.
S. S. Buckman Collection (ex J. Buckman), purchased 1911.
GSM 26762

Tragophylloceras ibex (Quenstedt)
Howarth & Donovan 1964, plate 49, fig. 2a,b.
Lower Lias, *ibex* Zone.
South of Paulton, Avon [Somerset].
Museum Collection
GSM 24443

Tragophylloceras undulatum (W. Smith)
Howarth & Donovan 1964, plate 48, fig. 7a, b.
Lower Lias, *ibex* Zone
Radstock, Avon [Somerset].
R. Tate Collection, purchased ?1870.
GSM 24441

Tragophylloceras undulatum (W. Smith)
Howarth & Donovan 1964, plate 49, fig. 1a,b.
Lower Lias, *ibex* Zone.
Radstock, Avon [Somerset].
R. Tate Collection, purchased ?1870.
GSM 24439

Tragophylloceras undulatum (W. Smith) microconch
Howarth & Donovan 1964, plate 48, fig. 9a, b, text-fig. 1d.
Lower Lias, *ibex* Zone.
Radstock, Avon [Somerset].
R. Tate Collection, purchased ?1870.
GSM 24430

Androgynoceras cf. **brevilobatum** (Trueman)
Spath 1938, pp. 155-156, text-fig. 17.
Lower Lias, *davoei* Zone.
Mickleton, Gloucestershire.
Geological Society Collection, presented 1911.
Geological Society Collection 4361.

Aegoceras striatum (Reinecke)
Wright 1881, plate XLIII, p. 378.
Liparoceras cheltiense (Murchison)
S. S. Buckman 1905c, plate 67a.
Liparoceras wrighti Spath HOLOTYPE
Spath 1938, p. 67.
Liparoceras (Liparoceras) wrighti Spath HOLOTYPE
Donovan 1954, p. 39.
Lower Lias, *davoei* Zone, *capricornus* Subzone.
Lyme Regis, Dorset.
Museum Collection
GSM 25024

Belemnites longissimus Miller LECTOTYPE
Phillips 1867, plate 13, fig. 31g′, g″, p. 66.
Lang 1928, p. 220.
Lower Lias.
Charmouth, Dorset.
E. C. H. Day Collection, purchased c.1870.
GSM 94536

Belemnites sp. deformed
Tate 1875, text-figs. 5, 5a, p. 504.
Lower Lias.
Radstock, Avon [Somerset].
R. Tate Collection, purchased 1870.
GSM 94516

Geoteuthis sp.
Huxley 1864, plate 2, figs. 1, 1a.
Lower Lias.
Lyme Regis, Dorset.
H. E. Norris Collection, purchased 1878.
GSM 87479

Leptaleoceras pseudoradians (Reynès)
Howarth 1957, plate 17, fig. 1.
Middle Lias, Eype Nodule Bed, *margaritatus* Zone, *stokesi* Subzone.
Down Cliff, Seatown, near Bridport, Dorset.
H. E. Norris Collection, purchased 1878.
GSM 22747

Tragophylloceras loscombi (J. Sowerby)
Howarth & Donovan 1964, text-fig. 1g.
Middle Lias, Eype Nodule Bed, *margaritatus* Zone, *stokesi* Subzone.
Cliff section below Golden Cap, Seaton, Dorset.
Survey Collection 1936.
GSM 102185

Ammonites margaritatus (Montfort)
Woodward 1893, p. 208
Amaltheus cf. **stokesi** (J. Sowerby)
Kellaway & Wilson 1941, plate 9, fig. 9, pp. 166-167.
Middle Lias, *margaritatus* Zone, *stokesi* Subzone.
Well near Brent Knoll station, Somerset.
Survey Collection, 1885.
GSM 62462

Lytoceras furcicrenatum S. S. Buckman HOLOTYPE
S. S. Buckman 1928, plate DCCLXXXIV A.
Middle Lias, *margaritatus* Zone.
Thorncombe Beacon, Eype, Symondsbury, Dorset.
S. S. Buckman Collection, purchased 1929.
GSM 49354

Amaltheus margaritatus Montfort
Howarth 1958, plate 3, fig. 6a, b.
Middle Lias, *margaritatus* Zone.
Hawsker Bottoms, Whitby, Yorkshire.
W. B. Clarkson Collection, purchased 1913.
GSM 26542

Pleuroceras salebrosum (Hyatt)
Howarth 1958, plate 5, fig. 12, pp. 33-34.
Middle Lias, *margaritatus* Zone.
Hallaig, Raasay, Inverness.
R. Tate Collection, purchased ?1875.
GSM 24784

Amaltheus lenticularis (Young & Bird)
Wright 1886, plate 82, figs. 14-15, pp. 482-483.
Amauroceras lenticulare (Young & Bird)
Donovan 1954, p. 51.
Howarth 1958, pp. 26-27.
Middle Lias, *spinatum* Zone, *apyrenum* Subzone.
Whitby, Yorkshire.
J. Leckenby Collection, presented 1866.
GSM 24807

Amaltheus solitarius (Simpson)
Tate & Blake 1876, plate 8, fig. 2, p. 295.
Paltopleuroceras apyrenum S. S. Buckman HOLOTYPE
S. S. Buckman 1911, p. 24d.
Pleuroceras apyrenum (S. S. Buckman) HOLOTYPE
Howarth 1955, p. 164.
Howarth 1958, plate 6, fig. 1a,b, pp. 35-36.
Dean, Donovan & Howarth 1961, plate 71, fig. 5a, b.
Middle Lias, *spinatum* Zone, *apyrenum* Subzone.
Eston, Cleveland [Yorkshire].
R. Tate Collection, purchased 1875.
GSM 24855

Pleuroceras quadratum Howarth PARATYPE
Howarth 1958, plate 8, fig. 4, p. 35.
Middle Lias, Marlstone Rock, *spinatum* Zone, *apyrenum* Subzone.
Chideock, Dorset.
E. C. H. Day Collection, purchased 1862.
GSM 24856

Pleuroceras quadratum Howarth PARATYPE
Howarth 1958, plate 8, fig. 3, p. 35.
Middle Lias, Marlstone Rock, *spinatum* Zone, *apyrenum* Subzone.
Chideock, Dorset.
E. C. H. Day Collection, purchased 1862.
GSM 24857

Ammonites regularis Simpson HOLOTYPE
Simpson 1855, p. 89.
Simpson 1884, p. 127.
Paltopleuroceras regulare (Simpson) HOLOTYPE
S. S. Buckman 1913, plate LXXVII.
Pleuroceras solare (Phillips)
Howarth 1958, pp. 28-30.
Pleuroceras regulare (Simpson) HOLOTYPE
Howarth 1962, p. 114.
Middle Lias, *spinatum* Zone, *apyrenum* Subzone.
Robin Hood's Bay or Hawsker, Yorkshire.
W. B. Clarkson Collection, purchased 1913.
GSM 26403

Amaltheus laevigatus Howarth HOLOTYPE
Howarth 1958, plate 4, fig. 1a,b, pp. 19-20.
Middle Lias, bed 25, *spinatum* Zone, *apyrenum* Subzone.
Hawsker Bottoms, Whitby, Yorkshire.
W. B. Clarkson Collection, purchased 1913.
GSM 26541

Argutarpites argutus S. S. Buckman HOLOTYPE
S. S. Buckman 1923, plate CCCLXIII
Middle Lias, *spinatum* Zone.
South Petherton, Somerset.
S. S. Buckman Collection, purchased 1924.
GSM 47162

Paltopleuroceras pseudocostatum (Hyatt)
S. S. Buckman 1889c, plate XXII, fig. 1.
Jackson 1922, p. 441.
Paltopleuroceras buckmanii (Moxon)
S. S. Buckman 1924, plate CIC C
Pleuroceras spinatum (Bruguière) **buckmani** (Moxon)
Howarth 1958, p. 39.
Middle Lias, *spinatum* Zone.
Thorncombe Beacon, Bridport, Dorset.
S. S. Buckman Collection (ex J. F. Jackson), purchased 1926.
GSM 47526

Ammonites buckmanii Moxon HOLOTYPE
Moxon 1841, plate 24, fig. 5.
Pleuroceras hawskerense (Young & Bird)
S. S. Buckman 1889c, p. 653.
Paltopleuroceras buckmanii (Moxon) HOLOTYPE
S. S. Buckman 1921, plate CIC B
Pleuroceras spinatum (Bruguière) **buckmani** (Moxon) HOLOTYPE of ssp.
Howarth 1958, pp. 39-41.
Middle Lias, Marlstone Rock-bed, *spinatum* Zone, *hawskerense* Subzone.
Alderton Hill, near Cheltenham, Gloucestershire.
S. S. Buckman Collection (ex J. Buckman), purchased 1923.
GSM 32031

Ammonites cf. **kurianus** Oppel
Buckman 1922a, p. 394.
Platyharpites platypleurus S. S. Buckman HOLOTYPE
S. S. Buckman 1927, plate DCXCVIII
Paltarpites platypleurus (S. S. Buckman) HOLOTYPE
Howarth 1957, p. 199.
Middle Lias, *spinatum* Zone.
Thorncombe Beacon, Bridport, Dorset.
S. S. Buckman Collection, purchased 1928.
GSM 49291

Pleuroceras gigas Howarth PARATYPE
Howarth 1958, plate 10, fig. 2a, b, pp 48-49.
Middle Lias, Marlstone, *spinatum* Zone, *?apyrenum* Subzone.
Duke's Pit, Woolsthorpe, Colsterworth, Leicestershire.
W. Fowler Collection, presented 1906.
GSM 49754

Pleuroceras spinatum (Bruguière) **buckmani** (Moxon) transitional to **P. yeovilense** Howarth
Howarth 1958, text-fig. 15-5, p. 45.
Middle Lias, *spinatum* Zone.
South Petherton, Somerset.
L. F. Spath Collection, purchased 1946.
GSM 73641

?Pleuroceras quadratum Howarth
Howarth 1958, plate 8, fig. 6a, b, p. 35.
Middle Lias, Marlstone, *spinatum* Zone, *apyrenum* Subzone.
Stow-on-the-Wold, Gloucestershire.
L. F. Spath Collection, purchased 1946.
GSM 73645

Pleuroceras gigas Howarth
Howarth 1958, plate 10, fig. 1a, b, pp. 48-49.
Middle Lias, *spinatum* Zone, *?apyrenum* Subzone.
Woolsthrope Ironstone Works, Colsterworth, Leicestershire.
Survey Collection 1885.
JR 3

Pleuroceras salebrosum (Hyatt)
Howarth 1958, plate 5, fig. 13.
Middle Lias, Marlstone, *spinatum* Zone, *apyrenum* Subzone.
Norton-sub-Hamdon, Somerset.
W. H. Hudleston Collection, presented by Miss C. A. Raisin 1920.
Y 2816

Pleuroceras transiens (Frentzen)
Versey 1958, p. 440.
Middle Lias drift in Cretaceous basal conglomerate.
Binvane Farm, Murlough Bay, Co. Antrim, Northern Ireland.
H. C. Versey Collection, presented 1958.
GSM 96788

TOARCIAN STAGE

Orthodactylites directus S. S. Buckman HOLOTYPE
S. S. Buckman 1926, plate DCLIV.
Dactylioceras directum (S. S. Buckman) HOLOTYPE
Arkell 1957, fig. 284, 2, p. L252.
Hains and Horton 1969, plate 9, fig. 3.
Upper Lias, *tenuicostatum* Zone.
Middleton Cheney, Northamptonshire.
S. S. Buckman Collection, purchased 1927.
GSM 47847

Paltarpites paltus S. S. Buckman PARATYPE
S. S. Buckman 1923, plate CCCLXII B.
Protogrammoceras paltum (S. S. Buckman) PARATYPE
Howarth 1973, p. 265.
Upper Lias, Junction Bed, *tenuicostatum* Zone, *paltum* Subzone.
Down Cliff, Thorncombe Beacon, Bridport, Dorset.
S. S. Buckman Collection, purchased 1924.
GSM 47161

Paltarpites paltus S. S. Buckman HOLOTYPE
S. S. Buckman 1922a, plate CCCLXII A.
Arkell 1957, fig. 289, 5, p. L256.
Géczy 1967, p. 121.
Hirano 1971. pp. 114, 115.
Protogrammoceras paltum (S. S. Buckman) HOLOTYPE
Howarth 1973, p. 265.
Paltarpites paltus S. S. Buckman HOLOTYPE
Gabilly 1976, pp. 71-75.
Upper Lias, Junction Bed, *tenuicostatum* Zone, *paltum* Subzone.
Thorncombe Beacon, Bridport, Dorset.
S. S. Buckman Collection, purchased 1924.
GSM 47160

Stephanoceras holandrei (d'Orbigny)
Tate & Blake 1876, pp. 172, 299. 300.
Dactylioceras (Dactylioceras) pseudocommune Fucini
Howarth 1973, plate 1, fig. 1, pp. 253, 254.
Upper Lias, Grey Shales, *tenuicostatum* Zone, *paltum* Subzone.
Hob Hill Mine, Saltburn, Cleveland [Yorkshire].
R. Tate Collection, purchased 1875.
GSM 22568

Ammonites acutus Tate
Tate 1875, p. 204.
Harpoceras acutum (Tate)
Wright 1884, plate 82, figs. 7, 8, p. 469.
Tiltoniceras acutum (Tate) LECTOTYPE
Donovan 1954, p. 51.
Hoffmann and Martin 1960, pp. 117-119.
Tiltoniceras antiquum (Wright)
Géczy 1967, p. 122.
Howarth 1973, pp. 266, 267.
Schlegelmilch 1976, plate 46, fig. 5.
Tiltoniceras acutum (Tate) LECTOTYPE
Gabilly 1976, p. 61.
Upper Lias, *tenuicostatum* Zone, upper *semicelatum* Subzone.
King's Sutton, near Banbury, Oxfordshire.
R. Tate Collection, purchased 1875.
GSM 24783

Kryptodactylites semicelatus (Simpson)
S. S. Buckman 1927, plate XXXI A, p. 41.
Dactylioceras (Kryptodactylites) semicelatum (Simpson)
Hoffmann and Martin 1960, p. 111.
Dactylioceras semicelatum (Simpson)
Sapunov 1963a, pp. 117, 118.
Upper Lias Grey Shale, *tenuicostatum* Zone, *semicelatum* Subzone.
Whitby, Yorkshire.
S. S. Buckman Collection, purchased 1929.
GSM 49310

Dactylioceras cf. **tenuicostatum** (Young & Bird)
S. S. Buckman 1910b, p. 83.
Upper Lias, *tenuicostatum* Zone, *semicelatum* Subzone.
Chideock, Dorset.
E. C. H. Day Collection, purchased 1862.
GSM 22475

Orthodactylites mitis S. S. Buckman HOLOTYPE
S. S. Buckman 1927, plate DCCXXXVIII.
Upper Lias, *tenuicostatum* Zone.
Byfield, Northamptonshire.
J. Pringle Collection, presented 1918.
GSM 38384

Xeinodactylites helianthoides (Yokoyama)
S. S. Buckman 1927, plate DCXCIX, p. 41.
Dactylioceras (Xeinodactylites) helianthoides Yokoyama
Hoffmann and Martin 1960, p. 113.
Upper Lias, Bed 6, *tenuicostatum* Zone.
Barrington Quarry, near Ilminster, Somerset.
Survey Collection (A. Templeman) 1921.
GSM 38013 [formerly AT 133]

Tenuidactylites tenuicostatus (Young & Bird)
S. S. Buckman 1926, p. 41.
S. S. Buckman 1927, plate CLVII A.
Sapunov 1963a, pp. 116, 117.
Upper Lias, Grey Shales, *tenuicostatum* Zone.
Whitby, Yorkshire.
S. S. Buckman Collection, purchased 1928.
GSM 49297

Dactylioceras directum (S. S. Buckman)
Edmunds and Oakley 1936, 1947, plate 6, fig. 2
Upper Lias, *tenuicostatum* Zone.
Adderbury, near Banbury, Oxfordshire.
Museum Collection.
GSM 22566

Harpoceras falciferoides S. S. Buckman HOLOTYPE
S. S. Buckman 1927, plate DCCXLIX.
Harpoceras (Harpoceras) falciferoides S. S. Buckman HOLOTYPE
Gabilly 1976, pp. 100, 101.
Upper Lias, *falciferum* Zone.
Ilminster, Somerset.
S. S. Buckman Collection, (ex T. Stock), purchased 1929.
GSM 49328

Harpoceratoides strangwaysi (J. Sowerby)
S. S. Buckman 1927, plate DCCXXXIX.
Gabilly 1976, p. 85.
Upper Lias, *falciferum* Zone, top of *exaratum* Subzone.
Barrington, near Ilminster, Somerset.
Survey Collection (A. Templeman) 1921.
GSM 44681 [formerly AT 120]

Eleganticeras pseudo-elegans S. S. Buckman HOLOTYPE
S. S. Buckman 1912, p. viii.
S. S. Buckman 1918a, plate CX.
Harpoceras (Eleganticeras) elegantulum (Young & Bird)
Weitschat 1973, p. 50.
Eleganticeras elegantulum (Young & Bird)
Gabilly 1976, p. 62.
Upper Lias, *falciferum* Zone, *exaratum* Subzone.
Whitby, Yorkshire.
S. S. Buckman Collection, purchased 1924.
GSM 47090

Ammonites pinguis Simpson HOLOTYPE
Simpson 1855, p. 100.
Simpson 1884, p. 141.
Whitbyiceras pingue (Simpson) HOLOTYPE
S. S. Buckman 1913, plate LXXX.
Arkell 1957, fig. 289, 10, p. L258.
Howarth 1962, p. 121.
Upper Lias, Jet Rock *falciferum* Zone, *exaratum* Subzone.
Near Whitby, Yorkshire.
W. B. Clarkson Collection, purchased 1913.
GSM 26408

Glyptarpites glyptus S. S. Buckman HOLOTYPE
S. S. Buckman 1927, plate DCCXL, pp. 8, 9.
Upper Lias, *falciferum* Zone, basal *falciferum* or top *exaratum* Subzone.
Barrington Upper Quarry, Ilminster, Somerset.
Survey Collection (A. Templeman) 1921.
GSM 38394 [formerly AT 518]

Simplicidactylites simplicicosta S. S. Buckman HOLOTYPE
S. S. Buckman 1927, p. 43.
Upper Lias, *falciferum* Zone, *falciferum* Subzone.
Barrington, near Ilminster, Somerset.
Survey Collection, (A. Templeman) 1921.
GSM 38304 [formerly AT 574]
[figured here, plate 1, fig. 2.]

Simplicidactylites simplicicosta S. S. Buckman PARATYPE
S. S. Buckman 1927, p. 43.
Upper Lias, *falciferum* Zone, *falciferum* Subzone.
Barrington, near Ilminster, Somerset.
Survey Collection (A. Templeman) 1921.
GSM 38303 [formerly AT 300a]

Anguidactylites anguiformis S. S. Buckman HOLOTYPE
S. S. Buckman 1922b, p. 453.
S. S. Buckman 1926, p. 41.
S. S. Buckman 1928, plate DCCLXIII.
Dactylioceras anguiforme (S. S. Buckman) HOLOTYPE
Howarth 1978, pp. 251, 253.
Upper Lias, *falciferum* Zone, *falciferum* Subzone.
Barrington, near Ilminster, Somerset.
Survey Collection (A. Templeman) 1921.
GSM 38014 [formerly AT 171]

Dactylioceras annulatum (J. Sowerby)
S. S. Buckman 1927, plate DCC.
Dactylioceras (Orthodactylites) semiannulatum Howarth
Howarth 1978, pp. 251, 253.
Upper Lias, *falciferum* Zone, *falciferum* Subzone.
Barrington, near Ilminster, Somerset.
Survey Collection (A. Templeman) 1921.
GSM 38302 [formerly AT 193]

Crassicoeloceras pingue S. S. Buckman HOLOTYPE
S. S. Buckman 1926, p. 42.
S. S. Buckman 1927, plate DCCXXVIII.
Nodicoeloceras crassoides (Simpson)
Howarth 1978, p. 258.
Upper Lias, *falciferum* Zone, *falciferum* Subzone.
Barrington Upper Quarry, near Ilminster, Somerset.
Survey Collection (A. Templeman) 1921.
GSM 38015 [formerly AT 198]

Vermidactylites vermis (Simpson)
S. S. Buckman 1927, plate LXVIII A.
Dactylioceras (?Orthodactylites) vermis (Simpson)
Howarth 1978, p. 253.
Upper Lias, *falciferum* Zone, *falciferum* Subzone.
Barrington, near Ilminster, Somerset.
Survey Collection (A. Templeman) 1921.
GSM 38016 [formerly AT 258]

Toxodactylites toxophorus S. S. Buckman HOLOTYPE
S. S. Buckman 1926, p. 42.
S. S. Buckman 1928, plate DCCLXXVI.
Upper Lias, *falciferum* Zone, *falciferum* Subzone.
Barrington, near Ilminster, Somerset.
Survey Collection (A. Templeman) 1921.
GSM 38017 [formerly AT 294]

Leptodactylites leptum S. S. Buckman HOLOTYPE
S. S. Buckman 1926, p. 42.
Upper Lias, *falciferum* Zone, *falciferum* Subzone.
Barrington, near Ilminster, Somerset.
Survey Collection (A. Templeman) 1921.
GSM 38018 [formerly AT 329]
[figured here, plate 1, fig. 10.]

Spinicoeloceras spicatum S. S. Buckman HOLOTYPE
S. S. Buckman 1926, p. 42.
S. S. Buckman 1928, plate DCCLXXVII.
Upper Lias, *falciferum* Zone, *falciferum* Subzone.
Barrington, near Ilminster, Somerset.
Survey Collection (A. Templeman) 1921.
GSM 38019 [formerly AT 330]

Lobodactylites lobatum S. S. Buckman HOLOTYPE
S. S. Buckman 1925, p. 42.
S. S. Buckman 1927, plate DCCXXX.
Nodicoeloceras lobatum (S. S. Buckman) HOLOTYPE
Howarth 1978, p. 259.
Upper Lias, Bed 24, *falciferum* Zone, *falciferum* Subzone.
Barrington Quarry, near Ilminster, Somerset.
Survey Collection (A. Templeman) 1921
GSM 38020 [formerly AT 350]

Tardarpoceras tardum S. S. Buckman HOLOTYPE
S. S. Buckman 1927, plate DCCXLI, p. 9.
S. S. Buckman 1928, p. 14.
Harpoceras (Harpoceras) falciferum (J. Sowerby)
Gabilly 1976, p. 95.
Upper Lias, Bed 22, *falciferum* Zone, *falciferum* Subzone.
Barrington Upper Quarry, near Ilminster, Somerset.
Survey Collection (A. Templeman) 1921.
GSM 38382 [formerly AT 287].

Nodicoeloceras crassoides (Simpson)
S. S. Buckman 1926, p. 42.
S. S. Buckman 1927, plate LXXXIX A.
Howarth 1978, pp. 256, 258.
Upper Lias, *falciferum* Zone, *falciferum* Subzone.
Barrington Upper Quarry, near Ilminster, Somerset.
Survey Collection (A. Templeman) 1921.
GSM 31616 [formerly AT 202]

Harpoceras falcula S. S. Buckman HOLOTYPE
S. S. Buckman 1926, plate DCLXXXII.
Upper Lias, *falciferum* Zone, *falciferum* Subzone.
Barrrington Upper Quarry, near Ilminster, Somerset.
Survey Collection (A. Templeman) 1921.
GSM 31620 [formerly AT 310]

Orthildaites orthus S. S. Buckman HOLOTYPE
S. S. Buckman 1923, plate CDXLIV.
Arkell 1957, fig. 291, 1, p. L259.
Orthildaites douvillei (Haug)
Gabilly 1976, fig. 34, pp. 119-125.
Upper Lias, *falciferum* Zone, *falciferum* Subzone.
Down Cliff, Chideock, Dorset.
S. S. Buckman Collection, purchased 1925.
GSM 37298

Hildoceratoides serpentinus (Reinecke)
S. S. Buckman 1926, plate CXXXVIII C.
Upper Lias, *falciferum* Zone, *falciferum* Subzone.
Cudworth, near Ilminster, Somerset.
Presented by A.P.I. Cotterell & Son, 1926.
GSM 37959

Lytoceras cornucopiae (Young & Bird)
S. S. Buckman 1896, p. 421.
Lobolytoceras siemensi (Denckmann)
S. S. Buckman 1923, plate CDXL.
Lobolytoceras perlobulatum S. S. Buckman HOLOTYPE
S. S. Buckman 1924, plate CDXL*.
Upper Lias, *falciferum* or *bifrons* Zone.
South Petherton, Somerset.
S. S. Buckman Collection, purchased 1925.
GSM 37297

Dactylioceras crassiusculum (Simpson)
S. S. Buckman 1910b, p. 83.
Upper Lias, *falciferum* Zone.
Chideock, Dorset.
Museum Collection.
GSM 22514

Phaularpites exiguus S. S. Buckman HOLOTYPE
S. S. Buckman 1928, plate DCCLXXV A, pp. 13, 14.
Harpoceras (Maconiceras) exiguum (S. S. Buckman) HOLOTYPE
Gabilly 1976, pp. 113-115.
Upper Lias, *falciferum* Zone, *falciferum* Subzone.
Moolham, Ilminster, Somerset.
S. S. Buckman Collection, purchased 1929.
GSM 49349

Phaularpites exiguus S. S. Buckman PARATYPE
S. S. Buckman 1928, plate DCCLXXV B, pp. 13, 14.
Harpoceras (Maconiceras) exiguum (S. S. Buckman) PARATYPE
Gabilly 1976, pp. 113-115.
Barrington, near Ilminster, Somerset.
Survey Collection (A. Templeman) 1921.
GSM 47917 [formerly AT 314]

Harpoceras falciferum (J. Sowerby)
S. S. Buckman 1928, plate DCCLXIV A.
Harpoceras (Harpoceras) falciferum (J. Sowerby)
Gabilly 1976, p. 95.
Upper Lias, *falciferum* Zone, *falciferum* Subzone.
Barrington Upper Quarry, near Ilminster, Somerset.
Survey Collection (A. Templeman) 1921.
GSM 48019 [formerly AT 342]

Harpoceras concinnum S. S. Buckman HOLOTYPE
S. S. Buckman 1927, plate DCCXLII.
Upper Lias, *falciferum* Zone, *falciferum* Subzone.
Barrington Upper Quarry, near Ilminster, Somerset.
Survey Collection (A. Templeman) 1921.
GSM 31623 [formerly AT 369]

Nodicoeloceras acanthus (d'Orbigny)
S. S. Buckman 1927, plate DCCXXIX A, B.
Sapunov 1963a, pp. 118-119.
Upper Lias, *falciferum* Zone, *falciferum* Subzone.
Shelway Lane, Barrington, near Ilminster, Somerset.
Survey Collection (A. Templeman) 1921.
GSM 31637 [formerly AT 568]

Murleyiceras gyrale S. S. Buckman HOLOTYPE
S. S. Buckman 1928, plate DCCLXXII.
Upper Lias, *falciferum* Zone, *falciferum* Subzone.
Catesby, Northamptonshire.
S. S. Buckman Collection (ex B. Thompson), purchased 1929.
GSM 49346

Arcidactylites arcus S. S. Buckman HOLOTYPE
S. S. Buckman 1926, plate DCLVII.
S. S. Buckman 1927, p. 44.
Dactylioceras commune (J. Sowerby)
Howarth 1978, p. 253.
Upper Lias, *bifrons* Zone.
Astrop Pits, King's Sutton, near Banbury, Oxfordshire.
Survey Collection 1918.
GSM 37972

Peronoceras praepositum S. S. Buckman HOLOTYPE
S. S. Buckman 1927, plate DCCI.
Dactylioceras commune (J. Sowerby)
Howarth 1978, p. 253.
Upper Lias, Alum Shale, *bifrons* Zone, *commune* Subzone.
Whitby, Yorkshire.
S. S. Buckman Collection, purchased 1928.
GSM 49292

Ammonites crassibundus Simpson HOLOTYPE
Simpson 1855, p. 55.
Simpson 1884, p. 87.
Dactylioceras crassibundum (Simpson) HOLOTYPE
Howarth 1962, plate 16, fig. 7a, b, p. 115.
Upper Lias, *bifrons* Zone, probably basal *commune* Subzone.
Whitby, Yorkshire.
W. B. Clarkson Collection, purchased 1913.
GSM 26407

Koinodactylites communis (J. Sowerby)
S. S. Buckman 1927, plate DCCVII, p. 43.
Dactylioceras commune (J. Sowerby)
Howarth 1978, p. 253.
Upper Lias, *bifrons* Zone, *commune* Subzone.
Whitby, Yorkshire.
S. S. Buckman Collection, purchased 1928.
GSM 49300

Nomodactylites temperatus S. S. Buckman HOLOTYPE
S. S. Buckman 1927, plate DCCXXXI, p. 43.
Upper Lias, *bifrons* Zone.
Whitby, Yorkshire.
S. S. Buckman Collection, purchased 1929.
GSM 49318

Curvidactylites curvicosta S. S. Buckman HOLOTYPE
S. S. Buckman 1927, plate DCCVIII, p. 43.
Maubeuge 1948, p. 2.
Dactylioceras commune (J. Sowerby)
Howarth 1978, p. 253.
Upper Lias, Alum Shale or above, *bifrons* Zone, *commune* Subzone.
Whitby, Yorkshire.
S. S. Buckman Collection, purchased 1928.
GSM 49301

Peronoceras fibulatum (J. de C. Sowerby)
S. S. Buckman 1926, plate DCLXXXIII.
Arkell 1957, fig. 286, 2, p. L253.
Upper Lias, *bifrons* Zone, *fibulatum* Subzone.
Whitby, Yorkshire.
S. S. Buckman Collection, purchased 1928.
GSM 49279

Porpoceras verticosum S. S. Buckman
Howarth 1978, p. 280.
Upper Lias, *bifrons* Zone, *fibulatum* Subzone.
Grantham, Lincolnshire.
Survey Collection (R. Gibbs) 1870.
GSM 22517

Porpoceras vortex (Simpson)
Howarth 1978, p. 280.
Upper Lias, *bifrons* Zone, *fibulatum* Subzone.
Grantham, Lincolnshire.
Survey Collection (R. Gibbs) 1870.
GSM 22515, 22516, 22518

Zugodactylites mutatus S. S. Buckman HOLOTYPE
S. S. Buckman 1927, plate DCCXX.
Zugodactylites braunianus (d'Orbigny)
Howarth 1978, pp. 268, 270, 271.
Upper Lias, *bifrons* Zone, *crassum* Subzone.
Vigo Brickyard, Northampton.
S. S. Buckman Collection, purchased 1929.
GSM 49312

Zugodactylites braunianus (d'Orbigny)
S. S. Buckman 1926, plate DCLVIII.
Arkell 1957, fig. 283, 2, p. L253.
Howarth 1978, p. 268.
Upper Lias, *bifrons* Zone, *crassum* Subzone.
Vigo Brickyard, Northampton.
S. S. Buckman Collection, purchased 1927.
GSM 47848

Frechiella subcarinata (Young & Bird)
S. S. Buckman 1923, plate XXIII A.
Upper Lias, *?bifrons* Zone.
Watton Cliff, Eype, Symondsbury, Dorset.
S. S. Buckman Collection, purchased 1924.
GSM 47106

Peridactylites consimilis S. S. Buckman HOLOTYPE
S. S. Buckman 1926, p. 42.
S. S. Buckman 1928, plate DCCLXXVIII.
Upper Lias, *bifrons* Zone.
Barrington, near Ilminster, Somerset.
Survey Collection (A. Templeman) 1921.
GSM 38021 [formerly AT 352]

Multicoeloceras multum S. S. Buckman HOLOTYPE
S. S. Buckman 1926-1927, pp. 42, 43.
S. S. Buckman 1928, plate DCCLXXXV.
Upper Lias, *bifrons* Zone.
Barrington, near Ilminster, Somerset.
Survey Collection (A. Templeman) 1921.
GSM 38022 [formerly AT 428]

Maconiceras vigoense S. S. Buckman HOLOTYPE
S. S. Buckman 1926, plate DCLXXXIV.
S. S. Buckman 1928, p. 13.
Harpoceras (Maconiceras) vigoense (S. S. Buckman) HOLOTYPE
Gabilly 1976, p. 110.
Upper Lias, *bifrons* Zone, *crassum* Subzone.
Vigo Brickyard, Northampton.
S. S. Buckman Collection, purchased 1928.
GSM 49280

Lobolytoceras perlobulatum S. S. Buckman
PARATYPE
S. S. Buckman 1925, plate CDXL A.
Upper Lias, *bifrons* Zone.
Trent, near Yeovil, Somerset.
S. S. Buckman Collection, purchased 1926.
GSM 47531

Parvidactylites parvus S. S. Buckman HOLOTYPE
S. S. Buckman 1927, p. 43.
S. S. Buckman 1928, plate DCCLXXIX.
Upper Lias, *bifrons* Zone, *crassum* Subzone.
Barrington, near Ilminster, Somerset.
Survey Collection, (A. Templeman) 1921.
GSM 38023 [formerly AT 578]

Hildoceras semicosta S. S. Buckman HOLOTYPE
S. S. Buckman 1926, plate DCLXXXV.
Hildoceras semipolitum S. S. Buckman
Upper Lias, grey stone at base of Cotswold Sand, *bifrons* Zone, *crassum* Subzone.
Excavation at gasworks, Nailsworth, Gloucestershire.
S. S. Buckman Collection, purchased 1928.
GSM 49281

Hildoceras walcotti (J. Sowerby)
S. S. Buckman 1928, plate DCCLXXIII A.
Upper Lias, *bifrons* Zone.
Trent, near Yeovil, Somerset.
S. S. Buckman Collection, purchased 1929.
GSM 49358

Hildoceras walcotti (J. Sowerby) NEOTYPE
S. S. Buckman 1928, plate DCCLXXIII.
Howarth 1962, p. 134.
Upper Lias, Alum Shales, *bifrons* Zone.
Whitby, Yorkshire.
S. S. Buckman Collection, purchased 1929.
GSM 49347

Nodicoeloceras group of **angelonii** (Ramaccioni)
Pinna and Levi-Setti 1971, fig. 18B, p. 86.
Upper Lias, *bifrons* Zone.
Barrington, Somerset.
S. S. Buckman Collection, purchased, date unknown.
GSM 62634

Catacoeloceras crassum (Young & Bird)
Howarth 1978, plate 8, fig. 6, p. 246.
Upper Lias, Leda ovum Beds, top *bifrons* Zone, *crassum* Subzone.
Leicestershire [?Nevill Holt area, Medbourne].
Presented by Lady Exeter, before 1865.
GSM 22519

Catacoeloceras confectum S. S. Buckman HOLOTYPE
S. S. Buckman 1923, plate CDXIII.
S. S. Buckman 1927, p. 44.
Arkell 1957, fig. 284, 4, p. L254
Behmel and Geyer 1966, p. 20.
Pinna 1966, p. 108.
Géczy 1967, pp. 94, 95.
Upper Lias, *variabilis* Zone.
North Nibley, Gloucestershire.
S. S. Buckman Collection, purchased 1924.
GSM 47198

Thysanoceras cornucopia (Young & Bird)
S. S. Buckman 1923, plates CCCXCI B, C.
Upper Lias, *variabilis* Zone.
North Nibley Knoll, Gloucestershire.
S. S. Buckman Collection, purchased 1924.
GSM 47182

Harpoceras bicarinatum Münster
Wright 1884, plate 82, figs. 9, 10, pp. 462, 463.
Polyplectus elegans (J. Sowerby)
Donovan 1954, p. 51.
Upper Lias, *variabilis* Zone.
Nailsworth, Gloucestershire.
J. Lycett Collection, purchased 1867.
GSM 22749

Haugia illustris (Denckmann)
S. S. Buckman 1898, pp. xxvi, xxvii.
Upper Lias, *variabilis* Zone.
Shepton Beauchamp, Somerset.
S. S. Buckman Collection, purchased 1906.
GSM 16249

Ammonites (Harpoceras) striatulum (J. de C. Sowerby)
Walker 1892, p. 440.
S. S. Buckman 1910b, p. 57.
Upper Lias, *thouarsense* Zone, *striatulum* Subzone.
West side of Quarry Hill, Chideock, Dorset.
S. S. Buckman Collection (ex J. F. Walker), purchased 1910.
GSM 24765 & 24766

Grammoceras striatulum (J. de C. Sowerby)
S. S. Buckman 1889b, p. 444.
Costigrammoceras costigerum S. S. Buckman HOLOTYPE
S. S. Buckman 1926, plate DCLXXXVI.
Grammoceras costigerum (S. S. Buckman) HOLOTYPE
Gabilly 1975, p. 114.
Upper Lias, lower part of the Cephalopod Bed, *thouarsense* Zone, *striatulum* Subzone.
Coaley Wood, Uley Bury, Gloucestershire.
S. S. Buckman Collection, purchased 1928.
GSM 49282

Grammoceras toarciense (d'Orbigny)
S. S. Buckman 1904, p. cxxxii.
Upper Lias, *thouarsense* Zone, *striatulum* Subzone.
Coaley Wood, Dursley, Gloucestershire.
S. S. Buckman Collection, purchased 1912.
GSM 27600

Haugia occidentalis (Haug)
S. S. Buckman 1889b, p. 446.
Upper Lias, *thouarsense* Zone, *striatulum* Subzone.
Little Sodbury, Avon [Gloucestershire].
S. S. Buckman Collection, purchased 1912.
GSM 27599

Grammoceras thouarsense (d'Orbigny)
S. S. Buckman 1927, plate DCCLXXIV.
Upper Lias, *thouarsense* Zone, *striatulum* Subzone.
Nibley Knoll, North Nibley, Gloucestershire.
S. S. Buckman Collection, purchased 1928.
GSM 49348

Ammonites (Grammoceras) thouarsense (d'Orbigny)
Walker 1892, p. 442.
S. S. Buckman 1910b, p. 57.
Upper Lias, *thouarsense* Zone, *striatulum* Subzone.
West side of Quarry Hill, Chideock, Dorset.
S. S. Buckman Collection (ex J. F. Walker), purchased 1910.
GSM 24763

Ammonites compactilis Simpson ?HOLOTYPE
Simpson 1855, p. 75.
Simpson 1884, p. 110.
Pseudolioceras compactile (Simpson) ?HOLOTYPE
S. S. Buckman 1911, plate XLI A.
Howarth 1962, p. 121.
Upper Lias, *thouarsense* Zone, *striatulum* Subzone.
Peak, Ravenscar, Yorkshire.
J. Lycett Collection, purchased 1864 or 1867.
GSM 24914

Grammoceras doerntense Denckmann
S. S. Buckman 1896, p. 712.
Upper Lias, *thouarsense* Zone, *?striatulum* Subzone.
Wellow, Avon [Somerset].
S. S. Buckman Collection, purchased 1910.
GSM 24758

Grammoceras striatulum (J. de C. Sowerby)
S. S. Buckman 1910b, p. 57.
Upper Lias, *thouarsense* Zone, *striatulum* Subzone.
West side of Quarry Hill, Chideock, Dorset.
S. S. Buckman Collection, purchased 1910.
GSM 24764

Ammonites cf. **radians** Reinecke
Lycett 1865, p. 10.
Upper Lias, *thouarsense* Zone, *fallaciosum* Subzone.
Frocester Hill, Frocester, Gloucestershire.
J. Lycett Collection, purchased 1867.
GSM 22824 & 22825

Pseudogrammoceras cotteswoldiae S. S. Buckman
S. S. Buckman 1904, p. cxlix.
Upper Lias (bed 11), *thouarsense* Zone, *fallaciosum* Subzone.
Sodbury, Avon [Gloucestershire].
S. S. Buckman Collection, purchased 1906.
GSM 16278

Hammatoceras cappucinum S. S. Buckman HOLOTYPE
S. S. Buckman 1921, plate CCVI A.
Upper Lias, *levesquei* Zone, *dispansum* Subzone.
Railway cutting at Cole, Pitcombe, near Bruton, Somerset.
S. S. Buckman Collection, purchased 1923.
GSM 32036

Phlyseogrammoceras dispansum (Lycett)
S. S. Buckman 1903, p. 447.
Upper Lias, *levesquei* Zone, *dispansum* Subzone.
Gravel pit at Overbury, Bredon Hill, Worcestershire.
S. S. Buckman Collection, purchased 1924.
Z 3490

Ammonites variabilis d'Orbigny **dispansus** Lycett HOLOTYPE of ssp.
Lycett 1860, p. 146.
Ammonites dispansus Lycett HOLOTYPE
Lycett 1865, p. 5.
Phlyseogrammoceras dispansum (Lycett) HOLOTYPE
S. S. Buckman plate CCCXL.
Arkell 1957 fig. 294, 4, p. L261.
Maubeuge 1949, pp. 2, 6.
Upper Lias, *levesquei* Zone, *dispansum* Subzone.
Frocester Hill, Gloucestershire.
J. Lycett Collection, purchased 1867.
GSM 24924

Phlyseogrammoceras electum S. S. Buckman HOLOTYPE
S. S. Buckman 1922a, plate CCCXCIV.
Upper Lias, *levesquei* Zone, *dispansum* Subzone.
Little Sodbury, Avon [Gloucestershire].
S. S. Buckman Collection, purchased 1924.
GSM 47183

Dumortieria arata S. S. Buckman
S. S. Buckman 1890, p. 180.
S. S. Buckman 1891, plate 39, figs. 1, 2.
Catulloceras subaratum Brasil
S. S. Buckman 1905a, p. clxxii.
S. S. Buckman 1907, p. 4.
Sapunov 1959, p. 25.
Pseudogrammoceras aratum (S. S. Buckman) PARATYPE
Gabilly 1975, pp. 123-125.
Upper Lias, marly limestone below the Yeovil Sands, *levesquei* Zone.
Trent, Dorset.
S. S. Buckman Collection (ex J. Buckman), purchased 1910.
GSM 6719

Dumortieria arata S. S. Buckman HOLOTYPE
S. S. Buckman 1891, plate 39, figs. 3-5.
Catulloceras aratum (S. S. Buckman) HOLOTYPE
S. S. Buckman 1892, p. 280.
S. S. Buckman 1907, p. 4.
Sapunov 1959, p. 25.
Pseudogrammoceras aratum (S. S. Buckman) LECTOTYPE
Gabilly 1975, pp. 122-125.
Upper Lias, *levesquei* Zone.
Penn Wood, King's Stanley, Gloucestershire.
S. S. Buckman Collection, purchased 1900.
GSM 6720

Catulloceras leesbergi (Branco)
S. S. Buckman 1891, plate 39, figs. 10, 11.
S. S. Buckman 1892, p. 279.
Upper Lias, *levesquei* Zone, *levesquei* Subzone.
Wotton-under-Edge, Gloucestershire.
S. S. Buckman Collection, purchased 1900.
GSM 6721

Catulloceras insigni-similis (Brauns)
S. S. Buckman 1891, plate 39, figs. 12-14.
S. S. Buckman 1892, p. 278.
Upper Lias, *levesquei* Zone, *levesquei* Subzone.
Breakheart Hill, Stinchcombe, Gloucestershire.
S. S. Buckman Collection, purchased 1900.
GSM 6722

Polymorphites senescens S. S. Buckman HOLOTYPE
S. S. Buckman 1892, plate 48, figs. 13-15, p. 268.
Upper Lias, *Terebratula haresfieldensis* Horizon, *levesquei* Zone.
Haresfield Hill, Gloucestershire.
S. S. Buckman Collection, purchased 1900.
GSM 6725

Walkeria arcuata S. S. Buckman
S. S. Buckman 1904, p. cxxxix.
Upper Lias, towards the top of the Yeovil Sands, *levesquei* Zone, *aalensis* Subzone.
Quarry Hill, Chideock, Dorset.
S. S. Buckman Collection, purchased 1910.
GSM 16281

Catulloceras psamminum S. S. Buckman
S. S. Buckman 1905a, p. clxxii.
Upper Lias, Yeovil Sands, *levesquei* Zone, *levesquei* Subzone.
Furzey Knap, East Coker, Somerset.
S. S. Buckman Collection, purchased 1906.
GSM 16255

Catulloceras dumortieri (Thiollière)
S. S. Buckman 1891, pp. 277-278.
S. S. Buckman 1892, plate 39, figs. 6-9.
S. S. Buckman 1910b, p. 69.
Upper Lias, Yeovil Sands, *levesquei* Zone, *levesquei* Subzone.
Burton Bradstock, Dorset.
S. S. Buckman Collection (ex J. E. Clark), purchased 1900.
GSM 6718

Dumortieria pseudoradiosa (Branco)
S. S. Buckman 1891, plate 41, figs. 1-3, p. 246.
Upper Lias, Yeovil Sands, *levesquei* Zone, *levesquei* Subzone.
Yeovil Junction, Dorset.
S. S. Buckman Collection (ex T. C. Maggs), purchased 1900.
GSM 6727

Dactylogammites digitatus S. S. Buckman HOLOTYPE
S. S. Buckman 1925, plate DLXXIII.
Upper Lias, *levesquei* Zone, *levesquei* Subzone.
Pipley Bottom, North Stoke, near Bath, Avon [Somerset].
S. S. Buckman Collection, purchased 1926.
GSM 47574

Ammonites moorei Lycett HOLOTYPE
Lycett 1857, plate 1, fig. 2a.
Harpoceras mactra Dumortier
Dumortier 1874, pp. 251, 252.
Harpoceras aalense Zieten
Wright 1883, plate 80, fig. 3.
Dumortieria moorei (Lycett) HOLOTYPE
S. S. Buckman 1891, plate 44, fig. 9, 255-258.
S. S. Buckman 1905a, p. clxxxii.
Donovan 1954, p. 50.
Dean, Donovan and Howarth 1961, plate 74, fig. 5.
Géczy 1967, pp. 149, 150.
Schegelmilch 1976, plate 51 fig. 5.
Upper Lias, *levesquei* Zone, *moorei* Subzone.
Frocester Hill, Gloucestershire.
J. Lycett Collection, purchased 1867.
GSM 25312

Table 2 Zones and subzones of the Middle Jurassic (after Arkell, 1956b, with modifications by Parsons, 1974, 1976b and Torrens, 1971).

	Zone	Subzone
Bathonian	*Clydoniceras discus*	*Clydoniceras discus* *Clydoniceras hollandi*
	Oxycerites aspidoides	
	Prohecticoceras retrocostatum	
	Morrisiceras morrisi	
	Tulites subcontractus	
	Procerites progracilis	
	Zigzagiceras zigzag	*Oxycerites yeovilensis* *Morphoceras macrescens* *Parkinsonia convergens*
Bajocian	*Parkinsonia parkinsoni*	*Parkinsonia bomfordi* *Strigoceras truellei*
	Strenoceras (Garantiana) garantiana	*Parkinsonia (Parkinsonia) acris* *Strenoceras (Pseudogarantiana) dichotoma*
	Strenoceras (Strenoceras) subfurcatum	*Strenoceras (Garantiana) baculatum* *Caumontisphinctes polygyralis* *Teloceras banksi*
	Stephanoceras humphriesianum	*Teloceras blagdeni* *Stephanoceras humphriesianum* *Dorsetensia romani*
	Emileia (Otoites) sauzei	
	Witchellia laeviuscula	*Witchellia laeviuscula* *Sonninia ovalis*
	Hyperlioceras discites	
	Graphoceras concavum	
	Ludwigia (Ludwigia) murchisonae	*Brasilia bradfordensis* *Ludwigia (Ludwigia) murchisonae* *Ancolioceras opalinoides*
	Leioceras opalinum	*Tmetoceras scissum* *Leioceras opalinum*

Dumortieria aff. **moorei** (Lycett)
Kellaway and Wilson 1941, plate 9, fig. 2, pp. 167, 168.
Upper Lias, Yeovil Sands, *levesquei* Zone, *moorei* Subzone.
Charlock Hill, Sherborne, Dorset.
J. Fowler Collection, purchased 1940.
GSM 62454

Dumortieria latescens S. S. Buckman
S. S. Buckman 1905a, p. clxxxv.
Upper Lias, sands in Cephalopod Bed, *levesquei* Zone, *moorei* Subzone.
North Stoke, near Bath, Avon [Somerset].
S. S. Buckman Collection, (ex E. Wilson) purchased 1906.
GSM 16254

Dumortieria linearis S. S. Buckman PARATYPE
S. S. Buckman 1905a, p. clxxxiii.
S. S. Buckman 1910b, p. 64.
Upper Lias, *levesquei* Zone, *moorei* Subzone.
Chideock, Dorset.
S. S. Buckman Collection, purchased 1912.
GSM 27604

Dumortieria rhodanica Haug
S. S. Buckman 1926, plate DCLXVIII A, B.
Upper Lias, *levesquei* Zone, *moorei* Subzone.
Pen Wood, King's Stanley, near Stroud, Gloucestershire.
S. S. Buckman Collection, purchased 1928.
GSM 49269

Ammonites leckenbyi Lycett HOLOTYPE
Lycett 1857, plate 2, fig. 7.
Lytoceras hircinum Schlotheim
Wright 1883, plate 74, figs. 4-5, pp. 415-416.
Pleurolytoceras hircinum (Schlotheim)
Donovan 1954, p. 49.
Upper Lias, *levesquei* Zone, *moorei* Subzone.
Frocester Hill, Gloucestershire.
J. Lycett Collection, purchased 1867.
GSM 24955

Xeinophylloceras xeinus S. S. Buckman HOLOTYPE
S. S. Buckman 1921, plate CCLXVI A-B.
Upper Lias, *levesquei* Zone, *moorei* Subzone.
Stoford, Somerset.
S. S. Buckman Collection, purchased 1922.
GSM 32065

Pleydellia aalensis (Zieten)
Dean, Donovan & Howarth 1961, plate 74, fig. 4.
Upper Lias, *levesquei* Zone, *aalensis* Subzone.
Haselbury Mill, Haselbury Plucknett, Somerset.
G. Kellaway and V. Wilson Collection, presented 1939.
GSM 69983

Pseudolioceras beyrichi (Schloenbach)
S. S. Buckman 1889a, p. 88.
Upper Lias (bed 15), *levesquei* Zone, *aalensis* Subzone.
Haresfield Hill, Gloucestershire.
S. S. Buckman Collection, purchased 1906.
GSM 16290

BAJOCIAN STAGE

Lioceras cf. **uncinatum** S. S. Buckman
Buckman *in* Richardson 1904, p. 231.
Inferior Oolite (derived), *opalinum* Zone.
Gravel pit at Charlton Kings, Cheltenham, Gloucestershire.
S. S. Buckman Collection, purchased 1924.
Z 3481

Lioceras uncinatum S. S. Buckman
S. S. Buckman *in* Richardson 1904, p. 231.
Inferior Oolite, *opalinum* Zone.
Kimsbury Court, Painswick, Gloucestershire.
S. S. Buckman Collection, purchased 1924.
Z 3480

Tmetoceras regleyi (Thiollière)
S. S. Buckman 1905, p. clxxi.
Richardson 1906, p. 122.
Tmetoceras scissum (Benecke)
Cave 1977, p. 111.
Inferior Oolite, *opalinum* Zone, *scissum* Subzone.
Pen Wood, King's Stanley, near Stroud, Gloucestershire.
S. S. Buckman Collection, purchased 1906.
GSM 16266

Tmetoceras circulare S. S. Buckman
S. S. Buckman 1905, p. clxx.
Inferior Oolite, *opalinum* Zone, *scissum* Subzone (? derived).
Bradford Abbas, Dorset.
S. S. Buckman Collection, purchased 1906.
GSM 16265

Bredyia crassornata S. S. Buckman PARATYPE
S. S. Buckman 1925, plate DLXXVII
Bredyia subinsignis (Oppel)
Senior 1977, plate 81, figs. 3, 4, text-figs. 2b, 3a, 6M, p. 682.
Inferior Oolite, *opalinum* Zone, *scissum* Subzone.
Burton Bradstock, Dorset.
S. S. Buckman Collection, purchased 1927.
GSM 47763

Bredyia subinsignis (Oppel)
Senior 1977, text-fig. 2d, p. 682.
Inferior Oolite, *opalinum* Zone, *scissum* Subzone.
Loders Cross NE quarry, Loders, Dorset.
G. Bomford Collection, presented 1948.
Zk 1401, 1402 (misquoted as Zx 1402)

Bredyia subinsignis (Oppel)
Senior 1977, text-fig. 20, p. 683.
Northampton Ironstone, *opalinum* Zone, *scissum* Subzone.
Duston, Northamptonshire.
Survey Collection (H. B. Woodward) 1893.
1160 HBW (misquoted as 1160 HW)

Bredyia subinsignis (Oppel)
Senior 1977, plate 84, figs. 9, 10, text-fig. 2q, p. 683.
Inferior Oolite, *opalinum* Zone, *scissum* Subzone.
Burton Bradstock, Dorset.
S. S. Buckman Collection, purchased 1890.
GSM 3666

Bredyia subinsignis (Oppel)
Senior 1977, p. 682.
Inferior Oolite, *opalinum* Zone, *scissum* Subzone.
Broad Windsor, Dorset.
Geological Society Collection (ex D. Sharpe 1854) presented 1911.
Geol. Soc. Coll. GSc 3307 [misquoted as GSM 3307]

Bredyia subinsignis (Oppel)
Senior 1977, p. 682.
Inferior Oolite, *opalinum* Zone, *scissum* Subzone.
Burton Bradstock, Dorset.
L. F. Spath Collection, purchased 1945.
GSM 72799

Bredyia subinsignis (Oppel)
Senior 1977, p. 682.
Inferior Oolite, *opalinum* Zone, *scissum* Subzone.
Upton Farm, Bridport, Dorset.
L. F. Spath Collection, purchased 1945.
GSM 72800, 72801

Bredyia subinsignis (Oppel)
Senior 1977, p. 683.
Inferior Oolite, *opalinum* Zone, *scissum* Subzone.
Newmarket, Nailsworth, Gloucestershire.
J. Lycett Collection, purchased 1867.
GSM 22813

Bredyia subinsignis (Oppel)
Senior 1977, p. 683.
Inferior Oolite, *opalinum* Zone, *scissum* Subzone.
Ravensgate, Cheltenham, Gloucestershire.
J. Lycett Collection, purchased 1867
GSM 25101

Bredyia subinsignis (Oppel)
Senior 1977, p. 683.
Inferior Oolite, *opalinum* Zone,*scissum* Subzone.
Duston, Northamptonshire.
W. H. Hudleston Collection, presented by C. A. Raisin 1920.
Y 3345-3347

Bredyia subinsignis (Oppel)
Senior 1977, p. 683.
Inferior Oolite, Pea Grit, *opalinum* Zone, *scissum* Subzone.
Leckhampton, Gloucestershire.
W. H. Hudleston Collection, presented by C. A. Raisin 1920.
Y 3444

Bredyia subinsignis (Oppel)
Senior 1977, plate 84, figs. 7, 8, p. 683.
Inferior Oolite, *opalinum* Zone, *scissum* Subzone.
South Petherton, Somerset.
J. G. Lowe Collection, presented 1862.
GSM 69945
[misquoted as from Sherborne, S. S. Buckman (J. Buckman) Collection.]

Bredyia subinsignis (Oppel)
Senior 1977, p. 683.
Inferior Oolite, *opalinum* Zone, *scissum* Subzone.
Oatley (Otley) Hill, Hook Norton, Oxfordshire.
L. Richardson Collection, presented 1925.
Z 3881

Bredyia subinsignis (Oppel)
Senior 1977, p. 683.
Inferior Oolite, *opalinum* Zone, *scissum* Subzone.
Gayton Ironstone Pit, Northamptonshire.
Survey Collection (J. W. Judd) 1869.
h 389

Ancolioceras cf. **substriatum** S. S. Buckman
Cave 1977, p. 112.
Inferior Oolite, Lower Limestone, *murchisonae* Zone, *opalinoides* Subzone.
Cross Hands, Sodbury, Avon [Gloucestershire].
Geological Society Collection (ex W. Lonsdale), presented 1911.
Geol Soc Coll 4144 [quoted as GSM 114894]

Ludwigia sp.
Cave 1977, p. 112.
Inferior Oolite, Pea Grit, *murchisonae* Zone, *murchisonae* Subzone.
Nailsworth, Gloucestershire.
W. H. Hudleston Collection, presented by Miss C. A. Raisin 1920.
GSM 114895 [formerly Y 3492]

Indeterminate graphoceratid
Cave 1977, p. 112.
Inferior Oolite, Pea Grit, *murchisonae* Zone, *murchisonae* Subzone.
Shipton Moyne No. 5 borehole, Gloucestershire.
Survey Collection.
Ba 3303

Strophogyria cosmia S. S. Buckman
Richardson 1904, p. 232.
Inferior Oolite, Lower Pea Grit, *murchisonae* Zone, *murchisonae* Subzone.
Barns Batch, Leckhampton, Gloucestershire.
S. S. Buckman Collection (ex C. Upton), purchased 1924.
Z 3483.

Pseudographoceras literatum S. S. Buckman
PARATYPE
S. S. Buckman 1904a, p. xci.
S. S. Buckman 1910b, p. 63.
Inferior Oolite, *murchisonae* Zone, *murchisonae* Subzone.
Quarry Hill, Chideock, Dorset.
S. S. Buckman Collection, purchased 1905.
GSM 12552

Crickia reflua S. S. Buckman PARATYPE
S. S. Buckman 1904a, p. lxxiv.
S. S. Buckman 1910b, p. 63.
Inferior Oolite, *murchisonae* Zone, *murchisonae* Subzone.
Quarry Hill, Chideock, Dorset.
S. S. Buckman Collection, purchased 1905.
GSM 12553

Ludwigia gradata S. S. Buckman PARATYPE
S. S. Buckman 1904a, p. lxxi.
Inferior Oolite, *murchisonae* Zone, *murchisonae* Subzone.
Haselbury Plucknett, Somerset.
S. S. Buckman Collection, purchased 1905.
GSM 12562

Grammoceras nannodes S. S. Buckman SYNTYPE
S. S. Buckman 1890, plate 33, figs. 13, 14.
Asthenoceras nannodes (S. S. Buckman) SYNTYPE
S. S. Buckman 1899, p. xlix.
S. S. Buckman 1907, p. 3.
Imlay 1973, pp. 56, 66.
Inferior Oolite, *murchisonae* Zone, *murchisonae* Subzone.
Stoford, Somerset.
S. S. Buckman Collection, purchased 1900.
GSM 6726

Pseudographoceras deletum S. S. Buckman
S. S. Buckman 1904a, p. xcii.
Inferior Oolite, *murchisonae* Zone.
Bradford Abbas, Dorset.
S. S. Buckman Collection, purchased 1906.
GSM 12620

Keeled ammonite
Hudleston 1887, p. 41.
Hammatoceras planinsigne Vacek
S. S. Buckman 1889c, p. 661.
Planammatoceras planiforme S. S. Buckman HOLOTYPE
S. S. Buckman 1922a, plates CCCLVI, CCCLVI*.
Arkell 1957, fig. 308, 2a; p. L267.
Hammatoceras (Planammatoceras) planiforme (S. S. Buckman) HOLOTYPE
Rieber 1963, p. 69.
Hammatoceras planiforme (S. S. Buckman) HOLOTYPE
Géczy 1966, pp. 31, 56-57.
Inferior Oolite, *murchisonae* Zone, *bradfordensis* Subzone.
Haselbury Plucknett, Somerset.
S. S. Buckman Collection (ex T. Wright), purchased 1924.
GSM 47156

Abbasites abbas S. S. Buckman HOLOTYPE
S. S. Buckman 1921, plate CCXXXVI.
Roché 1939, pp. 173, 174.
Erycites (Abbasites) abbas (S. S. Buckman) HOLOTYPE
Arkell 1957, fig. 309, p. L267.
Géczy 1966, p. 116.
Inferior Oolite, Paving Bed, *murchisonae* Zone, *bradfordensis* Subzone.
Bradford Abbas, Dorset.
S. S. Buckman Collection (ex D. S. Darell), purchased 1923.
GSM 32045

Ambersites aegrotus S. S. Buckman HOLOTYPE
S. S. Buckman 1921, plate CCXXXVII.
Roché 1939, p. 174.
Géczy 1966, p. 116.
Inferior Oolite, Ringens Beds, *murchisonae* Zone, *bradfordensis* Subzone.
Ambers Knoll, Sherborne, Dorset.
S. S. Buckman Collection, purchased 1923.
GSM 32046

Brasilina crinalis S. S. Buckman PARATYPE
S. S. Buckman 1904, p. lxxxiv.
Inferior Oolite *murchisonae* Zone, *bradfordensis* Subzone.
Sherborne, Dorset.
S. S. Buckman Collections, purchased 1905.
GSM 12581

Erycites sphaeroconicus S. S. Buckman HOLOTYPE
S. S. Buckman 1922a, plate CCCXV.
Inferior Oolite, *murchisonae* Zone, *bradfordensis* Subzone.
Marston Road Quarry, Sherborne, Dorset.
S. S. Buckman Collection, purchased 1924.
GSM 47130

Erycites partschi Prinz
S. S. Buckman 1921, plate CCXLVI.
Inferior Oolite, *murchisonae* Zone, *bradfordensis* Subzone.
Rockery [? ex Louse Hill], Bradford Abbas, Dorset.
S. S. Buckman Collection, purchased 1923.
GSM 32053

Ludwigella arcuata S. S. Buckman PARATYPE
S. S. Buckman 1904, p. lxxix.
Inferior Oolite, *murchisonae* Zone, *bradfordensis* Subzone.
Stoke Knap, Stoke Abbott, Dorset.
S. S. Buckman Collection, purchased 1905.
GSM 12524

Ludgwigella impolita S. S. Buckman PARATYPE
S. S. Buckman 1904, p. lxxxv.
Inferior Oolite, *murchisonae* Zone, *bradfordensis* Subzone.
Bradford Abbas, Dorset.
S. S. Buckman Collection, purchased 1905.
GSM 12521

Planifastigites platys S. S. Buckman HOLOTYPE
S. S. Buckman 1925 plate DLXXIX.
Inferior Oolite, Ringens Beds, *murchisonae* Zone, *bradfordensis* Subzone.
Ambers Knoll, Sherborne, Dorset.
S. S. Buckman Collection, purchased 1927.
GSM 47764

Parammatoceras obtectum S. S. Buckman HOLOTYPE
S. S. Buckman 1925, plate DLV.
Arkell 1957, fig. 308, 2b, p. L 267.
Imlay 1973, p. 61.
Inferior Oolite, Building Stone, *murchisonae* Zone, *bradfordensis* Subzone.
Quarry on east side of Stoke Knap, Stoke Abbott, Dorset.
S. S. Buckman Collection, purchased 1926.
GSM 47562

Praestrigites praenuntius S. S. Buckman HOLOTYPE
S. S. Buckman 1924, plate CDLXVI.
Arkell 1957, fig. 314, 3a, b, p. L271.
Géczy 1967, pp. 222-224.
Imlay 1973, p. 76.
Inferior Oolite, Ironshot Bed, *murchisonae* or *concavum* Zone.
Horn Park, Beaminster, Dorset.
S. S. Buckman Collection (ex D. S. Darell), purchased 1925.
GSM 37314

Dumortieria grammoceroides Haug
S. S. Buckman 1891, plate 46, figs. 4, 5.
Fontannesia luculenta S. S. Buckman HOLOTYPE
S. S. Buckman 1905a, p. clxxxix.
S. S. Buckman 1907, p. 4.
Imlay 1973, pp. 57, 58.
Inferior Oolite, *concavum* Zone.
Bradford Abbas, Dorset.
S. S. Buckman Collection, purchased 1900.
GSM 6723

Dumortieria grammoceroides Haug
S. S. Buckman 1891, plate 47, figs. 10, 12.
Fontannesia luculenta S. S. Buckman PARATYPE
S. S. Buckman 1905a, p. clxxxix.
S. S. Buckman 1907, p. 4.
Inferior Oolite, *concavum* Zone.
Bradford Abbas, Dorset.
S. S. Buckman Collection, purchased 1900.
GSM 6724

Ludwigella casta S. S. Buckman PARATYPES
S. S. Buckman 1904, p. lxxxix.
Inferior Oolite, Building Stone, *concavum* Zone.
Stoke Knap, Stoke Abbott, Dorset.
S. S. Buckman Collection, purchased 1905.
GSM 12522, 12523

Ludwigella micra S. S. Buckman PARATYPE
S. S. Buckman 1904, p. lxxxix.
Inferior Oolite, Fossil Bed, *concavum* Zone.
Bradford Abbas, Dorset.
S. S. Buckman Collection, purchased 1905.
GSM 12519

Graphoceras (Graphoceras) concavum (J. Sowerby)
Contini 1969, p. 61.
Inferior Oolite, *concavum* Zone.
Bradford Abbas, Dorset.
W. H. Hudleston Collection, presented by Miss C. A. Raisin 1920.
Y 3013

Graphoceras stigmosum S. S. Buckman PARATYPE
S. S. Buckman 1904, p. xcvii.
Inferior Oolite, *concavum* Zone.
Sandford Lane, Sherborne, Dorset.
S. S. Buckman Collection, purchased 1905.
GSM 12557

Graphoceras scriptitatum S. S. Buckman HOLOTYPE
S. S. Buckman 1923, plate, CCCLXXXVIII.
Inferior Oolite, middle part of Bradford Abbas Fossil Bed, *concavum* Zone.
Bradford Abbas, Dorset.
S. S. Buckman Collection, purchased 1924.
GSM 47181

Graphoceras undulatum S. S. Buckman PARATYPE
S. S. Buckman 1904, p. xcvii.
Inferior Oolite, Bradford Abbas Fossil Bed, *concavum* Zone.
Bradford Abbas, Dorset.
S. S. Buckman Collection, purchased 1905.
GSM 12558

Graphoceras v-scriptum S. S. Buckman
S. S. Buckman 1904, p. xcvi.
Inferior Oolite, *concavum* Zone.
Beaminster, Dorset.
S. S. Buckman Collection, purchased 1905.
GSM 12556

Graphoceras vibrata S. S. Buckman ?PARATYPE
S. S. Buckman 1904, p. lxxxviii.
Inferior Oolite, *concavum* Zone.
Bradford Abbas, Dorset.
S. S. Buckman Collection, purchased 1905.
GSM 12525

Depaoceras hamatum S. S. Buckman PARATYPE
S. S. Buckman 1904, p. lxxix.
Inferior Oolite, *concavum* Zone.
Halfway House, Nether Compton, Dorset.
S. S. Buckman Collection, purchased 1905.
GSM 12554

Docidoceras planulatum S. S. Buckman PARATYPE
S. S. Buckman 1921, plate CCLXIV, fig. 3.
Inferior Oolite, Bradford Abbas Fossil Bed, *discites* Zone.
Bradford Abbas, Dorset.
S. S. Buckman Collection, purchased 1923.
GSM 32063

Docidoceras planulatum S. S. Buckman HOLOTYPE
S. S. Buckman 1921, plate CCLXIV, figs. 1-2.
Imlay 1973, p. 79.
Inferior Oolite, middle part of Bradford Abbas Fossil Bed, *discites* Zone.
Bradford Abbas, Dorset.
S. S. Buckman Collection (ex J. Euckman Collection), purchased 1923.
GSM 32062

Docidoceras cylindroides S. S. Buckman PARATYPE
S. S. Buckman 1921, plate CXXXIII B.
Inferior Oolite, middle part of Bradford Abbas Fossil Bed, *discites* Zone.
Bradford Abbas, Dorset.
S. S. Buckman Collection, purchased 1923.
GSM 32059

Deltostrigites deltotus S. S. Buckman HOLOTYPE
S. S. Buckman 1924, plate CDLXVII.
Praestrigites deltotus (S. S. Buckman) HOLOTYPE
Imlay 1973, pp. 75, 76.
Inferior Oolite, Bradford Abbas Fossil Bed, *discites* Zone.
Bradford Abbas, Dorset.
S. S. Buckman Collection, purchased 1926.
GSM 37315

Hammatoceras amaltheiforme (Vacek)
S. S. Buckman 1889c, p. 661.
Euaptetoceras euaptetum S. S. Buckman HOLOTYPE
S. S. Buckman 1922a, plate CCXCIX.
Eudmetoceras euaptetum (S. S. Buckman) HOLOTYPE
Arkell 1957, fig. 308, 1c, p. L267.
Euaptetoceras euaptetum S. S. Buckman HOLOTYPE
Bayer 1969, pp. 214-215.
Westermann 1969, pp. 66-68, 70–71.
Inferior Oolite, *concavum* or *discites* Zone.
Bradford Abbas, Dorset.
S. S. Buckman Collection, purchased 1924.
GSM 47119

Eudmetoceras eudmetum S. S. Buckman HOLOTYPE
S. S. Buckman 1920, plate CLXXIX.
Arkell 1957, fig. 308, 1a, b, p. L267.
Inferior Oolite, middle part of Bradford Abbas Fossil Bed, *discites* Zone.
Bradford Abbas, Dorset.
S. S. Buckman Collection, purchased 1923.
GSM 32025

Hammatoceras sp.
S. S. Buckman 1920, cited in explanation of plate CLXXIX.
Eudmetoceras eudmetum S. S. Buckman PARATYPE
S. S. Buckman 1925, plate CLXXIX A.
Inferior Oolite, middle part of Bradford Abbas Fossil Bed, *discites* Zone.
Bradford Abbas, Dorset.
S. S. Buckman Collection (ex J. Buckman Collection), purchased 1926.
GSM 47525

Euaptetoceras infernense (Roman)
S. S. Buckman 1923, plate CCCXCVI A.
Inferior Oolite, middle part of Bradford Abbas Fossil Bed, *discites* Zone.
Railway cutting, Bradford Abbas, Dorset.
S. S. Buckman Collection, purchased 1924.
GSM 47184

Darellia concinna S. S. Buckman HOLOTYPE
S. S. Buckman 1904, p. cxiv.
Inferior Oolite, *discites* Zone.
Dundry, Avon [Somerset].
S. S. Buckman Collection, purchased 1905.
GSM 12549

Hammatoceras climacomphalum (Vacek)
S. S. Buckman 1889c, pp. 660-661.
Euaptetoceras infernense (Roman).
S. S. Buckman 1924, plate CCCXCVI B.
Inferior Oolite, middle part of Bradford Abbas Fossil Bed, *discites* Zone.
Railway cutting, Bradford Abbas, Dorset.
S. S. Buckman Collection, purchased 1925.
GSM 47530

Eudmetoceras prosphues S. S. Buckman HOLOTYPE
S. S. Buckman 1923, plate CCXCVII.
Inferior Oolite, middle part of Bradford Abbas Fossil Bed, *discites* Zones.
Bradford Abbas, Dorset.
S. S. Buckman Collection, purchased 1924.
GSM 47185

Eudmetoceras amplectens S. S. Buckman PARATYPE
S. S. Buckman 1920, plate CLXXX B, fig. 2.
Inferior Oolite, Bradford Abbas Fossil Bed, *discites* Zone.
Bradford Abbas, Dorset.
S. S. Buckman Collection (ex J. Buckman Collection), purchased 1923.
GSM 32026

Hyperlioceras aff. **rudidiscites** S. S. Buckman
Kent and Barker 1938, p. 169.
Hyperlioceras cf. **rudidiscites** S. S. Buckman
Parsons 1976, p. 52.
Lincolnshire Limestone, *discites* Zone.
Quarry near the "Bowling Green", Wragby Road, Greetham, Lincoln.
P. E. Kent Collection, presented 1947.
Zk 772

Hyperlioceras incisum S. S. Buckman PARATYPE
S. S. Buckman 1904, p. cxxvi.
Inferior Oolite, *discites* Zone.
Burton Bradstock, Dorset.
S. S. Buckman Collection (?ex D. S. Darell), purchased 1905.
GSM 12559

Hyperlioceras discitiforme S. S. Buckman PARATYPE
S. S. Buckman 1904, p. cxxiv.
Inferior Oolite, *discites* Zone.
Burton Bradstock, Dorset.
S. S. Buckman Collection (ex D. S. Darell), purchased 1905.
GSM 12575

Hyperlioceras deflexum S. S. Buckman PARATYPE
S. S. Buckman 1904, p. cxxii.
Inferior Oolite, Bradford Abbas Fossil Bed, *discites* Zone.
Bradford Abbas, Dorset.
S. S. Buckman Collection (?ex D. S. Darell), purchased 1905.
GSM 12571

Hyperlioceras discites (Waagen)
S. S. Buckman 1893, p. 493.
Inferior Oolite, *discites* Zone.
Sandford Lane, Sherborne, Dorset.
S. S. Buckman Collection, purchased 1906.
GSM 16295

Nannoceras nannomorphum S. S. Buckman HOLOTYPE
S. S. Buckman 1923, plate CDXLV.
Inferior Oolite, Bradford Abbas, Fossil Bed, *discites* Zone.
Bradford Abbas Dorset.
S. S. Buckman Collection, purchased 1925.
GSM 37299

Hyperlioceras rudidiscites S. S. Buckman
Senior and Earland-Bennet 1973, fig. 3, pp. 323-324.
Cave Oolite, *discites* Zone.
Eastfield quarry, South Cave, Humberside [Yorkshire].
D. Ward Collection, presented 1968.
GSM 112733

Deltoidoceras subdiscoideum S. S. Buckman
Kent and Barker 1938, p. 169.
Hyperlioceras cf. **subdiscoideum** (S. S. Buckman)
Parsons 1976, p. 52.
Lincolnshire Limestone, *discites* Zone.
Quarry near the "Bowling Green", Wragby Road, Greetham, Lincoln.
P. E. Kent Collection, presented 1947.
Zk 770

Deltotoceras subsectum S. S. Buckman
Kent and Barker 1938, p. 169.
Hyperlioceras subsectum (S. S. Buckman)
Parsons 1976, p. 52.
Lincolnshire Limestone, *discites* Zone.
Quarry near the "Bowling Green", Wragby Road, Greetham, Lincoln.
P. E. Kent Collection, presented 1947.
Zk 773

Kleistoxyites protrusus S. S. Buckman HOLOTYPE
S. S. Buckman 1922a, plate CCCXVII.
Inferior Oolite, *discites* Zone.
Bradford Abbas, Dorset.
S. S. Buckman Collection, purchased 1924.
GSM 47132

Braunsina? angulifera S. S. Buckman PARATYPE
S. S. Buckman 1904, p. ci.
Inferior Oolite, Fossil Bed, *discites* Zone.
Bradford Abbas, Dorset.
S. S. Buckman Collection, purchased 1905.
GSM 12532

Braunsina elegantula S. S. Buckman PARATYPE
S. S. Buckman 1904, p.c.
Inferior Oolite, *discites* Zone.
Bradford Abbas, Dorset.
S. S. Buckman Collection, purchased 1905.
GSM 12530

Graphoceras mirabile S. S. Buckman PARATYPE
S. S. Buckman 1904, p. xcvii.
Inferior Oolite, *discites* Zone.
Dundry, Avon [Somerset].
S. S. Buckman Collection (ex E. Wilson), purchased 1912.
GSM 27626

Lioceras concavum (J. Sowerby)
S. S. Buckman 1893b, p. 500.
Graphoceras? inclusum S. S. Buckman PARATYPE
S. S. Buckman 1904, p. xcviii.
Inferior Oolite, *discites* Zone.
Frogden Quarry, Oborne, Dorset.
S. S. Buckman Collection, purchased 1905.
GSM 27625

Docidoceras cylindroides S. S. Buckman HOLOTYPE
S. S. Buckman, 1919, plate CXXXIII A.
Arkell 1957, fig. 341, 4, p. L287.
Inferior Oolite, upper part of Bradford Abbas Fossil Bed, *discites* Zone.
Bradford Abbas, Dorset.
S. S. Buckman Collection (ex D. S. Darell), purchased 1923.
GSM 32000

Docidoceras biforme S. S. Buckman HOLOTYPE
S. S. Buckman 1922a, plate CCLXXVI.
Inferior Oolite, Blue Beds, *discites* Zone.
Halfway House, Compton, Sherborne, Dorset.
S. S. Buckman Collection (ex T. Wright Collection), purchased 1924.
GSM 47110

Docidoceras perfectum S. S. Buckman HOLOTYPE
S. S. Buckman 1922a, plate CCCXIV.
Inferior Oolite, *discites* Zone.
Louse Hill, Nether Compton, Sherborne, Dorset.
S. S. Buckman Collection, purchased 1924.
GSM 47129

Sonninia crassibullata S. S. Buckman PARATYPE
S. S. Buckman 1893a, plate 80, fig. 3.
Inferior Oolite, *discites* Zone.
Bradford Abbas, Dorset.
S. S. Buckman Collection, purchased 1905.
GSM 12597

Sonninia camura S. S. Buckman
S. S. Buckman 1893b, plate 99, fig. 6.
Inferior Oolite, *discites* Zone.
Bradford Abbas, Dorset.
S. S. Buckman Collection, purchased 1905.
GSM 12594

Euhoploceras sp. (group of **regularis-costigera**)
Kent and Barker 1938, pp. 169, 170.
Lincolnshire Limestone.
Barnstone Cement Co. Quarry, Waltham station, Leicestershire.
P. E. Kent Collection, presented 1947.
Zk 774

Sonninia (Euhoploceras) acanthodes S. S. Buckman
Barker and Torrens 1971.
Inferior Oolite, Lincolnshire Limestone, *discites* Zone.
Botany Pit, Geddington, Northamptonshire.
H. S. Torrens Collection, presented 1971.
Zr 7339

Sonninia densicostata S. S. Buckman
S. S. Buckman 1893a, plate 88, figs. 8, 9a, p. 375.
Inferior Oolite, *discites* Zone.
Stoke Knap, near Beaminster, Dorset.
Museum Collection.
GSM 25122

Sonninia cf. **dominans** S. S. Buckman
S. S. Buckman 1894, plate 97, fig. 6, p. 440.
Inferior Oolite, *discites* Zone.
Bradford Abbas, Dorset.
S. S. Buckman Collection, purchased 1905.
GSM 12600

Sonninia locuples S. S. Buckman PARATYPE
S. S. Buckman 1893a, plate 93, fig. 4.
Inferior Oolite, *discites* Zone.
Bradford Abbas, Dorset.
S. S. Buckman Collection, purchased 1905.
GSM 12598

Sonninia gibbera S. S. Buckman PARATYPE
S. S. Buckman 1893a, plate 88, figs. 2, 3.
Inferior Oolite, *discites* Zone.
Bradford Abbas, Dorset.
S. S. Buckman Collection, purchased 1905.
GSM 12589

Sonninia gibbera S. S. Buckman PARATYPE
S. S. Buckman 1893a, plate 88, fig. 1.
Inferior Oolite, *discites* Zone.
Bradford Abbas, Dorset.
S. S. Buckman Collection, purchased 1905.
GSM 12588

Sonninia parvicostata S. S. Buckman PARATYPE
S. S. Buckman 1892, plate 75, fig. 5, p. 339.
Inferior Oolite, *discites* Zone.
Bradford Abbas, Dorset.
S. S. Buckman Collection, purchased 1905.
GSM 12592

Sonninia spinosa S. S. Buckman PARATYPE
S. S. Buckman 1894, plate 103, fig. 23, p. 365.
Inferior Oolite, *discites* Zone.
Bradford Abbas, Dorset.
S. S. Buckman Collection, purchased 1905.
GSM 12601

Sonninia substriata S. S. Buckman PARATYPE
S. S. Buckman 1892, plate 71, fig. 8.
Inferior Oolite, *discites* Zone.
Bradford Abbas, Dorset.
S. S. Buckman Collection, purchased 1905.
GSM 12599

Sonninia substriata S. S. Buckman PARATYPE
S. S. Buckman 1894, plate 103, fig. 12.
Inferior Oolite, Building Stone, *discites* Zone.
Stoke Knap, Stoke Abbott, Beaminster, Dorset.
S. S. Buckman Collection, purchased 1905.
GSM 12591

Sonninia simplex S. S. Buckman PARATYPE
S. S. Buckman 1892, plate 70, fig. 4.
Inferior Oolite, *discites* Zone.
Bradford Abbas, Dorset.
S. S. Buckman Collection, purchased 1905.
GSM 12593

Sonninia subdecorata S. S. Buckman PARATYPE
S. S. Buckman 1893, plate 84, fig. 11.
Inferior Oolite, *discites* Zone.
Bradford Abbas, Dorset.
S. S. Buckman Collection, purchased 1905.
GSM 12590

Stokeia subacuta S. S. Buckman PARATYPE
S. S. Buckman 1904, p. cxxviii.
Inferior Oolite, *discites* Zone.
Dundry, Avon [Somerset].
S. S. Buckman Collection, purchased 1905.
GSM 12587

Trilobiticeras trilobitoides S. S. Buckman HOLOTYPE
S. S. Buckman 1919, plate CXL.
Trilobiticeras triloboides [sic] S. S. Buckman HOLOTYPE
Roman 1938, p. 200.
Trilobiticeras trilobitoides S. S. Buckman
Arkell 1957, fig.339, 1, p. L287.
Inferior Oolite, upper part of Bradford Abbas Fossil Bed, *discites* Zone.
Bradford Abbas, Dorset.
S. S. Buckman Collection, purchased 1923.
GSM 32004

Trilobiticeras platygaster S. S. Buckman HOLOTYPE
S. S. Buckman 1922a, plate CCLXXVII A, figs. 1-3.
Westermann 1954, pp. 122-123.
Inferior Oolite, middle of Bradford Abbas Fossil Bed, *discites* Zone.
Bradford Abbas, Dorset.
S. S. Buckman Collection, purchased 1924.
GSM 47111

Trilobiticeras platygaster S. S. Buckman PARATYPE
S. S. Buckman 1922a, plate CCLXXVII B, figs. 1-3.
Inferior Oolite, middle of Bradford Abbas Fossil Bed, *discites* Zone.
Bradford Abbas, Dorset.
S. S. Buckman Collection, purchased 1924.
GSM 47112

Witchellia sp.
S. S. Buckman 1893b, p. 499.
Zugella connata S. S. Buckman HOLOTYPE
S. S. Buckman 1927, plate DCCL.
S. S. Buckman 1928, pp. 12, 13.
Witchellia connata (S. S. Buckman) HOLOTYPE
Imlay 1973, pp. 69, 70.
Inferior Oolite, *discites* Zone.
Clatcombe Farm (Upper Clatcombe), Sherborne, Dorset.
S. S. Buckman Collection purchased 1929.
GSM 49329

Ammonites corrugatus J. de C. Sowerby
?J. Buckman 1844, pp. 28, 80 (*fide* S. S. Buckman)
Zugophorites zugophorus S. S. Buckman HOLOTYPE
S. S. Buckman 1922a, plate CCCXLI, figs. 1, 2.
Imlay 1973, p. 70.
Inferior Oolite, Gryphite Grit, *laeviuscula* Zone.
Leckhampton Hill, Cheltenham, Gloucestershire.
S. S. Buckman Collection (ex J. Buckman), purchased 1924.
GSM 47145

Lissoceras semicostulatum S. S. Buckman HOLOTYPE
S. S. Buckman 1923, plate CD.
Sapunov 1963b, pp. 152, 162.
Imlay 1973, p. 77.
Inferior Oolite, middle part of Sandford Fossil Bed, *laeviuscula* Zone.
Sandford Lane, near Sherborne, Dorset.
S. S. Buckman Collection (ex D. S. Darell), purchased 1924.
GSM 47188

Dundryites pavimentarius S. S. Buckman HOLOTYPE
S. S. Buckman 1927, plate DCCLI.
S. S. Buckman 1928, p. 12.
Inferior Oolite, *laeviuscula* Zone.
Leckhampton Hill, Cheltenham, Gloucestershire.
S. S. Buckman Collection, purchased 1929.
GSM 49330

Dundryites albidus S. S. Buckman HOLOTYPE
S. S. Buckman 1927, plate DCLXXXVII.
S. S. Buckman 1928, p. 12.
Inferior Oolite, Lower White Ironshot, *laeviuscula* Zone.
Dundry, Avon [Somerset].
S. S. Buckman Collection (ex E. Wilson), purchased 1928.
GSM 49283

Sonninia arenata (Quenstedt)
S. S. Buckman 1893, p. 494.
Fissilobiceras phlyctaenoides S. S. Buckman HOLOTYPE
S. S. Buckman 1923, plate CCCLXXXVII, figs. 1, 2.
Inferior Oolite, lower part of Sandford Fossil Bed, *laeviuscula* Zone.
Sandford Lane, Sherborne, Dorset.
S. S. Buckman Collection (ex D. S. Darell), purchased 1924.
GSM 47180

Harpoceras fissilobatum Waagen
S. S. Buckman 1881, p. 603.
Sonninia
S. S. Buckman 1893, p. 494.
Fissilobiceras fissilobatum (Waagen)
S. S. Buckman 1919, p. xv.
S. S. Buckman 1920, plates CLXXXI A, B.
Euhoploceras (Fissilobiceras) fissilobatum (Waagen)
Morton 1975, p. 53.
Inferior Oolite, lower part of Sandford Fossil Bed, *laeviuscula* Zone.
Sandford Lane, Sherborne, Dorset.
S. S. Buckman Collection (ex J. Buckman), purchased 1923.
GSM 32027

Hebetoxyites clypeus S. S. Buckman PARATYPE
S. S. Buckman 1924, plate CDXCVI B.
Imlay 1973, p. 77.
Inferior Oolite, middle part of Sandford Fossil Bed, *laeviuscula* Zone.
Sandford Lane, Sherborne, Dorset.
S. S. Buckman Collection, purchased 1926.
GSM 47538

Ammonites discus J. Sowerby
J. Buckman 1876, p.7.
Hebetoxyites clypeus S. S. Buckman HOLOTYPE
S. S. Buckman 1924, plate CDXCVI A
Inferior Oolite, middle part of Sandford Fossil Bed, *laeviuscula* Zone.
Sandford Lane, Sherborne, Dorset.
S. S. Buckman Collection (ex D. S. Darell), purchased 1926.
GSM 47537

Hebetoxyites incongruens S. S. Buckman HOLOTYPE
S. S. Buckman 1924, plate CDXCVII.
Inferior Oolite, Sandford Fossil Bed, *laeviuscula* Zone.
Sandford Lane, Sherborne, Dorset.
S. S. Buckman Collection, purchased 1926.
GSM 47539

Ammonites truelli compressus J. Sowerby
S. S. Buckman 1896b, p. 701.
Hebetoxyites hebes S. S. Buckman HOLOTYPE
S. S. Buckman 1924, plate CDLXXV.
Arkell 1957, fig. 314, 2, p. L272.
Imlay 1973, p. 77.
Inferior Oolite, Lower White Ironshot, *laeviuscula* Zone.
Dundry, Avon [Somerset]
S. S. Buckman Collection, purchased 1925.
GSM 37323

Hebetoxyites macilentus S. S. Buckman HOLOTYPE
S. S. Buckman 1924, plate CDXCVIII.
Inferior Oolite, *laeviuscula* or *sauzei* Zone.
Stoford, Somerset.
S. S. Buckman Collection, purchased 1926.
GSM 47540

Witchellia aff. **sutneri** (Branco)
S. S. Buckman 1893b, pp. 492-494.
Gelasinites gelasinus S. S. Buckman HOLOTYPE
S. S. Buckman 1925, plates DXCIII A, B.
Inferior Oolite, lower part of Sandford Fossil Bed, *laeviuscula* Zone.
Sandford Lane Quarrry, Sherborne, Dorset.
S. S. Buckman Collection, purchased 1927.
GSM 47776

Macerites aurifer S. S. Buckman HOLOTYPE
S. S. Buckman 1928, plates DCCLXVI, p. 11.
Inferior Oolite, Upper White Ironshot, *laeviuscula* Zone.
Dundry, Avon [Somerset].
S. S. Buckman Collection, purchased 1929.
GSM 49341

Mollistephanus mollis S. S. Buckman HOLOTYPE
S. S. Buckman 1922a, plate CCCXLIV.
Roché 1939, p. 174.
Inferior Oolite, *laeviuscula* Zone.
Coombe (Clatcombe), Sherborne, Dorset.
S. S. Buckman Collection (ex T. C. Maggs), purchased 1924.
GSM 47148

Ammonites humphriesianus J. de C. Sowerby
Woodward 1894, p. 111.
Emileites malenotatus S. S. Buckman HOLOTYPE
S. S. Buckman 1927, plate DCCII, pp. 46-48.
Trilobiticeras (Emileites) malenotatus (S. S. Buckman) HOLOTYPE
Parsons 1977, p. 110.
Inferior Oolite, Lower White Ironshot, *laeviuscula* Zone.
Dundry, Avon [Somerset]. [Buckman's corrected locality; Tate gave the locality as being 'Rodborough, near Stroud, Gloucestershire' and was followed in this by Woodward.]
S. S. Buckman Collection (ex R. Tate per H. B. Woodward), purchased 1928.
GSM 49293

Sonninia zurcheri Douvillé
S. S. Buckman & Wilson 1896, p. 692.
Pelekodites pelekus S. S. Buckman HOLOTYPE
S. S. Buckman 1923, plate CCCXCIX.
S. S. Buckman 1928, p. 12.
Arkell 1957, fig. 311, 4, p. L270.
Westermann 1969, p. 115.
Inferior Oolite, White Ironshot, *laeviuscula* Zone.
Rackledown, Dundry, Avon [Somerset].
S. S. Buckman Collection (ex J. W. D. Marshall), purchased 1924.
GSM 47187

Spatulites spatians S. S. Buckman HOLOTYPE
S. S. Buckman 1928, plate DCCLXV, p. 12.
Pelekodites (Spatulites) spatians (S. S. Buckman) HOLOTYPE
Westermann 1969, p. 128.
Inferior Oolite, *laeviuscula* Zone.
Dundry, Avon [Somerset].
S. S. Buckman Collection, purchased 1929.
GSM 49340

Witchellia laeviuscula (J. de C. Sowerby)
S. S. Buckman 1927, plate DCCXLV.
Inferior Oolite, *laeviuscula* Zone.
Frogden Quarry, Oborne, Dorset.
S. S. Buckman Collection, purchased 1929.
GSM 49324

Ammonites laeviusculus J. de C. Sowerby
J. Buckman, 1844, pp. 27, 90.
Witchellia sp.
S. S. Buckman 1895, pp. 411, 418-419.
Witchellia patefactor S. S. Buckman HOLOTYPE
S. S. Buckman 1923, plate CDX.
Inferior Oolite, Perna Bed, *laeviuscula* Zone and Subzone.
Cold Comfort, Cheltenham, Gloucestershire.
S. S. Buckman Collection (ex J. Buckman), purchased 1924.
GSM 47195

Witchellia sp.
S. S. Buckman 1889b, p. 658.
Witchellia glauca S. S. Buckman HOLOTYPE
S. S. Buckman 1925, plate DXCIV.
Inferior Oolite, *laeviuscula* Zone and Subzone.
Frogden Quarry, Oborne, Dorset.
S. S. Buckman Collection, purchased 1927.
GSM 47777

Witchellia falcata S. S. Buckman HOLOTYPE
S. S. Buckman 1926, plate DCLXXXVIII.
Inferior Oolite, *laeviuscula* Zone and Subzone.
Frogden Quarry, Oborne, Dorset.
S. S. Buckman Collection, purchased 1928.
GSM 49284

Witchellia actinophora S. S. Buckman HOLOTYPE
S. S. Buckman 1926, plate DCLXXXIX.
Inferior Oolite, *laeviuscula* Zone and Subzone.
Frogden Quarry, Oborne, Dorset.
S. S. Buckman Collection, purchased 1928.
GSM 49285

Witchellia platymorpha S. S. Buckman PARATYPE
S. S. Buckman 1926, plate DLXXX C.
Inferior Oolite, *laeviuscula* Zone and Subzone.
Frogden Quarry, Oborne, Dorset.
S. S. Buckman Collection, purchased 1928.
GSM 49278

Rubrileiites ruber S. S. Buckman HOLOTYPE
S. S. Buckman 1926, plate DCXLII
Witchellia rubra (S. S. Buckman) HOLOTYPE
Morton 1975, pp. 59-61.
Inferior Oolite, *laeviuscula* Zone and Subzone.
Frogden Quarry, Oborne, Dorset.
S. S. Buckman Collection, purchased 1927.
GSM 47839

Stiphromorphites nodatipinguis S. S. Buckman HOLOTYPE
S. S. Buckman 1923, plate CCCXCVIII.
Sonninia nodatipinguis (S. S. Buckman) HOLOTYPE
Imlay 1973, p. 62.
Inferior Oolite, *laeviuscula* Zone.
Clatcombe, Sherborne, Dorset.
S. S. Buckman Collection (ex D. S. Darell), purchased 1924.
GSM 47186

Emileia catamorpha S. S. Buckman HOLOTYPE
S. S. Buckman 1923, plate CDXIV.
S. S. Buckman 1927, p. 47.
Roman 1938, p. 199.
Inferior Oolite, lower part of Sandford Fossil Bed, *laeviuscula* Zone and Subzone.
Sandford Lane, Sherborne, Dorset.
S. S. Buckman Collection (ex D. S. Darell), purchased 1924.
GSM 47199

Emileia brocchi (J. Sowerby)
Arkell and Playford 1954, text-fig. 13 right.
Inferior Oolite, *laeviuscula* Zone.
Milborne Wick, Somerset.
S. S. Buckman Collection, purchased 1910.
GSM 24743

Emileia subcadonica S. S. Buckman HOLOTYPE
S. S. Buckman 1927, plate DCCXI.
Emileia (Emileia) subcadonica S. S. Buckman HOLOTYPE
Parsons 1977, p. 105.
Inferior Oolite, *laeviuscula* Zone, *ovalis* Subzone.
Dundry, Avon [Somerset].
S. S. Buckman Collection, purchased 1929.
GSM 49304

Emileia (Otoites) douvillei Parsons PARATYPE
Parsons 1977, text-fig. 1, pp. 103, 104.
Inferior Oolite, *laeviuscula* Zone, *ovalis* Subzone.
Dundry, Avon [Somerset].
Museum Collection.
GSM 25189

Emileia multifida S. S. Buckman HOLOTYPE
S. S. Buckman 1927, plate DCCXXXIII.
Imlay 1973, pp. 80, 81.
Inferior Oolite, upper part of Sandford Fossil Bed, *laeviuscula* Zone and Subzone.
Sandford Lane, Sherborne, Dorset.
S. S. Buckman Collection, ex D. S. Darell, purchased 1929.
GSM 49320

Emileia contrahens S. S. Buckman HOLOTYPE
S. S. Buckman 1927, plates DCCXLIV A, B.
Inferior Oolite, lower middle part of Sandford Fossil Bed, *laeviuscula* Zone and Subzone.
Sandford Lane Quarry, Sherborne, Dorset.
S. S. Buckman Collection, ex J. Buckman, purchased 1929.
GSM 49323

Cadomoceras sp.
S. S. Buckman and Wilson 1896, p. 698.
Cadomoceras carinatum S. S. Buckman HOLOTYPE
S. S. Buckman 1923, plate CDLVI.
Inferior Oolite, Ironshot Bed, *sauzei* Zone.
Dundry, Avon [Somerset].
S. S. Buckman Collection, purchased 1924.
GSM 37306

Cadomoceras sp.
S. S. Buckman and Wilson 1896, p. 698.
Cadomoceras ellipticum S. S. Buckman PARATYPE
S. S. Buckman 1923, plate CDLV, fig. 3.
Inferior Oolite, *sauzei* Zone.
Dundry, Avon [Somerset].
S. S. Buckman Collection, purchased 1925.
GSM 37305

Cadomoceras costellatum S. S. Buckman HOLOTYPE
S. S. Buckman 1923, plate CDLVII
Inferior Oolite, Sandford Fossil Bed, middle *brocchii* Bed, *laeviuscula* Zone.
Sandford Lane, Sherborne, Dorset.
S. S. Buckman Collection, purchased 1925.
GSM 37307

Toxamblyites arcifer S. S. Buckman HOLOTYPE
S. S. Buckman 1924, plate CDLXXIII figs. 1-3.
Arkell 1957, fig. 315, 8 a,b; p. L273
Toxalambites [sic] **arcifer** S. S. Buckman HOLOTYPE
Sturani 1971, p. 94
Inferior Oolite, Ironshot Bed, *sauzei* Zone.
Dundry, Avon [Somerset].
S. S. Buckman Collection, ex T. Wright, purchased 1925.
GSM 37321

Sonninia mesacanthus Waagen
S. S. Buckman 1893b, p. 485
Papilliceras mesacanthum (Waagen)
S. S. Buckman 1925, plates DLVII A, B.
Inferior Oolite, Irony Bed, *sauzei* Zone.
East Hill Quarry, Bradford Abbas, Dorset.
S. S. Buckman Collection, ex D. S. Darrell, purchased 1926.
GSM 47564

Witchellia laeviuscula mutation
S. S. Buckman 1889b, p. 558
Anolkoleiites plenus S. S. Buckman HOLOTYPE
S. S. Buckman 1926, plate DCLIX
Inferior Oolite, ?*sauzei* Zone
Frogden Quarry, Oborne, Dorset.
S. S. Buckman Collection, purchased 1927
GSM 47849

Oppelia praeradiata
S. S. Buckman 1893, p. 484
Amblyoxyites amblys S. S. Buckman HOLOTYPE
S. S. Buckman 1822a, plate CCCIII, figs. 1,2.
Bradfordia amblys (S. S. Buckman) HOLOTYPE
Arkell 1957, fig. 318, 1c; p. L275
Inferior Oolite, *sauzei* Zone.
Stoford, Somerset.
S. S. Buckman Collection, purchased 1924.
GSM 47121

Frogdenites spiniger S. S. Buckman HOLOTYPE
S. S. Buckman 1921, plate CCXV; p. 42
Arkell 1957, fig. 341, 2a, b, p. L287
Inferior Oolite, *sauzei* Zone
Frogden Quarry, Oborne, Dorset
S. S. Buckman Collection, ex D. S. Darell Collection, purchased 1923.
GSM 32039

Hyalinites hyalinus S. S. Buckman HOLOTYPE
S. S. Buckman 1924 plate DXIX, figs. 1, 2.
Inferior Oolite, upper part of Sandford Fossil Bed, *sauzei* Zone.
Sandford Lane, Sherborne, Dorset.
S. S. Buckman Collection, ex. T. C. Maggs Collection, purchased 1926.
GSM 47548

Kallistephanus kalus S. S. Buckman HOLOTYPE
S. S. Buckman 1921, plate CCXXX, figs. 1, 2.
Inferior Oolite, upper part of Sandford Fossil Bed, *sauzei* Zone.
Sandford Lane, Sherborne, Dorset.
S. S. Buckman Collection, ex D. S. Darell Collection, purchased 1923.
GSM 32043

Kumatostephanus perjucundus
S. S. Buckman HOLOTYPE
S. S. Buckman 1927, plates DCCXII A, B.
Roché 1939, pp. 174-175
Inferior Oolite, *sauzei* Zone.
Milborne Wick, Somerset.
S. S. Buckman Collection, purchased 1929.
GSM 49305

Kumatostephanus kumaterus
S. S. Buckman HOLOTYPE
S. S. Buckman 1922a, plates CCCXLV A, B.
Roché 1939, p. 175.
Arkell 1957, fig. 342, 2, p. L290.
Inferior Oolite, *sauzei* Zone.
Sandford Lane, Sherborne, Dorset.
S. S. Buckman Collection, purchased 1924.
GSM 47149

Labyrinthoceras gibberulum S. S. Buckman HOLOTYPE
S. S. Buckman 1922a, plate CCLXXVIII, figs. 1, 2.
Inferior Oolite, base of Ironshot Bed, *sauzei* Zone.
Dundry, Avon [Somerset].
S. S. Buckman Collection, purchased 1924.
GSM 47113

Labyrinthoceras extensum S. S. Buckman HOLOTYPE
S. S. Buckman 1921, plate CCXIV, figs. 1, 2.
Inferior Oolite, *sauzei* Zone.
South Main Road Quarry, Dundry, Avon [Somerset].
S. S. Buckman Collection, ex E. Wilson Collection, purchased 1923.
GSM 32038

Sphaeroceras perexpansum S. S. Buckman
PARATYPE
S. S. Buckman 1882, p. 142.
Labyrinthoceras intricatum S. S. Buckman HOLOTYPE
S. S. Buckman 1919, plate CXXXV, figs. 1-4.
Inferior Oolite, *sauzei* Zone.
Sherborne, Dorset.
S. S. Buckman, ex J. Buckman Collection, purchased 1923.
GSM 32001

Labyrinthoceras amphilaphes S. S. Buckman
HOLOTYPE
S. S. Buckman 1922a, plate CCLXXIX.
Inferior Oolite, Ironshot Bed, *sauzei* Zone.
Dundry, Avon [Somerset].
S. S. Buckman, ex T. Stock Collection, purchased 1924.
GSM 47114

Labyrinthoceras intricatum S. S. Buckman
PARATYPE
S. S. Buckman 1927, plate CXXXVA, figs. 1-3.
Inferior Oolite, *sauzei* Zone.
Clatcombe, Sherborne, Dorset.
S. S. Buckman Collection, ex D. S. Darell Collection, purchased 1928.
GSM 49296

Ammonites truelli compressus J. Sowerby
S. S. Buckman & Wilson 1896, p. 701.
Leptostrigites languidus S. S. Buckman PARATYPE
S. S. Buckman 1924, plate CDLXXVIIB, fig. 1.
Inferior Oolite, Upper White Ironshot, *sauzei* Zone.
South Main Road Quarry, Dundry, Avon [Somerset].
S. S. Buckman Collection, purchased 1925.
GSM 37325

Strigoceras sp.
S. S. Buckman 1893b, p. 494.
Leptostrigites languidus S. S. Buckman HOLOTYPE
S. S. Buckman 1924, plate CDLXXVIIA.
Strigoceras (Leptostrigites) languidum (S. S. Buckman) HOLOTYPE
Imlay 1973, p. 76.
Inferior Oolite, upper part of Sandford Fossil Bed, *sauzei* Zone.
Sandford Lane, Sherborne, Dorset.
S. S. Buckman Collection, purchased 1925.
GSM 37324

Nannina undifera S. S. Buckman HOLOTYPE
S. S. Buckman 1927, plate DCCLIII
S. S. Buckman 1928, p. 13.
Inferior Oolite, *sauzei* Zone
Clatcombe, Sherborne, Dorset
S. S. Buckman Collection, purchased 1929
GSM 49332

Ammonites sauzei d'Orbigny
J. Buckman 1881, p. 62.
Otoites contractus (J. de C. Sowerby)
S. S. Buckman 1920, plate CLVIII.
Otoites contractus contractus (J. de C. Sowerby)
NEOTYPE
Westermann 1954, plate 1 fig. 4; pp. 89-94.
Inferior Oolite, top of Sandford Fossil Bed, *sauzei* Zone.
Sandford Lane, Sherborne, Dorset.
S. S. Buckman, ex J. Buckman Collection, purchased 1923
GSM 32013

Otoites contractus (J. de C. Sowerby) **spaniopleurus** Westermann PARATYPE
Westermann 1954, plate 2 fig. 3; pp. 95-96
Inferior Oolite, *sauzei* Zone.
Dundry, Avon [Somerset]
W. H. Hudleston Collection, presented 1920.
Y 3322 [quoted by Westermann as Q 3332]

Otoites delicatus S. S. Buckman HOLOTYPE
S. S. Buckman 1919, plate CXLI.
Westermann 1954, plate 4, fig. 3; pp. 116-118.
Inferior Oolite, middle of Sandford Fossil Bed, *sauzei* Zone.
Sandford Lane, Sherborne, Dorset.
S. S. Buckman, ex D. S. Darell Collection, purchased 1923.
GSM 32005

Stepheoceras freycineti (Bayle)
S. S. Buckman 1910b, p. 73.
Rhytostephanus rhytus S. S. Buckman HOLOTYPE
S. S. Buckman 1921, plates CCL A, B.
Roché 1939, p. 182.
Stephanoceras rhytus (S. S. Buckman) HOLOTYPE
Imlay 1973, p. 88.
Inferior Oolite, Red Bed, *sauzei* Zone.
Burton Bradstock, Dorset.
S. S. Buckman Collection, purchased 1923.
GSM 32056

Skirroceras macrum (Quenstedt)
S. S. Buckman 1921, plate CCXLVIII.
Inferior Oolite, upper part of Sandford Fossil Bed, *sauzei* Zone.
Sandford Lane, Sherborne, Dorset.
S. S. Buckman ex D. S. Darell Collection, purchased 1923.
GSM 32055

Stephanoceras bayleanum
S. S. Buckman and Wilson 1896, p. 680.
Oecostephanus dolichoecus S. S. Buckman HOLOTYPE
S. S. Buckman 1921, plate CCLXV
Stephanoceras (Skirroceras) dolichoecus (S. S. Buckman) HOLOTYPE
Imlay 1973, p. 89.
Inferior Oolite, Ironshot Bed, *sauzei* Zone.
Northern Main Road Quarry, Butcher's Arms, Dundry, Avon [Somerset].
S. S. Buckman Collection, purchased 1923.
GSM 32064

Ammonites humphriesianus (J. de C. Sowerby)
J. Buckman 1874, p. 148.
Skirroceras leptogyrale S. S. Buckman HOLOTYPE
S. S. Buckman 1924, plate DXVI.
Cadomites leptogyrale (S. S. Buckman) HOLOTYPE
Roché 1939, p. 183.
Stephanoceras (Skirroceras) leptogyrale (S. S. Buckman) HOLOTYPE
Imlay 1973, p. 88.
Inferior Oolite, upper part of Sandford Fossil Bed, *sauzei* Zone.
Sandford Lane, Sherborne, Dorset.
S. S. Buckman Collection, ex D. S. Darell Collection, purchased 1926.
GSM 47547

Oecotraustes spiniger S. S. Buckman PARATYPE
S. S. Buckman 1910b, pp. 95-96.
Inferior Oolite, *sauzei* Zone.
Dundry, Avon [Somerset].
S. S. Buckman Collection, purchased 1910.
GSM 24731

Papilliceras papillatum S. S. Buckman HOLOTYPE
S. S. Buckman 1920, plates CL A, B.
Sonninia (Papilliceras) papillata (S. S. Buckman) HOLOTYPE
Arkell 1957, fig. 311, 5; p. L 268.
Imlay 1973, p. 68.
Inferior Oolite, top of Sandford Fossil Bed, *sauzei* Zone.
Sandford Land, Sherborne, Dorset.
S. S. Buckman Collection, ex J. Buckman Collection, purchased 1923.
GSM 32009

Papilliceras micracanthicum S. S. Buckman HOLOTYPE
S. S. Buckman 1925, plate DCXI.
Inferior Oolite, *sauzei* Zone.
Northern Main Road Quarry, Dundry, Avon [Somerset].
S. S. Buckman Collection, purchased 1927.
GSM 47782

Papilliceras acantherum S. S. Buckman HOLOTYPE
S. S. Buckman 1921, plates CCV A, B.
Sonninia (Papilliceras) acantherum (S. S. Buckman) HOLOTYPE
Imlay, 1973, p. 68.
Inferior Oolite, top of Sandford Fossil Bed, *sauzei* Zone.
Sandford Lane, Sherborne, Dorset.
S. S. Buckman, ex D. S. Darell Collection, purchased 1923.
GSM 32035

Sonninites felix S. S. Buckman HOLOTYPE
S. S. Buckman 1923, plate CDXXVIII A.
Inferior Oolite, upper part of Sandford Fossil Bed, *sauzei* Zone.
Sandford Lane, Sherborne, Dorset.
S. S. Buckman ex D. S. Darell Collection, purchased 1925.
GSM 37290

Sonninia aff. **patella**
S. S. Buckman 1893b, p. 494
Sonninites felix S. S. Buckman PARATYPE
S. S. Buckman 1923, plate CDXXVIII B.
Westermann 1969, p. 114.
Inferior Oolite, upper part of Sandford Fossil Bed, *sauzei* Zone.
Sandford Lane, Sherborne, Dorset.
S. S. Buckman Collection, purchased 1925.
GSM 37291

Sherbornites undifer S. S. Buckman HOLOTYPE
S. S. Buckman 1923, plate CDXXVII.
Inferior Oolite, lower middle part of Sandford Fossil Bed, *sauzei* Zone.
Sandford Lane, Sherborne, Dorset.
S. S. Buckman ex D. S. Darell Collection, purchased 1925.
GSM 37289

Sherbornites adricus (Waagen)
S. S. Buckman 1926, plate DCLXIX.
Inferior Oolite, middle part of Sandford Fossil Bed, *sauzei* Zone.
Sandford Lane, Sherborne, Dorset.
S. S. Buckman Collection, purchased 1928.
GSM 49270

Ammonites corrugatus J. de C. Sowerby
S. S. Buckman 1889d, pp. 202-203.
Sonninia corrugata (J. de C. Sowerby)
S. S. Buckman & Wilson 1896, p. 680
S. S. Buckman 1926, plate CDXIIA.
Gillet 1937, p. 35.
Inferior Oolite, *sauzei* Zone
Northern Main Road Quarry, Butcher's Arms, Dundry, Avon [Somerset].
S. S. Buckman Collection, purchased 1927.
GSM 47761

Ammonites corrugatus J. de C. Sowerby
S. S. Buckman 1889d, p. 202.
Sonninia corrugata (J. de C. Sowerby)
S. S. Buckman 1923, plate CDXII.
Gillet 1937, p. 34.
Inferior Oolite, Ironshot Bed, *sauzei* Zone.
Dundry, Avon [Somerset]
S. S. Buckman Collection, purchased 1925.
GSM 47197

Ammonites variabilis d'Orbigny
?J. Buckman 1874, p. 146.
Sonninites alsaticus (Haug)
S. S. Buckman 1924, plate DXXVIII.
Inferior Oolite, Brown Ironshot, *sauzei* Zone.
Clatcombe, Sherborne, Dorset.
S. S. Buckman ex D. S. Darell Collection, purchased 1924.
GSM 47552

Sonninites alsaticus (Haug)
S. S. Buckman 1925, plate DXXVIII A [misprinted **Sonnites** on plate, see corrigenda 1927, p. 52].
Inferior Oolite, Brown Ironshot, *sauzei* Zone.
Clatcombe, Sherborne, Dorset.
S. S. Buckman ex D. S. Darell Collection, purchased 1927
GSM 47762

Sonninia propinquans (Bayle)
S. S. Buckman 1922a, plate CCXCVIII.
Inferior Oolite, top of Sandford Fossil Bed, *sauzei* Zone.
Sandford Lane, Sherborne, Dorset.
S. S. Buckman ex D. S. Darell Collection, purchased 1924.
GSM 47118

Sonninites celans S. S. Buckman HOLOTYPE
S. S. Buckman 1924, plate CDLXI
Inferior Oolite, *sauzei* Zone
Near Sherborne, Dorset.
S. S. Buckman ex D. S. Darell Collection, purchased 1925
GSM 37310

Strigites strigifer S. S. Buckman HOLOTYPE
S. S. Buckman 1924, plate CDLXIX A.
Strigoceras strigifer (S. S. Buckman) HOLOTYPE
Roché 1939, p. 166.
Inferior Oolite, *sauzei* Zone.
Clatcombe, Sherborne, Dorset.
S. S. Buckman ex D. S. Darell Collection, purchased 1925.
GSM 37316

Strigites strigifer S. S. Buckman PARATYPE
S. S. Buckman 1924, plate CDLXIX B.
Strigoceras pseudostrigifer (Maubeuge)
Sturani 1971, p. 119.
Inferior Oolite, *Astarte spissa* Bed, *sauzei* Zone.
Milborne Wick, Somerset.
S. S. Buckman ex L. Richardson Collection, purchased 1925.
GSM 37317

Labyrinthoceras perexpansum (S. S. Buckman)
S. S. Buckman 1921, plates CXXXIV C, D.
Arkell 1957, fig. 347, 4a; p. L292 [figured erroneously as holotype].
Inferior Oolite, *sauzei* Zone.
Clatcombe, Sherborne, Dorset.
S. S. Buckman Collection, ex D. S. Darell, purchased 1923.
GSM 32041

Emileia vagabunda S. S. Buckman HOLOTYPE
S. S. Buckman 1927, plates DCCXXIII A, B.
Inferior Oolite, *sauzei* Zone.
Rollingbank Quarry, Cleeve Hill, Cheltenham, Gloucestershire.
S. S. Buckman Collection, purchased 1929.
GSM 49313

Emileia bulligera S. S. Buckman HOLOTYPE
S. S. Buckman 1927, plates DCCXXXII A-C.
Imlay 1973, p. 80.
Inferior Oolite, *sauzei* Zone
Sandford Lane, Sherborne, Dorset
S. S. Buckman Collection, purchased 1929
GSM 49319

Emileia brocchi (J. Sowerby)
S. S. Buckman 1927, plates DCCX C, D.
Imlay 1973, p. 80.
Inferior Oolite, *sauzei* Zone.
Sandford Lane, Sherborne, Dorset.
S. S. Buckman Collection, purchased 1929.
GSM 49303

Ammonites eudesianus d'Orbigny
?J. Buckman 1875, p. 146.
Metrolytoceras metretum S. S. Buckman HOLOTYPE
S. S. Buckman 1923, plate CDXXIX
Arkell 1957, fig. 226, 6, p. L196.
Inferior Oolite, *sauzei* Zone.
Near Sherborne, Dorset.
S. S. Buckman Collection, ex D. S. Darell, purchased 1925.
GSM 37292

Stegoxyites parcicarinatus S. S. Buckman HOLOTYPE
S. S. Buckman 1924, plate CDLXXIV
Oecotraustes? (Stegoxyites) parcicarinatus (S. S. Buckman) HOLOTYPE
Arkell 1957, fig. 323; p. L276.
Stegoxytes [sic] **parcicarinatus** S. S. Buckman HOLOTYPE
Sturani 1971, pp. 97-98.
Inferior Oolite, lower part of Roadstone, *humphriesianum* Zone, *romani* Subzone.
Frogden Quarry, Oborne, Dorset.
S. S. Buckman Collection, purchased 1925.
GSM 37322

Phaulostephanus paululus S. S. Buckman HOLOTYPE
S. S. Buckman 1927, plate DCCLIV.
Cadomites paululus (S. S. Buckman) HOLOTYPE
Roché 1939, p. 217.
Stephanoceras (Phaulostephanus) paululum (S. S. Buckman) HOLOTYPE
Arkell 1957, fig. 343, p. L289.
Imlay 1973, p. 89.
Inferior Oolite, *humphriesianum* Zone, *romani* Subzone.
Clatcombe, Sherborne, Dorset.
S. S. Buckman Collection, ex D. S. Darrell Collection, purchased 1929.
GSM 49333

Stepheoceras plagium S. S. Buckman HOLOTYPE
S. S. Buckman 1921, plate CCXXIX.
Cadomites plagius (S. S. Buckman) HOLOTYPE
Roché 1939, p. 186.
Inferior Oolite, *humphriesianum* Zone, *romani* Subzone.
Clatcombe, Sherborne, Dorset.
S. S. Buckman Collection, ex D. S. Darell Collection, purchased 1922.
GSM 32042

Stephanoceras blagdeni (J. Sowerby)
S. S. Buckman 1881, p. 595.
Teloceras labrum S. S. Buckman HOLOTYPE
S. S. Buckman 1922a, plates CCCL A, B.
Cadomites labrus (S. S. Buckman) HOLOTYPE
Roché 1939, p. 208.
Inferior Oolite, lower part of Roadstone, *humphriesianum* Zone and Subzone
Frogden Quarry, Oborne, Dorset.
S. S. Buckman Collection, purchased 1924.
GSM 47150

Ammonites gervillii J. Sowerby
J. Buckman 1881, p. 63.
Sphaeroceras gervillii (J. Sowerby)
S. S. Buckman 1881, p. 597.
Chondroceras delphinus S. S. Buckman HOLOTYPE
S. S. Buckman 1923, plate CDXXXI.
Inferior Oolite, *humphriesianum* Zone, *humphriesianum* Subzone
Milborne Wick, Somerset.
S. S. Buckman Collection, ex J. Buckman, purchased 1925.
GSM 37293

Chondroceras gervillii (J. Sowerby)
S. S. Buckman 1881, pp. 593, 597
S. S. Buckman 1927, plate DCCXXIV.
Arkell 1957, fig. 247, a, b; p. L292. [Figured erroneously as Holotype]
Inferior Oolite, *humphriesianum* Zone, *humphriesianum* Subzone.
Oborne, Dorset.
S. S. Buckman Collection, ex J. Buckman Collection, purchased 1929.
GSM 49314

Chondroceras grandiforme S. S. Buckman HOLOTYPE
S. S. Buckman 1922a, plate CCCLVII.
Inferior Oolite, *humphriesianum* Zone, *humphriesianum* Subzone.
Near Sherborne, Dorset.
S. S. Buckman Collection, ex D. S. Darell Collection, purchased 1924.
GSM 47157

Kreterosphinctes kreter S. S. Buckman HOLOTYPE
S. S. Buckman 1927, plate DCCLV.
Cadomites kreter (S. S. Buckman) HOLOTYPE
Roché 1939, p. 196.
Inferior Oolite, Red Bed, *humphriesianum* Zone, *humphriesianum* Subzone.
Burton Bradstock, Dorset.
S. S. Buckman Collection, purchased 1929.
GSM 49334

Stepheoceras humphriesianum (J. de C. Sowerby)
S. S. Buckman 1921, plate CCXXXVIII.
Inferior Oolite, *humphriesianum* Zone, *humphriesianum* Subzone.
Clatcombe, Sherborne, Dorset.
S. S. Buckman Collection, ex J. Buckman Collection, purchased 1923.
GSM 32047

Stephanoceras braikenridgii (J. Sowerby)
S. S. Buckman 1881, p. 595.
Epalxites formosus S. S. Buckman HOLOTYPE
S. S. Buckman 1920, plate CL1, figs. 1-3.
Roché 1939, p. 219.
Itinsaites formosus (S. S. Buckman) HOLOTYPE
Westermann 1954, plate 23, fig. 1; text-fig. 107; pp. 259-260.
Normannites formosus (S. S. Buckman) HOLOTYPE
Sturani 1971, pp. 131-132.
Normannites (Itinsaites) formosus (S. S. Buckman) HOLOTYPE
Imlay, 1973, p. 84.
Inferior Oolite, *humphriesianum* Zone, *humphriesianum* Subzone.
Frogden Quarry, Oborne, Dorset.
S. S. Buckman Collection, purchased 1923.
GSM 32010

Stephanoceras braikenridgii (J. Sowerby)
S. S. Buckman 1891, p. 595.
Masckeites densus S. S. Buckman HOLOTYPE
S. S. Buckman 1920, plate CLII.
Normannites densus (S. S. Buckman) HOLOTYPE
Roché 1939, p. 221.
Maskeites densus S. S. Buckman HOLOTYPE
Westermann 1954, plate 32, fig. 1; text-fig. 142; pp. 332-334.
Westermann 1956, text-fig. 3b; pp. 251-252.
Stephanoceras (Normannites) densum (S. S. Buckman) HOLOTYPE
Morton 1971, p. 284.
Normannites (Masckeites?) densus (S. S. Buckman) HOLOTYPE
Imlay 1973, p. 85.
Inferior Oolite, *humphriesianum* Zone, *humphriesianum* Subzone.
Clatcombe, Sherborne, Dorset.
S. S. Buckman Collection, ex J. Buckman, purchased 1922.
GSM 32011

Normannites orbignyi S. S. Buckman
S. S. Buckman 1927, plate DCCXXXIV.
Normannites (Normannites) orbignyi orbignyi S. S. Buckman NEOTYPE
Westermann 1954, plate 5 fig. 3; pp. 135-141.
Imlay 1973,pp. 82, 83.
Inferior Oolite, *humphriesianum* Zone, *humphriesianum* Subzone.
Clatcombe, Sherborne, Dorset.
S. S. Buckman Collection, ex D. S. Darell Collection, purchased 1929.
GSM 49321

Poecilomorphus angulinus S. S. Buckman HOLOTYPE
S. S. Buckman 1927, plate DCCLVII; p. 10.
Imlay 1973, p. 75.
Inferior Oolite, *humphriesianum* Zone, *humphriesianum* Subzone.
Milborne Wick, Somerset.
S. S. Buckman Collection, ex D. S. Darell Collection, purchased 1929.
GSM 49336

Poecilomorphus regulatus S. S. Buckman HOLOTYPE
S. S. Buckman 1927, plate DCCXLVI; p. 10.
Imlay 1973, p. 75.
Inferior Oolite, *humphriesianum* Zone, *humphriesianum* Subzone.
Clatcombe Farm, Sherborne, Dorset.
S. S. Buckman Collection, purchased 1929.
GSM 49325

Poecilomorphus primiferus S. S. Buckman HOLOTYPE
S. S. Buckman 1927, plates DCCLVI A, B,; p. 10.
Imlay 1973, p. 75.
Inferior Oolite, *humphriesianum* Zone, *humphriesianum* Subzone.
Clatcombe, Sherborne, Dorset.
S. S. Buckman Collection ex D. S. Darell, purchased 1929.
GSM 49335

Dorsetensia liostraca S. S. Buckman
S. S. Buckman 1893b, p. 502.
Inferior Oolite, *humphriesianum* Zone, *humphriesianum* Subzone.
Milborne Wick, Somerset.
S. S. Buckman Collection, purchased 1910.
GSM 24720

Dorsetensia liostraca S. S. Buckman
S. S. Buckman 1892a, plate 56, fig. 1.
Inferior Oolite, *humphriesianum* Zone.
Oborne, Dorset.
S. S. Buckman Collection, purchased 1900
GSM 6715

Dorsetensia subtecta S. S. Buckman SYNTYPE
S. S. Buckman 1892a, plate 54, fig. 3.
Inferior Oolite, *humphriesianum* Zone.
Oborne, Dorset.
S. S. Buckman Collection, purchased 1900.
GSM 6717

Dorsetensia tecta S. S. Buckman SYNTYPE
S. S. Buckman 1892a, plate 56, fig. 5.
Inferior Oolite, *humphriesianum* Zone.
Oborne, Dorset.
S. S. Buckman Collection, purchased 1900.
GSM 6716

Perisphinctes pygmaeum (d'Orbigny)
S. S. Buckman 1881, p. 602.
Nannolytoceras sp.
S. S. Buckman 1905b, p. 151.
Nannolytoceras subovale S. S. Buckman HOLOTYPE
S. S. Buckman 1922a, plate CCCXXIV A.
Inferior Oolite, Irony Bed, *humphriesianum* Zone, *blagdeni* Subzone.
Louse Hill, Compton, Sherborne, Dorset.
S. S. Buckman Collection, purchased 1924.
GSM 47137

Nannolytoceras pygmaeum (d'Orbigny)
S. S. Buckman 1922a, plate CCCXXIII.
Inferior Oolite, Irony Bed, *humphriesianum* Zone, *blagdeni* Subzone.
Louse Hill, Sherborne, Dorset.
S. S. Buckman Collection, purchased 1924.
GSM 47136

Nannolytoceras subovale S. S. Buckman PARATYPE
S. S. Buckman 1922a, plate CCCXXIVB.
Inferior Oolite, Irony Bed, *humphriesianum* Zone, *blagdeni* Subzone.
Louse Hill, Compton, Sherborne, Dorset.
S. S. Buckman Collection, ex D. S. Darell Collection, purchased 1924.
GSM 47138

Stemmatoceras (Stemmatoceras) triptolemus (Morris and Lycett)
Arkell and Playford 1954, p. 583.
Scarborough Limestone, *humphriesianum* Zone, *blagdeni* Subzone.
Scarborough, Yorkshire.
J. Lycett Collection, purchased 1867.
GSM 25254

Chondroceras grandiforme S. S. Buckman
Arkell 1952, text-fig. 20, 5a, b; p. 77.
Inferior Oolite, *humphriesianum* Zone, *blagdeni* Subzone.
Milborne Wick, Somerset.
Mrs E. Warne Collection, ex J. Buckman, purchased 1867.
GSM 25286

Oppelia (umbilicate sp.)
S. S. Buckman 1893b, p. 497.
Oppelina umbilicata S. S. Buckman HOLOTYPE
S. S. Buckman 1926, plate DCLXXI.
Inferior Oolite, *humphriesianum* Zone, *blagdeni* Subzone.
Lower Clatcombe, Sherborne, Dorset.
S. S. Buckman Collection, purchased 1928.
GSM 49272

Cosmoceras subfurcatum (Schlotheim)
S. S. Buckman 1881, pp. 600-601.
Strenoceras apleurum S. S. Buckman HOLOTYPE
S. S. Buckman 1921, plate CCXXXIX.
Inferior Oolite, *subfurcatum* Zone.
Frogden Quarry, Oborne, Dorset.
S. S. Buckman Collection, purchased 1923.
GSM 32048

Sphaeroceras brongniarti (J. Sowerby)
S. S. Buckman 1881, p. 597.
Sphaeroceras tutthum S. S. Buckman HOLOTYPE
S. S. Buckman 1921, plate CCLVIII.
Sphaeroceras auritum Parona
Sturani 1971, p. 143.
Inferior Oolite, *subfurcatum* Zone.
Sherborne, Dorset.
S. S. Buckman Collection, ex J. Buckman, purchased 1923.
GSM 32060

Ammonites cadomensis Defrance
S. S. Buckman 1881, p. 607.
Cadomoceras simulacrum S. S. Buckman HOLOTYPE
S. S. Buckman 1924, plate CDLVIII.
Cadomoceras nepos Parona
Sturani 1971, pp. 123-124.
Inferior Oolite, *subfurcatum* Zone
Frogden Quarry, Oborne, Dorset
S. S. Buckman Collection, ex T. C. Maggs, purchased 1925
GSM 37308

Cadomoceras costatum S. S. Buckman HOLOTYPE
S. S. Buckman 1920, plate CLXXXIX.
Inferior Oolite, White Bed, *subfurcatum* Zone.
Burton Bradstock, Dorset.
S. S. Buckman Collection, ex D. S. Darell Collection, purchased 1923.
GSM 47105

Perisphinctes martinsii S. S. Buckman
S. S. Buckman 1881, p. 602.
Pseudobigotella otiophora S. S. Buckman HOLOTYPE
S. S. Buckman 1920, plate CXCI.
Inferior Oolite, above Irony Bed, *subfurcatum* Zone.
Louse Hill, Nether Compton, Dorset.
S. S. Buckman Collection, purchased 1923.
GSM 32028

Plectostrigites symplectus S. S. Buckman HOLOTYPE
S. S. Buckman 1924, plate CDLXXI*.
Inferior Oolite, Roadstone, *subfurcatum* Zone.
Frogden Quarry, Oborne, Dorset.
S. S. Buckman Collection, purchased 1925.
GSM 37319

Hlawiceras platyrrymum S. S. Buckman HOLOTYPE
S. S. Buckman 1921, plate CCXL.
Garantiana (Hlawiceras) platyrrymum
(S. S. Buckman) HOLOTYPE
Arkell 1957, fig. 384, 3; p. L309.
Inferior Oolite, Rotten Bed, *subfurcatum* Zone.
Louse Hill, Nether Compton, Dorset.
S. S. Buckman Collection, purchased 1923.
GSM 32049

Oppelina pulchra S. S. Buckman HOLOTYPE
S. S. Buckman 1926, plate DCLXX.
Arkell 1951, p. 69.
Oecotraustes pulcher (S. S. Buckman) HOLOTYPE
Sturani 1971, p. 117.
Inferior Oolite, upper part of Roadstone, *subfurcatum* Zone, *banksi* Subzone.
Frogden Quarry, Oborne, Dorset.
S. S. Buckman Collection, purchased 1928.
GSM 49271

Ancyloceras bifurcatum (Quenstedt)
S. S. Buckman 1881, p. 607.
Rhabdodites rhabdodes S. S. Buckman HOLOTYPE
S. S. Buckman 1923, plate CCCLXXIV.
Inferior Oolite, upper part of Roadstone, *subfurcatum* Zone, *banksi* Subzone.
Frogden Quarry, Oborne, Dorset.
S. S. Buckman Collection, purchased 1924.
GSM 47170

Gibbistephanus gibbosus S. S. Buckman HOLOTYPE
S. S. Buckman 1928, plates DCCLXXX A, B.
Inferior Oolite, Upper Roadstone, *subfurcatum* Zone, *banksi* Subzone.
Frogden Quarry, Oborne, Dorset.
S. S. Buckman Collection, ex D. S. Darell Collection, purchased 1929.
GSM 49350

Teloceras multinodus (Quenstedt)
S. S. Buckman 1928, plates DCCLXXXVIII A, B.
Inferior Oolite, upper part of Roadstone, *subfurcatum* Zone, *banksi* Subzone.
Frogden Quarry, Oborne, Dorset.
S. S. Buckman Collection, purchased 1929.
GSM 49355

Leptosphinctes leptus S. S. Buckman HOLOTYPE
S. S. Buckman 1920, plate CLX.
Roman 1938, text-fig. 35; pp. 239, 261.
Arkell 1957, fig. 396, 1; p. L314.
Leptosphinctes (Leptosphinctes) leptus S. S. Buckman HOLOTYPE
Pavia 1971, p. 128.
Imlay 1973, pp. 91, 92.
Inferior Oolite, upper part of Roadstone, *subfurcatum* Zone, *banksi* Subzone.
Frogden Quarry, Oborne, Dorset.
S. S. Buckman Collection, ex D. S. Darell Collection, purchased 1923.
GSM 32014

Leptosphinctes cleistus S. S. Buckman HOLOTYPE
S. S. Buckman 1920, plate CLXI.
Roman 1938, p. 261.
Roché 1939, p. 238.
Cleistosphinctes cleistus (S. S. Buckman) HOLOTYPE
Arkell 1957, fig. 396, 2; p. L314.
Arkell 1958, p. 168.
Leptosphinctes (Cleistosphinctes) cleistus S. S. Buckman HOLOTYPE
Sturani 1971, pp. 173-4.
Pavia 1971, p. 133.
Inferior Oolite, *subfurcatum* Zone.
Frogden Quarry, Oborne, Dorset.
S. S. Buckman Collection, ex D. S. Darell, purchased 1923.
GSM 32015

Leptosphinctes coronarius S. S. Buckman HOLOTYPE
S. S. Buckman 1921, plate CCII.
Roché 1939, pp. 237-238.
Inferior Oolite, *subfurcatum* Zone.
Frogden Quarry, Oborne, Dorset.
S. S. Buckman Collection, purchased 1923.
GSM 32033

Caumontisphinctes polygyralis S. S. Buckman HOLOTYPE
S. S. Buckman 1920, plate CLXIII.
Roman 1938, p. 239.
Arkell 1956, p. 145.
Arkell 1957, fig. 384, 9; p. L309.
Sturani 1971, pp. 165-166.
Caumontisphinctes (Caumontisphinctes) polygyralis S. S. Buckman HOLOTYPE
Pavia 1971, p. 116.
Inferior Oolite, *subfurcatum* Zone, *polygyralis* Subzone.
Lower Clatcombe, Sherborne, Dorset.
S. S. Buckman Collection, purchased 1923.
GSM 32017

Caumontisphinctes phaulus S. S. Buckman HOLOTYPE
S. S. Buckman 1920, plate CLXIX.
Caumontisphinctes (Infraparkinsonia) phaulus (S. S. Buckman) HOLOTYPE
Sturani 1971, p. 168.
Pavia 1971, p. 118.
Inferior Oolite, *subfurcatum* Zone.
Lower Clatcombe, Sherborne, Dorset.
S. S. Buckman Collection, purchased 1923.
GSM 32019

Caumontisphinctes nodatus S. S. Buckman HOLOTYPE
S. S. Buckman 1921, plate CCXLII.
Roché 1939, pp. 238-239.
Inferior Oolite, *subfurcatum* Zone.
Lower Clatcombe, Sherborne, Dorset.
S. S. Buckman Collection, purchased 1923.
GSM 32050

Caumontisphinctes bifurcus S. S. Buckman HOLOTYPE
S. S. Buckman 1920, plate CXCII.
Caumontisphinctes (Caumontisphinctes) bifurcus S. S. Buckman HOLOTYPE
Pavia 1971, p. 117.
Inferior Oolite, upper part of Roadstone, *subfurcatum* Zone.
Frogden Quarry, Oborne, Dorset.
S. S. Buckman Collection, purchased 1923.
GSM 32029

Cadomites septicostatus S. S. Buckman HOLOTYPE
S. S. Buckman 1923, plate CDXXXII A.
Roché 1939, p. 216.
Inferior Oolite, *subfurcatum* Zone, *polygyralis* Subzone.
Lower Clatcombe, Sherborne, Dorset.
S. S. Buckman Collection, purchased 1925.
GSM 37294

Cadomoceras homalogaster S. S. Buckman HOLOTYPE
S. S. Buckman 1925, plates DXLIII A, B, B*.
Inferior Oolite, *subfurcatum* Zone, *polygyralis* Subzone.
Frogden Quarry, Oborne, Dorset.
S. S. Buckman Collection, purchased 1926.
GSM 47555

Baculatoceras baculatum (Quenstedt)
S. S. Buckman 1925, plate DLXXXI.
Inferior Oolite, upper part of Roadstone, *subfurcatum* Zone, *baculatum* Subzone.
Frogden Quarry, Oborne, Dorset.
S. S. Buckman Collection, ex D. S. Darrell Collection, purchased 1927.
GSM 47765.

Vermisphinctes reparator S. S. Buckman HOLOTYPE
S. S. Buckman 1923, plate CCCLXVI.
Inferior Oolite, upper part of Shell Bed, *garantiana* Zone.
Vetney (now Vinney) Cross, Loders, Dorset.
S. S. Buckman Collection, purchased 1924.
GSM 47164

Stomphosphinctes stomphus S. S. Buckman HOLOTYPE
S. S. Buckman 1921, plate CCXLVII.
Leptosphinctes (Prorsisphinctes) stomphus (S. S. Buckman) HOLOTYPE
Krystyn 1972, pp. 268-269.
Imlay 1973, p. 92.
Inferior Oolite, Shell Bed, *garantiana* Zone.
Vetney (now Vinney) Cross, Loders, Dorset.
S. S. Buckman Collection, ex D. S. Darell, purchased 1923.
GSM 32054

Prorsisphinctes meseres S. S. Buckman HOLOTYPE
S. S. Buckman 1923, plate CDXLVI
Leptosphinctes (Prorsisphinctes) meseres (S. S. Buckman) HOLOTYPE
Krystyn 1972, pp. 266-267.
Imlay 1973, p. 92.
Inferior Oolite, Shell Bed, *garantiana* Zone.
Vetney (now Vinney) Cross, Loders, Dorset.
S. S. Buckman Collection, purchased 1910.
GSM 24688

Prorsisphinctes meseres S. S. Buckman
S. S. Buckman 1927, plates CDXLVI A, B.
Leptosphinctes (Prorsisphinctes) meseres (S. S. Buckman)
Imlay 1973, p. 92.
Inferior Oolite, Shell Bed, *garantiana* Zone.
Vetney (now Vinney) Cross, Loders, Dorset.
S. S. Buckman Collection, ex T. Wright, purchased 1929.
GSM 49317

Prorsisphinctes omphalicus S. S. Buckman HOLOTYPE
S. S. Buckman 1922a, plate CCCXXVI.
Inferior Oolite, Shell Bed, *garantiana* Zone.
Vetney (now Vinney) Cross, Loders, Dorset.
S. S. Buckman Collection, purchased 1911.
GSM 26752

Bajocisphinctes bajociensis (Siemiradzki)
S. S. Buckman 1927, plate DCCXIII.
Inferior Oolite, *garantiana* Zone.
Clifton Maybank, Dorset.
S. S. Buckman Collection, ex J. Buckman, purchased 1929.
GSM 49306

Bajocisphinctes curvatus S. S. Buckman HOLOTYPE
S. S. Buckman 1927, plate DCCXVI.
Inferior Oolite, Upper Beds, *garantiana* Zone.
Quarry near railway, Clifton Maybank, Dorset.
S. S. Buckman Collection, ex D. S. Darell, purchased 1929.
GSM 49316

cf. **Cadomites-Polyplectites**
Westermann 1975, pp. 44, 45.
Inferior Oolite, Astarte Bed, *garantiana* Zone.
Burton Cliff, Burton Bradstock, Dorset.
W. H. Hudleston Collection, presented by Miss C. A. Raisin 1920.
Y3224, 3226

Odontolkites longidens (Quenstedt)
S. S. Buckman 1925, plate DLXXXII
Garantiana (Garantiana) parkinsoni (J. Sowerby) **longidens** (Quenstedt)
Arkell 1957, fig. 383; p. L309 [figured as being Quenstedt's type]
Inferior Oolite, Astarte Bed, *garantiana* Zone.
Burton Bradstock, Dorset.
S. S. Buckman Collection, ex D. S. Darell, purchased 1927.
GSM 47766

Parkinsonia rarecostata S. S. Buckman
S. S. Buckman 1910b, p. 67.
Parkinsonia interrupta (Bruguière)
S. S. Buckman 1923, plate CCCXXXVII A.
Inferior Oolite, Astarte Bed, *garantiana* Zone.
Burton Bradstock, Dorset.
S. S. Buckman Collection, purchased 1924.
GSM 47142

Parkinsonia rarecostata S. S. Buckman
S. S. Buckman 1922a, plate CCCLII.
Inferior Oolite, Shell Bed, *garantiana* Zone.
Burton Bradstock, Dorset.
S. S. Buckman Collection, ex D. S. Darell, purchased 1924.
GSM 47152

Garantiana garantiana (d'Orbigny)
S. S. Buckman 1922a, plate CCCLVIII.
Arkell 1933, p. 233.
Inferior Oolite, Astarte Bed, *garantiana* Zone.
Burton Bradstock, Dorset.
S. S. Buckman Collection, purchased 1924.
GSM 47158

Diplesioceras diplesium S. S. Buckman HOLOTYPE
S. S. Buckman 1920, plate CLXXVII.
Arkell 1957, fig. 311, 8ab; p. L271.
Inferior Oolite, Shell Bed, *garantiana* Zone.
Vetney (now Vinney) Cross, Loders, Dorset.
S. S. Buckman Collection, purchased 1923.
GSM 32024

Strigites septicarinatus S. S. Buckman HOLOTYPE
S. S. Buckman 1924, plate CDLXX.
Strigoceras septicarinatus (S. S. Buckman) HOLOTYPE
Roché 1939, pp. 166-167.
Inferior Oolite, Shell Bed, *garantiana* Zone.
Burton Bradstock, Dorset.
S. S. Buckman Collection, purchased 1925.
GSM 37318

Plagiamites campylus S. S. Buckman HOLOTYPE
S. S. Buckman 1925, plate DLXXXIV.
Inferior Oolite, Astarte Bed, *garantiana* Zone.
Burton Bradstock, Dorset.
S. S. Buckman Collection, ex D. S. Darell, purchased 1926.
GSM 47768

Plagiamites cyphus S. S. Buckman HOLOTYPE
S. S. Buckman 1925, plate DLXXXII.
Inferior Oolite, Astarte Bed, *garantiana* Zone.
Burton Bradstock, Dorset.
S. S. Buckman Collection, ex D. S. Darell, purchased 1926.
GSM 47767

Spiroceras toxoconicum S. S. Buckman HOLOTYPE
S. S. Buckman 1924, plate CDXCII.
Imlay 1973, p. 55.
Inferior Oolite, Shell Bed, *garantiana* Zone.
Vetney (now Vinney) Cross, Loders, Dorset.
S. S. Buckman Collection, ex D. S. Darell, purchased 1926.
GSM 47533

Morphoceras dimorphum (d'Orbigny)
S. S. Buckman 1910b, p. 73.
Dimorphinites dimorphus (d'Orbigny)
S. S. Buckman 1923, plate CCCLXXVII.
Morphoceras? (Dimorphinites) dimorphum (d'Orbigny)
Arkell 1957, fig. 386, 1; p. L311.
Inferior Oolite, *parkinsoni* Zone, *truellei* Subzone.
Burton Bradstock, Dorset.
S. S. Buckman Collection, ex D. S. Darell, purchased 1924.
GSM 47173

Lobosphinctes intersertus S. S. Buckman HOLOTYPE
S. S. Buckman 1923, plate CDXLVII
Arkell 1957, fig. 397, 5; p. L314.
Lobosphinctes? intersertus S. S. Buckman HOLOTYPE
Arkell 1958, pp. 173, 174.
Procerites (Lobosphinctes) intersertus (S. S. Buckman) HOLOTYPE
Pavia 1971, p. 139.
Inferior Oolite, *parkinsoni* Zone, *truellei* Subzone.
Burton Bradstock, Dorset.
S. S. Buckman Collection, ex D. S. Darell, purchased 1925.
GSM 37311

Strigoceras truellei (d'Orbigny)
S. S. Buckman 1924, plate CDLXXII.
Inferior Oolite, *parkinsoni* Zone, *truellei* Subzone.
Burton Bradstock, Dorset.
S. S. Buckman Collection, purchased 1926.
GSM 37320

Stegeostephanus stegeus S. S. Buckman HOLOTYPE
S. S. Buckman 1922a, plates CCCXII, CCCXII*.
Cadomites stegeus (S. S. Buckman) HOLOTYPE
Roché 1939, pp. 203, 204.
Wendt 1963, p. 131.
Inferior Oolite, *parkinsoni* Zone, *truellei* Subzone.
Bradford Abbas, Dorset.
S. S. Buckman Collection, ex J. Buckman, purchased 1924.
GSM 47127

Oecoptychoceras grossouvrei (Brasil)
S. S. Buckman 1920, plate CLXXV.
Inferior Oolite, Terebratula Bed, *parkinsoni* Zone, *truellei* Subzone.
Burton Bradstock, Dorset.
S. S. Buckman Collection, ex D. S. Darell Collection, purchased 1923.
GSM 32022

Oecoptychius grossouvrei (Brasil)
S. S. Buckman 1898, p. 456.
S. S. Buckman 1919, p. 7.
Oecoptychoceras subrefractum S. S. Buckman HOLOTYPE
S. S. Buckman 1920, plate CLXXVI.
Arkell 1957, fig. 347, 2; p. L292.
Inferior Oolite, *parkinsoni* Zone, *truellei* Subzone.
Broad Windsor, Dorset.
S. S. Buckman Collection, ex F. Stubbington Collection, purchased 1923.
GSM 32023

Bigotites trifurcatus S. S. Buckman HOLOTYPE
S. S. Buckman 1926, plate DCXXII.
Inferior Oolite, *parkinsoni* Zone, *truellei* Subzone.
Burton Bradstock, Dorset.
S. S. Buckman Collection, ex D. S. Darell Collection, purchased 1927.
GSM 47826

Pleuroxyites pleurifer S. S. Buckman HOLOTYPE
S. S. Buckman 1924, plate CDLXXVIII.
Oppelia (Oppelia) pleurifer (S. S. Buckman) HOLOTYPE
Pavia 1971, pp. 98-99.
Inferior Oolite, *parkinsoni* Zone, *truellei* Subzone.
Burton Bradstock, Dorset.
S. S. Buckman Collection, ex D. S. Darell Collection, purchased 1925.
GSM 37326

Phanerosphinctes costulatosus S. S. Buckman HOLOTYPE
S. S. Buckman 1923, plate CCCLXXXVI.
Procerites costulatosus (S. S. Buckman) HOLOTYPE
Arkell 1958, plate 21 fig. 8; text-fig. 69-1; pp. 185-188, 235.
Krystyn 1972, p. 271.
Inferior Oolite, *parkinsoni* Zone, *truellei* Subzone, or *zigzag* Zone.
Railway cutting, Bradford Abbas, Dorset.
S. S. Buckman Collection, purchased 1924.
GSM 47179

Phanerosphinctes phanerus S. S. Buckman HOLOTYPE
S. S. Buckman 1921, plate CCXI.
Inferior Oolite, *parkinsoni* Zone, *truellei* Subzone.
Burton Bradstock, Dorset.
S. S. Buckman Collection, ex D. S. Darell Collection, purchased 1923.
GSM 32037

Perisphinctes martinsii (d'Orbigny)
S. S. Buckman 1881, p. 602.
Vermisphinctes vermiformis S. S. Buckman HOLOTYPE
S. S. Buckman 1920, plate CLXII.
Roman 1938, p. 239.
Leptosphinctes (Vermisphinctes) vermiformis (S. S. Buckman) HOLOTYPE
Arkell 1957, fig. 396, 3; p. L314.
Pavia 1971, p. 133.
Inferior Oolite, Halfway House Bed, *parkinsoni* Zone, *truellei* Subzone.
Halfway House, Nether Compton, near Sherborne, Dorset.
S. S. Buckman Collection, purchased 1923.
GSM 32016

Prorsisphinctes pseudomartinsi (Siemiradzki)
S. S. Buckman 1921, plate CC.
Roman 1938, p. 261.
Inferior Oolite, Astarte Bed, *parkinsoni* Zone, *truellei* Subzone.
Burton Bradstock, Dorset.
S. S. Buckman Collection, ex D. S. Darell Collection, purchased 1923.
GSM 32032

Strigoceras gracile (Quenstedt)
S. S. Buckman 1925, plate DLXXXV.
Inferior Oolite, *parkinsoni* Zone, *truellei* Subzone.
Burton Bradstock, Dorset.
S. S. Buckman Collection, purchased 1927.
GSM 47769

Haselburgites admirandus S. S. Buckman HOLOTYPE
S. S. Buckman 1920, p. 30.
S. S. Buckman 1921, plates CCIII A, B.
Roman 1932, p. 241.
Inferior Oolite, *parkinsoni* Zone, *truellei* Subzone.
Quarry near the church, Haselbury Plucknett, Somerset.
S. S. Buckman Collection, purchased 1923.
GSM 32034.

Durotrigensia eimensis (Wetzel)
S. S. Buckman 1928, plate DCCLXVIII
Inferior Oolite, *parkinsoni* Zone.
Burton Bradstock, Dorset.
S. S. Buckman Collection; purchased 1929.
GSM 49342

Cosmoceras parkinsoni (J. Sowerby)
S. S. Buckman 1881, pp. 593, 600.
Durotrigensia parkinsoni (J. Sowerby)
S. S. Buckman 1928, plates DCCLXXXIA, B, C.
Inferior Oolite, *parkinsoni* Zone, *truellei* Subzone.
Railway cutting, Bradford Abbas, Dorset.
S. S. Buckman Collection, purchased 1929.
GSM 49351

Cadomites daubenyi Gemmellaro
S. S. Buckman 1910b, p. 73.
Polystephanus daubenyi (Gemmellaro)
S. S. Buckman 1922, plate CCCXI.
Inferior Oolite, *parkinsoni* Zone, *truellei* Subzone.
Burton Bradstock, Dorset.
S. S. Buckman Collection, ex D. S. Darell Collection, purchased 1924.
GSM 47126

Parkinsonia sp.
Cave 1977, p. 112.
Inferior Oolite, *parkinsoni* Zone.
Rodborough Hill, Gloucestershire.
Museum Collection.
GSM 25217

Harpoxyites harpophorus S. S. Buckman HOLOTYPE
S. S. Buckman 1924, plate CDLXXX.
Inferior Oolite, *parkinsoni* Zone.
Loders, near Bridport, Dorset.
S. S. Buckman Collection, purchased 1925.
GSM 37327

Gonoxyites goniophorus S. S. Buckman HOLOTYPE
S. S. Buckman 1924, plate CDLXXXI.
Inferior Oolite, *parkinsoni* Zone.
East Hill, Bradford Abbas, Dorset.
S. S. Buckman Collection, ex J. Buckman Collection, purchased 1925.
GSM 37328

Morphoceras defrancii (d'Orbigny)
S. S. Buckman 1910b, p. 73.
Dimorphinites defrancii (d'Orbigny)
S. S. Buckman 1924, plate DX.
Inferior Oolite, *parkinsoni* Zone, *truellei* Subzone.
Burton Bradstock, Dorset.
S. S. Buckman Collection, ex D. S. Darell Collection, purchased 1926.
GSM 47542

Haselburgites schloenbachi (Schlippe)
S. S. Buckman 1924, plate CDXCIII.
Parkinsonia bomfordi Arkell
Arkell 1956, pp. 157, 159.
Inferior Oolite, *parkinsoni* Zone, *bomfordi* Subzone.
Burton Bradstock, Dorset.
S. S. Buckman Collection, purchased 1926.
GSM 47534

BATHONIAN STAGE

Ebrayiceras filicosta Wetzel
Arkell 1955, plate 17, fig. 6; p. 141.
Inferior Oolite, *zigzag* Zone.
Quarry 150 yards SSE of Yeovil Junction Station, Clifton Maybank, Dorset.
Survey Collection (V. Wilson) 1938.
VW 1171.

Ebrayiceras jactatum S. S. Buckman HOLOTYPE
S. S. Buckman 1920, pp. 23-24.
S. S. Buckman 1928, plate DCCLXIX.
Arkell 1955, plate 17, fig. 2; p. 141.
Sturani 1966, p. 38.
Morphoceras jactatum (S. S. Buckman) HOLOTYPE
Hahn 1970, pp. 40-41.
Mangold 1970b, pp. 96-98.
Inferior Oolite, *zigzag* Zone.
Burton Bradstock, Dorset.
S. S. Buckman Collection, purchased 1929.
GSM 49343

Ebrayiceras pseudoanceps (Ebray)
S. S. Buckman 1920, plate CLXXIV.
Arkell 1955, plate 17, fig. 8; p. 139.
Inferior Oolite, *zigzag* Zone.
Crewkerne Station, Somerset.
S. S. Buckman Collection, ex D. S. Darell Collection, purchased 1923.
GSM 32021

Ebrayiceras ocellatum S. S. Buckman HOLOTYPE
S. S. Buckman 1920, plate CLXXIII.
Ebrayiceras pseudo-anceps (Ebray)
Arkell 1955, plate 17, fig. 7; p. 139.
Arkell 1957, fig. 386, 2; p. L311.
Inferior Oolite, *zigzag* Zone.
Broad Windsor, Dorset.
S. S. Buckman Collection, purchased 1923.
GSM 32020

Ebrayiceras pseudo-anceps (Ebray)
Arkell 1955, plate 17, fig. 11; pp. 139-140.
Inferior Oolite, *zigzag* Zone.
Crewkerne Station, Somerset.
S. S. Buckman Collection, purchased 1889.
GSM 3567

Ebrayiceras rursum S. S. Buckman
Arkell 1955, plate 17, fig. 15; p. 140.
Inferior Oolite, *zigzag* Zone.
Burton Bradstock, Dorset.
S. S. Buckman Collection, purchased 1889.
GSM 3643

Ebrayiceras rursum S. S. Buckman
S. S. Buckman 1920, pp. 23-24.
S. S. Buckman 1927, plate DCCLVIII.
Arkell 1955, plate 17, fig. 14; p. 140.
Sturani 1966, p. 39.
Hahn 1970, pp. 45-46.
Mangold 1970, b, p. 102.
Inferior Oolite, *zigzag* Zone.
Burton Bradstock, Dorset.
S. S. Buckman Collection, ex D. S. Darell Collection, purchased 1929.
GSM 49337

Morphoceras macrescens (S. S. Buckman)
Arkell 1955, plate 17, fig. 3; pp. 133-134.
Inferior Oolite, *zigzag* Zone.
Broad Windsor, Dorset.
S. S. Buckman Collection, purchased 1890.
GSM 3641

Morphoceras macrescens (S. S. Buckman)
Arkell 1955, p. 134.
Inferior Oolite, *zigzag* Zone.
Vitney Cross (now Vinney Cross), Loders, near Bridport, Dorset.
W. H. Hudleston Collection, presented by Miss C. A. Raisin 1920.
Y 3759

Patemorphoceras macrescens S. S. Buckman HOLOTYPE
S. S. Buckman 1923, plate CCCLXXVI.
Morphoceras macrescens (S. S. Buckman) HOLOTYPE
Arkell 1955, plate 16, fig. 4; pp. 133-134.
Hahn 1970, pp. 35-37.
Morphoceras macrescens macrescens (S. S. Buckman) HOLOTYPE
Mangold 1970b, pp. 69-72.
Inferior Oolite, *zigzag* Zone.
Grange Quarry, Broad Windsor, Dorset.
S. S. Buckman Collection, purchased 1924.
GSM 47172

Morphoceras multiforme Arkell
Arkell 1955, plate 16, fig. 2; pp. 132-133.
Inferior Oolite, *zigzag* Zone.
Broad Windsor, Dorset.
S. S. Buckman Collection, purchased 1910.
GSM 24714

Morphoceras multiforme Arkell
Arkell 1955, p. 133.
Inferior Oolite, *zigzag* Zone.
Burton Cliff, Burton Bradstock, Dorset.
Museum Collection.
GSM 25230

Morphoceras multiforme Arkell
Arkell 1955, p. 133.
Inferior Oolite, *zigzag* Zone.
Burton Bradstock, Dorset.
S. S. Buckman Collection, purchased 1910.
GSM 24715

Patemorphoceras patescens S. S. Buckman HOLOTYPE
S. S. Buckman 1922a, plate CCCLI.
Morphoceras patescens (S. S. Buckman) HOLOTYPE
Arkell 1955, plate 17, fig. 5; p. 133.
Sturani 1966, p. 36.
Hahn 1970, pp. 37-39.
Mangold 1970b, pp. 75-77.
Inferior Oolite, *zigzag* Zone.
Grange Quarry, Broad Windsor, Dorset.
S. S. Buckman Collection, ex D. S. Darell Collection, purchased 1924.
GSM 47151

Morphoceras patescens (S. S. Buckman)
Arkell 1955, p. 133.
Inferior Oolite, *zigzag* Zone.
Near Bridport, Dorset.
S. S. Buckman Collection, purchased 1918.
GSM 25231

Polysphinctites replictus S. S. Buckman HOLOTYPE
S. S. Buckman 1922a, plate CCCLIX.
Morphoceras replictum (S. S. Buckman) HOLOTYPE
Arkell 1955, plate 16, fig. 10; pp. 136-137.
Inferior Oolite, *zigzag* Zone.
Burton Bradstock, Dorset.
S. S. Buckman Collection, ex D. S. Darell Collection, purchased 1924.
GSM 47159

Oecotraustes (Oecotraustes) costiger S. S. Buckman
Arkell 1951a, plate 7 fig. 3; p. 67.
Inferior Oolite, Crackment Limestone, *zigzag* Zone.
Bradford Abbas, Dorset.
Museum Collection.
GSM 25102

Oecotraustes (Oecotraustes) costiger S. S. Buckman
Arkell 1951a, plate 7, fig. 4; p. 67.
Inferior Oolite, Crackment Limestone, *zigzag* Zone.
Bradford Abbas, Dorset.
S. S. Buckman Collection, purchased 1890.
GSM 3645

Oecotraustes (Oecotraustes) nodiger S. S. Buckman HOLOTYPE
Arkell 1951a, plate 7 fig. 7; p. 68.
Stefanov 1961, p. 346.
Inferior Oolite, Crackment Limestone, *zigzag* Zone.
Bradford Abbas, Dorset.
S. S. Buckman Collection, purchased 1907
GSM 69959

Oppelia (Oxycerites) fallax (Guéranger)
Arkell 1951a, plate 5 fig. 1; pp. 56, 60.
Inferior Oolite, *zigzag* Zone.
Yeovil, Somerset.
J. Lycett Collection, purchased 1867.
GSM 25311

Harpoxyites fallax (Guéranger)
S. S. Buckman 1924, plate CDXCIX.
Oppelia (Oxycerites) fallax (Guéranger)
Arkell 1951a, plate 8 fig. 11; pp. 56, 60.
Inferior Oolite, *zigzag* Zone.
Burton Bradstock, Dorset.
S. S. Buckman Collection, ex D. S. Darell Collection, purchased 1926.
GSM 47541

Polysphinctites polysphinctus S. S. Buckman
Arkell 1955, plate 16, fig. 8; p. 138; text-fig. 50, p. 136.
Inferior Oolite, *zigzag* Zone.
Burton Bradstock, Dorset.
L. F. Spath Collection, purchased 1945.
GSM 72829

Polysphinctites polysphinctus S. S. Buckman HOLOTYPE
S. S. Buckman 1922a, plate CCCXXIIA.
Arkell 1955, plate 16, fig. 7; p. 138.
Hahn 1970, pp. 56-57.
Inferior Oolite, *zigzag* Zone.
Burton Bradstock, Dorset.
S. S. Buckman Collection, ex D. S. Darell Collection, purchased 1924.
GSM 47133

Polysphinctites polysphinctus S. S. Buckman PARATYPE
S. S. Buckman 1922a, plate CCCXXIIB.
Arkell 1955, p. 138.
Arkell 1957, fig. 387, 1; p. L311 [as holotype]
Inferior Oolite, *zigzag* Zone.
Grange Quarry, Broad Windsor, Dorset.
S. S. Buckman Collection, purchased 1924.
GSM 47134

Parkinsonia (Parkinsonia) pachypleura S. S. Buckman
Arkell 1956a, plate 18, fig. 1; p. 150.
Inferior Oolite, Crackment Limestone, *zigzag* Zone.
Trench near Ven House, Milborne Port, Somerset.
Survey Collection (G. A. Kellaway), 1938.
GK 277

Parkinsonia (Parkinsonia) pachypleura S. S. Buckman
Arkell 1956a, p. 150.
Inferior Oolite, Crackment Limestone, *zigzag* Zone.
Trench near Ven House, Milborne Port, Somerset.
Survey Collection (G. A. Kellaway), 1938.
GK 274, 275

Parkinsonia (Parkinsonia) pachypleura S. S. Buckman
Arkell 1956a, text-fig. 57-6 on p. 154; p. 150.
Inferior Oolite, Crackment Limestone, *zigzag* Zone.
Trench near Ven House, Milborne Port, Somerset.
Survey Collection (G. A. Kellaway), 1938.
GK 291

Parkinsonia (Parkinsonia?) subtilis Arkell HOLOTYPE
Arkell 1956a, plate 18 fig. 6; pp. 152-153; text-fig. 57, 4.
Inferior Oolite, Crackment Limestone, *zigzag* Zone..
Trench near Ven House, Milborne Port, Somerset.
Survey Collection (G. A. Kellaway) 1938.
GK 278

Gonolkites convergens S. S. Buckman HOLOTYPE
S. S. Buckman 1925, plates DXLVI A, B.
Parkinsonia (Gonolkites) convergens (S. S. Buckman) HOLOTYPE
Arkell 1956a, plate 18 fig. 8; plate 19 fig. 1; text-fig. 57, 2; pp. 153, 154.
Arkell 1957, fig. 384, 7; p. L309.
Westermann 1958, pp. 68, 69.
Sturani 1966, pp. 31, 32.
Hahn 1970, pp. 16, 17.
Krystyn 1972, pp. 260-262.
Inferior Oolite, *zigzag* Zone, *convergens* Subzone.
Grange Quarry, Broadwindsor, Dorset.
S. S. Buckman Collection, ex D. S. Darell, purchased 1926.
GSM 47557

Parkinsonia (Gonolkites) convergens (S. S. Buckman)
Arkell 1956a, p. 156.
Inferior Oolite, *zigzag* Zone, *convergens* Subzone.
Broadwindsor, Dorset.
S. S. Buckman Collection, purchased 1889.
GSM 3545

Parkinsonia (Gonolkites) convergens (S. S. Buckman)
Arkell 1956a, p. 156.
Inferior Oolite, Crackment Limestone, *zigzag* Zone, *convergens* Subzone.
Trench near Ven House, Milborne Port, Somerset.
Survey Collection (G. A. Kellaway) 1938.
GK 272

Parkinsonia (Gonolkites) convergens (S. S. Buckman)
Arkell 1956a, p. 156.
Inferior Oolite, *zigzag* Zone, *convergens* Subzone.
Burton Bradstock, Dorset.
S. S. Buckman Collection, purchased 1890.
GSM 3651

Parkinsonia (Gonolkites) convergens (S. S. Buckman)
Arkell 1956a, p. 156.
Inferior Oolite, *zigzag* Zone, *convergens* Subzone.
Crewkerne Station, Somerset.
S. S. Buckman Collection, purchased 1910.
GSM 24683

Parkinsonia (Gonolkites) subgaleata (S. S. Buckman)
Arkell 1956a, p. 159, text-fig. 58.
Inferior Oolite, Crackment Limestone, *zigzag* Zone, *convergens* Subzone.
Trench near Ven House, Milborne Port, Somerset.
Survey Collection (G. A. Kellaway) 1938.
GK 279

Parkinsonia (Gonolkites) subgaleata (S. S. Buckman)
Arkell 1956a, plate 18 fig. 7, plate 19 fig. 3, p. 156.
Inferior Oolite, Crackment Limestone, *zigzag* Zone, *convergens* Subzone.
Sherborne, Dorset.
S. S. Buckman Collection, purchased 1890.
GSM 3650

Haselburgites subgaleatus S. S. Buckman HOLOTYPE
S. S. Buckman 1928, plate DCCXC.
Parkinsonia (Gonolkites) subgaleata (S. S. Buckman) HOLOTYPE
Arkell 1956a, p. 156, text-fig. 58.
Inferior Oolite, *zigzag* Zone, *convergens* Subzone.
Grange Quarry, Broad Windsor, Dorset.
S. S. Buckman Collection, purchased 1929.
GSM 49356

Procerites euryodos (Schmidt)
S. S. Buckman 1920, plate CLIII.
Zigzagiceras euryodos (Schmidt)
Arkell 1958, plate 21 fig. 1; p. 179.
Inferior Oolite, *zigzag* Zone.
Crewkerne Station, Somerset.
S. S. Buckman Collection, ex D. S. Darell Collection, purchased 1923.
GSM 32012

Zigzagiceras plenum Arkell
Arkell 1958, plate 22, fig. 7; p. 179.
Inferior Oolite, *zigzag* Zone.
Powerstock Station, Dorset
L. F. Spath Collection, purchased 1945
GSM 72827

Procerozigzag crassizigzag (S. S. Buckman)
Arkell 1958, plate 20, fig. 9; pp. 179-180.
Inferior Oolite, *zigzag* Zone.
Broad Windsor, Dorset.
S. S. Buckman Collection, purchased 1910.
GSM 24747

Zigzagiceras pollubrum S. S. Buckman HOLOTYPE
S. S. Buckman 1921, plate CCLIX A, B.
Procerozigzag crassizigzag (S. S. Buckman)
Arkell 1958, p. 180.
Inferior Oolite, Crackment Limestone, *zigzag* Zone.
Hall's (Vicarage) Quarry, Bradford Abbas, Dorset.
S. S. Buckman Collection, ex D. S. Darell Collection, purchased 1926.
GSM 32061

'Stephanoceras' crassizigzag var. α S. S. Buckman
S. S. Buckman 1892b, p. 449.
Zigzagiceras pollubrum S. S. Buckman
S. S. Buckman 1925, plate CCLIX C.
Inferior Oolite, *zigzag* Zone.
Grange Quarry, Broad Windsor, Dorset.
S. S. Buckman Collection, ex D. S. Darell Collection, purchased 1926.
GSM 47527

Stephanoceras crassizigzag var.α S. S. Buckman
HOLOTYPE
S. S. Buckman 1892b p. 449.
Zigzagiceras crassizigzag (S. S. Buckman) HOLOTYPE
S. S. Buckman 1922a, plate CCCXXXV.
Arkell 1933, p. 260.
Procerozigzag crassizigzag (S. S. Buckman) HOLOTYPE
Arkell 1958, plate 20, fig. 8; pp. 179-180.
Sturani 1966, pp. 49-50.
Zigzagiceras (Procerozigzag) crassizigzag
(S. S. Buckman) HOLOTYPE
Krystyn 1972, p. 270.
Inferior Oolite, *zigzag* Zone.
Crewkerne Station, Somerset.
S. S. Buckman Collection, ex D. S. Darell Collection, purchased 1924.
GSM 47141

Procerozigzag crassizigzag (S. S. Buckman)
Arkell 1958, p. 180.
Inferior Oolite, *zigzag* Zone.
West of Beaminster, Dorset.
Museum Collection.
GSM 25581

Zigzagiceras rhabdouchus S. S. Buckman HOLOTYPE
S. S. Buckman 1922a, plates CCC A, B, B*.
Procerozigzag pseudoprocerus (S. S. Buckman)
Arkell 1958, plate 20, fig. 10; p. 181.
Inferior Oolite, *zigzag* Zone.
Grange Quarry, Broad Windsor, Dorset.
S. S. Buckman Collection, ex D. S. Darell Collection, purchased 1924.
GSM 47120

Procerozigzag pseudoprocerus (S. S. Buckman)
Arkell 1958, plate 20, fig. 2; p. 181.
Inferior Oolite, *zigzag* Zone.
Broad Windsor, Dorset.
S. S. Buckman Collection, purchased 1890.
GSM 69989

?Procerozigzag pseudoprocerus (S. S. Buckman)
Arkell 1958, p. 181
Inferior Oolite, *zigzag* Zone.
Broad Windsor, Dorset.
S. S. Buckman Collection, purchased 1890.
GSM 69988

Procerozigzag pseudoprocerus (S. S. Buckman)
Arkell 1958, plate 20, fig. 4; p. 181.
Inferior Oolite, *zigzag* Zone.
West of Beaminster, Dorset.
Museum Collection.
GSM 25580

Procerites schloenbachi (de Grossouvre)
Arkell 1958, plate 21, fig. 9; p. 183.
Inferior Oolite, *zigzag* Zone.
Burton Bradstock, Dorset.
J. Lycett Collection purchased 1867.
GSM 25233

Procerites costulatosus (S. S. Buckman)
Arkell 1958, p. 189.
Inferior Oolite, ?*zigzag* Zone.
Broad Windsor, Dorset.
S. S. Buckman Collection, purchased 1890.
GSM 3669

Procerites tmetolobus S. S. Buckman
HOLOTYPE
S. S. Buckman 1923, plate CDXVI
Arkell 1958, plate 23 fig. 1; text-fig. 69-5; pp. 191-192.
Stephanov 1961, pp. 348-349.
Inferior Oolite, *zigzag* zone.
Allotment Quarry, Burton Broadstock, Dorset.
S. S. Buckman Collection, purchased 1924.
GSM 47200

Procerites tmetolobus S. S. Buckman
Arkell 1958, plate 23 fig. 3; p. 191
Inferior Oolite, *zigzag* Zone
Broad Windsor, Dorset
S. S. Buckman Collection, purchased 1889.
GSM 3543

Procerites incognitus Arkell HOLOTYPE
Arkell 1958, plate 26, fig. 5; p. 197.
Inferior Oolite, Crackment Limestone, *Parkinsonia convergens* Bed, *zigzag* Zone.
Trench near Ven House Milborne Port, Somerset.
Survey Collection (G. A. Kellaway), 1938.
GK 276

Procerites subprocerus (S. S. Buckman)
Arkell 1958, plate 22, fig. 4; 183-185.
Inferior Oolite, Crackment Limestone, *zigzag* Zone.
Trench near Ven House, Milborne Port, Somerset.
Survey Collection (G. A. Kellaway), 1938.
GK 273

?Procerites subprocerus (S. S. Buckman)
Arkell 1958, p. 185.
Inferior Oolite, Crackment Limestone, *zigzag* Zone
Trench near Ven House, Milborne Port, Somerset.
Survey Collection (G. A. Kellaway), 1938.
GK 280

Procerites subprocerus (S. S. Buckman)
Arkell 1958, pp. 183-185.
Inferior Oolite, Crackment Limestone, *zigzag* Zone.
Milborne Port, Somerset.
Survey Collection (J. Rhodes), 1885.
JR 636

Gonolkites vermicularis S. S. Buckman HOLOTYPE
S. S. Buckman 1925, plate DXLVII.
Parkinsonia (Durotrigensia?) vermicularis
(S. S. Buckman) HOLOTYPE
Arkell 1956a, text-fig. 57, 3; p. 160.
The Scroff, basal Lower Fuller's Earth, *zigzag* Zone.
Burton Bradstock, Dorset.
S. S. Buckman Collection, purchased 1926.
GSM 47558

Zigzagiceras sp.
Richardson 1910, p. 426.
Parkinsonites fullonicus S. S. Buckman HOLOTYPE
S. S. Buckman 1922a, plates CCCII, CCCII*.
Arkell, 1933, p. 280.
Procerites fullonicus (S. S. Buckman) HOLOTYPE
Wetzel 1937, pp. 110, 111.
Arkell 1958, plate 24, fig. 1; text-fig. 69, 6; pp. 189, 190.
Sturani 1966, p. 43.
Procerites laeviplex (Quenstedt)
Hahn 1970, pp. 48-50.
Basal Lower Fuller's Earth, *knorri* Clays, *zigzag* Zone.
Railway cutting, Combe Hay, near Bath, Avon [Somerset].
L. Richardson Collection, presented 1914.
GSM 26985

Procerites fullonicus (S. S. Buckman)
Cave 1977, p. 112.
Basal Lower Fuller's Earth, *zigzag* Zone.
Kingscote, Gloucestershire.
L. Richardson Collection, presented 1933.
GSM 52180

Planisphinctes planilobus S. S. Buckman HOLOTYPE
S. S. Buckman 1922a, plate CCCXXVII.
Arkell 1933, p. 255.
Arkell 1957, fig. 404; p. L317.
Siemiradzkia (Planisphinctes) planilobus (S. S. Buckman) HOLOTYPE
Arkell 1958, plate 33, fig. 7; pp. 230, 235.
Sturani 1966, pp. 39, 40.
Stefanov 1972, pp. 31, 33.
Fuller's Earth, *zigzag* Zone.
Burton Bradstock, Dorset.
S. S. Buckman Collection, ex D. S. Darell, purchased 1924.
GSM 47140

Oppelia fusca Roman
Solly and Walker 1891, p. 119
Gonoxyites limosus S. S. Buckman HOLOTYPE
S. S. Buckman 1925, plate DCXIII
Oppelia (Oxycerites) limosa (S. S. Buckman) HOLOTYPE
Arkell 1951, Plate 5, fig. 7; pp. 60-61.
Oxycerites (Limoxyites) nivernensis (Grossouvre)
Westermann 1958, p. 46.
Oxycerites limosus (S. S. Buckman) HOLOTYPE
Hahn 1968, pp. 33-36.
Basal Fuller's Earth Clay, *zigzag* Zone.
Black Rocks, Eype,. near Bridport, Dorset.
S. S. Buckman Collection, ex J. F. Walker Collection, purchased 1927.
GSM 47783

Oppeliidae indet.
Arkell 1952, p. 73.
Top part of Lower Fuller's Earth
Stream, south east of church, Halstock, Dorset.
Survey Collection (F. B. A. Welch) 1936.
BW 1439, 1441

Oppeliidae indet.
Arkell 1952, p. 73.
Top part of Lower Fuller's Earth
850 yards (773.50m) east of Whitevine Farm,
Survey Collection (F. B. A. Welch) 1936.
BW 1436, 1437

Oecotraustes (Paroecotraustes) cf. **serrigerus** Waagen
Arkell 1951a, pp. 69-70.
Fuller's Earth Rock, Polyzoa Bed
Lane cutting, near Maperton, Somerset
L. Richardson Collection, presented 1933
GSM 52178

Oecotraustes (Paroecotraustes) cf. **serrigerus** Waagen
Arkell 1951a, plate 8, fig. 4, pp. 69-70.
Fuller's Earth Rock, Polyzoa Bed.
Lane cutting, Maperton, Somerset.
L. Richardson Collection, presented 1933.
GSM 52179

Oecotraustes serrigerus Waagen
Arkell 1958, p. 245.
Oecotraustes (Paroecotraustes) waageni Stefanov
Stefanov 1966, p. 56.
Torrens 1969, pp. 68-69.
Fuller's Earth.
Chippenham U.D.C. water borehole, Patterdown, near Chippenham, Wiltshire Depth 270 feet (82.27m).
Survey Collection 1953.
Bi 9651

Oecostraustes (Paroecotraustes) splendens Arkell
Arkell 1951a, plate 8, fig. 2; p. 71.
Hahn 1968, p. 56.
?Fuller's Earth.
Doulting, Somerset.
L. Richardson Collection, presented 1933.
GSM 52183

Oppelia fusca (Quenstedt)
Richardson 1911, p. 228.
Oppelia (Oxycerites) limosa (S. S. Buckman)
Arkell 1951a, p. 61.
Torrens 1969 p. 74.
Chipping Norton Limestone, *zigzag* Zone.
Oakham Quarry, near Great Rollright, Oxfordshire.
L. Richardson Collection, purchased 1925.
Z 3872

Oppelia fusca (Quenstedt)
Richardson 1929, p. 95.
Oppelia (Oxycerites) limosa (S. S. Buckman)
Arkell 1951a, plate 6, fig. 5; p. 61.
Torrens 1969, p. 74.
Chipping Norton Limestone, *zigzag* Zone.
Lower Swell, near Stow-on-the-Wold, Gloucestershire.
F. B. A. Welch Collection, presented 1925.
GSM 37524

Ammonites waterhousei Morris & Lycett HOLOTYPE
Morris and Lycett 1851, plate 1, fig. 4, p. 13.
Oxycerites waterhousei (Morris & Lycett) HOLOTYPE
S. S. Buckman 1924, plate CDLXXVI.
Arkell 1933, p. 275.
Oppelia (Oxycerites) waterhousei (Morris & Lycett) HOLOTYPE
Cox and Arkell 1950, p. 91.
Arkell 1951a, plate 5, fig. 4, text-fig. 16, 4; p. 66.
Torrens 1969, p. 70.
Great Oolite, ?the Scroff, *zigzag* Zone.
Minchinghampton, Gloucestershire.
J. Lycett Collection, purchased 1867.
GSM 25619

Phaulozigzag phaulomorphus S. S. Buckman HOLOTYPE
S. S. Buckman 1926, plate DCXLIII.
Arkell 1933, p. 260.
Procerites (Phaulozigzag) phaulomorphus (S. S. Buckman)
Arkell 1957, fig. 398; p. L315.
Arkell 1958, text-fig. 64, pp. 175, 203, 204.
Westermann 1958, p. 77.
Sturani 1966, p. 45.
Fuller's Earth, ?*zigzag* Zone.
Grange Quarry, Broad Windsor, Dorset.
S. S. Buckman Collection, purchased 1927.
GSM 47840

Procerites sp.
Torrens 1968, p. 431.
Liostrea acuminata Beds, *progracilis* Zone.
Motorway cutting, near Dodington Ash, Avon [Gloucestershire].
Survey Collection (L. A. Joseph) 1965.
LAJ 45, 46

Procerites (Gracilisphinctes) aff. **progracilis** Cox & Arkell, fine-ribbed variety.
Arkell 1958, plate 28, fig. 1; text-fig. 72 no. 3; pp. 198-199.
Stonesfield Slate, *progracilis* Zone.
Eyford, Gloucestershire.
S. S. Buckman Collection, purchased 1903.
GSM 8255

Procerites (Gracilisphinctes) progracilis Cox & Arkell juv.
Arkell 1958, p. 199.
Stonesfield, Slate, *progracilis* Zone.
Stonesfield, Oxfordshire.
Geological Society Collection (C. Lyell 1824), presented 1911.
GSa 4574

Procerites (Gracilisphinctes) mirabilis Arkell PARATYPE
Arkell 1958, plate 28, fig. 6; p. 201.
Stonesfield Slate, *progracilis* Zone.
Stonesfield, Oxfordshire.
Geological Society Collection, presented 1911.
GSa 4588

Ammonites elegans?
J. Buckman 1844, p. 71.
Micromphalites oxus S. S. Buckman HOLOTYPE
S. S. Buckman 1926, plate DCXLIV.
Oppelia (Oxycerites) oxus (S. S. Buckman) HOLOTYPE
Arkell 1951a, plate 6, fig. 8; text-fig. 16, no. 2; pp. 66-67.
Sturani 1966, p. 25.
Stonesfield Slate, *progracilis* Zone.
Seven furlongs W by S of Eyford, Gloucestershire.
S. S. Buckman Collection, ex J. Buckman Collection, purchased 1927.
GSM 47841

Micromphalites micromphalus (Phillips)
S. S. Buckman 1923, plate CDLIII.
Arkell 1951a, p. 47.
Great Oolite Series, Stonesfield Slate, *progracilis* Zone.
Stonesfield, Oxfordshire.
Earl of Enniskillen Collection, presented 1853.
GSM 25607

?Procerites (Gracilosphinctes) vineta Arkell
Arkell 1958, plate 28, fig. 5; p. 203.
Stonesfield Slate, *progracilis* Zone.
Naunton, Gloucestershire.
W. H. Hudleston Collection, presented by Miss C. A. Raisin 1930.
Y 3495

Tulphorites praeclarus S. S. Buckman HOLOTYPE
S. S. Buckman 1921, p. 45.
S. S. Buckman 1922a, plate CCCLXVIII.
Tulites praeclarus (S. S. Buckman) HOLOTYPE
Arkell 1952, text-fig. 29; pp. 93, 95.
Torrens 1969, p. 70.
Torrens 1970, p. 137 [Number misquoted as GSM 47116]
Fuller's Earth Rock, Thornford Beds, *subcontractus* Zone.
Troll quarry, near Thornford, Dorset.
S. S. Buckman ex J. Buckman Collection, purchased 1924.
GSM 47166

Tulites praeclarus (S. S. Buckman)
Arkell 1952, p. 95.
Fuller's Earth Rock, *subcontractus* Zone.
Alham Lane quarry, near Doulting, Somerset.
L. Richardson Collection, purchased 1931.
Zd 4746

Tulphorites tulotus S. S. Buckman HOLOTYPE
S. S. Buckman 1921, p. 45.
S. S. Buckman 1922a, plates CCCLXIX A, B.
Arkell 1933, p. 258.
Roman 1938, p. 204.
Arkell 1952, plate 9, fig. 5; pp. 93, 95.
Fuller's Earth Rock, Thornford Beds, *subcontractus* Zone.
Troll quarry, near Thornford, Dorset.
S. S. Buckman ex J. Buckman Collection, purchased 1924.
GSM 47167

Tulites modiolaris (William Smith)
Arkell 1952, p. 97.
Fuller's Earth Rock, *subcontractus* Zone.
Thornford, Dorset.
Survey Collection (J. Rhodes) 1885.
JR 551

Tulites modiolaris (William Smith)
Spath 1932, text-fig. 1A; p. 11.
Arkell 1952, p. 97.
Fuller's Earth Rock.
Laycock railway cutting, Sherborne, Dorset.
L. Richardson Collection, presented 1915.
GSM 28221

Tulites modiolaris (William Smith)
Arkell 1952, p. 97.
Fuller's Earth Rock, *subcontractus* Zone.
Troll quarry, Thornford, Dorset.
F. B. A. Welch Collection, presented 1933.
Ze 1902

Sphaeromorphites sphaeroidalis S. S. Buckman HOLOTYPE
S. S. Buckman 1921, p. 49.
S. S. Buckman 1923, plate CCCLXVII.
Roman 1938, p. 204.
Tulites modiolaris (William Smith)
Arkell 1952, text-fig. 23, p. 97.
Fuller's Earth Rock, Thornford Beds, *subcontractus* Zone.
Troll Quarry, Thornford, Dorset.
S. S. Buckman, ex D. S. Darell Collection, purchased 1924.
GSM 47165

Madarites madarus S. S. Buckman HOLOTYPE
S. S. Buckman 1921, p. 46.
S. S. Buckman 1922a, plates CCLXX1 A, B.
Roman 1938, p. 204.
Tulites modiolaris (William Smith)
Arkell 1952, plate 9, fig. 1; pp. 95-96.
Great Oolite, *subcontractus* Zone.
Minchinhampton, Gloucestershire.
Museum Collection.
GSM 25615

Ammonites subcontractus Morris and Lycett SYNTYPE
Morris and Lycett 1851, plate 2, figs. 1, 1A; p. 11.
Tulites subcontractus (Morris and Lycett) LECTOTYPE
S. S. Buckman 1921, p. 45.
S. S. Buckman 1922a, plate CCLXX.
Cox and Arkell 1950, p. 92.
Arkell 1952, pp. 97-98.
Arkell 1954, plate 12, fig. 5.
Arkell 1956, plate 36, fig. 3.
Westermann 1958, p. 63.
Torrens 1969, p. 70.
Hahn 1971, pp. 76-78.
Great Oolite, *subcontractus* Zone.
Minchinhampton, Gloucestershire.
J. Lycett Collection, purchased 1867.
GSM 25610

Tulites subcontractus (Morris and Lycett)
Arkell 1952, p. 98.
Fuller's Earth Rock, Top Bed, *subcontractus* Zone.
Maperton, Somerset.
L. Richardson Collection, purchased 1931.
Zd 4315

Tulites subcontractus (Morris and Lycett)
Arkell 1952, text-fig. 30, p. 98.
Fuller's Earth Rock, Thornford Beds, *subcontractus* Zone.
Troll quarry, near Thornford, Dorset.
Survey Collection (V. Wilson) 1945.
BW 803

Tulites subcontractus (Morris and Lycett)
Arkell 1952, p. 98.
Fuller's Earth Rock, *subcontractus* Zone.
Laycock railway cutting, Sherborne, Dorset.
L. Richardson Collection, purchased 1931.
Zd 4740

Ammonites subcontractus Morris and Lycett juv.
Morris and Lycett 1851, plate 2, fig. 2; p. 11.
Tulites sp. juv.
Cox and Arkell 1950, p. 92.
Great Oolite, *subcontractus* Zone.
Minchinhampton, Gloucestershire.
J. Lycett Collection, purchased 1867.
GSM 25613

Rugiferites rugifer S. S. Buckman HOLOTYPE
S. S. Buckman 1921, p. 46.
S. S. Buckman 1923, plate CCCXXXVIII A.
Roman 1938, p. 204.
Tulites (Rugiferites) rugifer (S. S. Buckman) HOLOTYPE
Arkell 1954, plate 13, fig. 1; p. 104,
Arkell 1957, fig. 348. p. L 292.
Stefanov 1963, p. 180.
Hahn 1971, pp. 80-81.
Fuller's Earth Rock, Thornford Beds, *Rhynchonella* Bed, *subcontractus* Zone.
Troll quarry, near Thornford, Dorset.
S. S. Buckman, ex J. Buckman Collection, purchased 1924.
GSM 47144

Rugiferites rugifer S. S. Buckman PARATYPE
S. S. Buckman 1921, p. 46.
S. S. Buckman 1922a, plate CCCXXXVIII.
Tulites (Rugiferites) rugifer (S. S. Buckman) PARATYPE
Arkell 1954, plate 13, fig. 6; p. 104.
Fuller's Earth Rock, Thornford Beds, *subcontractus* Zone.
Sherborne, Dorset.
S. S. Buckman ex F. H. Butler Collection, purchased 1924.
GSM 47143

Pleurophorites polypleurus S. S. Buckman
HOLOTYPE
S. S. Buckman 1921, p. 47.
S. S. Buckman 1923, plate CCCLXX.
Rugiferites polypleurus (S. S. Buckman) HOLOTYPE
Arkell 1951b, p. 9.
Roman 1938, p. 204.
Tulites (Rugiferites) polypleurus (S. S. Buckman)
HOLOTYPE
Arkell 1954, pp. 104-105.
Stefanov 1963, p. 181.
Hahn 1971, pp. 81-82.
Fuller's Earth Rock, Thornford Beds, *subcontractus* Zone.
Troll quarry, Thornford, Dorset.
S. S. Buckman ex J. Buckman Collection, purchased 1924.
GSM 47168

Ammonites bullatus d'Orbigny
Lycett 1863, plate 31, fig. 1; p. 3.
Bullatimorphites bullatimorphus S. S. Buckman
HOLOTYPE
S. S. Buckman 1921, p. 47.
S. S. Buckman 1922a, plate CCLXXV.
Arkell 1933, p. 275.
Roman 1938, p. 204.
Cox and Arkell 1950, p. 92.
Arkell and Donovan 1951, p. 241.
Arkell 1957, fig. 349, 5; p. L292.
Stefanov 1963, p. 181.
Torrens 1967, p. 88.
Torrens 1969, p. 68.
Hahn 1971, p. 96.
Cave 1977, pp. 143, 175.
Probably from Upper Fuller's Earth, Tresham Rock, *retrocostatum* Zone.
Tiltups End, south of Nailsworth, Gloucestershire [labelled "Tiltups Inn"].
J. Lycett Collection, purchased 1867.
GSM 25620

Madarites glabretus S. S. Buckman HOLOTYPE
S. S. Buckman 1921, p. 52.
Arkell, Richardson and Pringle 1944, p. 344.
Tulites glabretus (S. S. Buckman) HOLOTYPE
Arkell 1952, text-fig. 32, pp. 100, 102.
Torrens 1967, p. 69.
Great Oolite, near base of White Limestone.
Cutting between Bucknell and Ardley Wood, NW of Bicester, Oxfordshire.
Survey Collection (J. Pringle) 1909.
GSM 31364 [formerly Pl 866]

Tulites mustela Arkell HOLOTYPE
Arkell 1954, plate 13, fig. 4; p. 103.
Hahn 1971, pp. 78-79.
Fuller's Earth Rock, lower part, *subcontractus* Zone.
Dancing Cross quarry, Maperton, Somerset.
V. Wilson & G. A. Kellaway Collection, presented 1939.
GSM 69979

Tulophorites aff. **tulotus** S. S. Buckman
Richardson 1929, p. 119.
Tulites mustela Arkell PPARATYPE
Arkell 1954, plate 12, fig.-tl; p. 103.
Torrens 1969, p. 69.
Great Oolite, near base of White Limestone.
Quarry ½ mile (801m) NW of Salperton church, Gloucestershire.
L. Richardson Collection, presented 1928.
GSM 48482

Tulites cadus S. S. Buckman
Arkell 1952, p. 93.
Fuller's Earth Rock, *subcontractus* Zone.
Railway cutting, Laycock, Sherborne, Dorset.
L. Richardson Collection, purchased 1931.
Zd 4737

Tulites sp.
Torrens 1968, p. 431.
Motorway cutting, near Dodington Ash, Gloucestershire.
Fuller's Earth, loose ?ex Cross Hands Rock (*subcontractus* or *morrisi* Zone).
Survey Collection (L. A. Joseph) 1965.
LAJ 217

Oecotraustes (Paroecotraustes) splendens Arkell
Arkell 1951a, plate 8, fig. 3; p. 71.
Stefanov 1966, pp. 57-58.
Hahn 1968, p. 56.
Fuller's Earth Rock.
South side of lane, Thornford, Dorset.
Rev. J. Fowler Collection, presented 1940.
GSM 73163

Tulites cadus S. S. Buckman HOLOTYPE
S. S. Buckman 1921, p. 45.
S. S. Buckman 1922a, plates CCLXVIII A, B.
Arkell 1952, text-fig. 28, pp. 91-93.
Torrens 1969, p. 70.
Tulites (Tulites) cadus S. S. Buckman HOLOTYPE
Hahn 1971, pp. 73-74.
Great Oolite, *morrisi* Zone.
Minchinhampton, Gloucestershire.
S. S. Buckman Collection, ex J. Buckman Collection, purchased 1924.
GSM 47107

Tulites cadus S. S. Buckman PARATYPE
S. S. Buckman 1922a, plate CCLXVIII C.
Arkell 1952, p. 93.
Fuller's Earth Rock, Milborne Beds, *morrisi* Zone.
Milborne Wick, Somerset.
S. S. Buckman Collection, ex D. S. Darell Collection, purchased 1924.
GSM 47108

Tulites cadus S. S. Buckman
Arkell 1952, pp. 91-93.
Fuller's Earth Rock, *subcontractus* Zone.
Alham Lane Quarry, Doulting, Somerset.
L. Richardson Collection, purchased 1931.
Zd 4744

Tulites pumilis Arkell PARATYPE
Arkell 1954, plate 12, fig. 4; p. 103.
Fuller's Earth Rock.
Pitman's Leaze quarry, NE of Thornford church, Dorset.
Survey Collection (V. Wilson) 1945.
VW 804

Tulites pumilis Arkell var.
Arkell 1954, plate 12, fig. 7, p. 103.
Fuller's Earth Rock, Milborne Beds, *morrisi* Zone.
Troll (or Trill) quarry, Thornford, Dorset.
F. B. A. Welch Collection, presented 1933.
Ze 1901

Tulites tula S. S. Buckman HOLOTYPE
S. S. Buckman 1921, p. 45.
S. S. Buckman 1922a, plate CCLXIX.
Arkell 1933, p. 257.
Roman 1938, plate 18, fig. 193; p. 203.
Arkell 1952, text-fig. 22; p. 93.
Basse 1952, pl. 11, fig. 2.
Arkell 1957, fig. 349, 6; p. L292.
Luppov and Drushchits 1958, plate 30, fig. 8.
Stefanov 1963, p. 180.
Fuller's Earth Rock, Milborne Beds, *morrisi* Zone.
S. S. Buckman Collection, ex D. S. Darell Collection, purchased 1924.
GSM 47109

Bullatimorphites serpenticonus Arkell HOLOTYPE
Arkell 1954, text-fig. 38, p. 111.
Fuller's Earth Rock,
Near Thornford, Dorset.
Survey Collection (J. Rhodes) 1885.
JR 550

Ammonites macrocephalus Schlotheim
Morris & Lycett 1851, plate 2, figs. 3, 3A; p. 12.
Ammonites morrisi Oppel HOLOTYPE
Oppel 1857, p. 478.
Ammonites viator d'Orbigny
Lycett 1863, p. 121.
Morrisites morrisi (Oppel) HOLOTYPE
S. S. Buckman 1921, p. 48.
S. S. Buckman 1922a, plate CCLXXIII.
Pionoceras morrisi (Oppel) HOLOTYPE
Lissajous 1923, pp. 103-105.
Morrisites morrisi (Oppel) HOLOTYPE
Roman 1938, pp. 204-205.
Morrisiceras morrisi (Oppel) HOLOTYPE
Cox & Arkell 1950, p. 93.
Arkell 1951a, p. 11.
Arkell 1954, plate 14, fig. 3; pp. 119-120.
Torrens 1970, p. 143.
Morrisiceras (Morriceras) morrisi (Oppel) HOLOTYPE
Hahn 1971, pp. 88-90.
Cross Hands Rock, *morrisi* Zone.
Minchinhampton, Gloucestershire.
J. Lycett Collection, purchased 1867.
GSM 25617

Macrocephalites morrisi (Oppel)
Richardson 1911, p. 111.
Morrisiceras morrisi (Oppel)
Arkell 1954, p. 121.
Torrens 1969, pp. 69-70.
Cross Hands Rock, *morrisi* Zone.
Stony Furlong railway cutting, Chedworth, Gloucestershire.
L. Richardson Collection, presented 1938.
GSM 52177

Morrisiceras morrisi (Oppel)
Arkell 1954, p. 121.
Fuller's Earth Rock, *morrisi* Zone.
1000 yards (910m.) SE of Englishcombe church, Avon [Somerset].
Survey Collection (G. A. Kellaway) 1947.
GK 1229

Morrisiceras morrisi (Oppel)
Arkell 1954, p. 121.
Fuller's Earth Rock, *morrisi* Zone.
Alham Lane Quarry, Doulting, Somerset.
L. Richardson Collection, purchased 1931.
Zd 4745

Morrisiceras morrisi (Oppel)
Arkell 1954, p. 121.
Fuller's Earth Rock, *morrisi* Zone.
Laycock railway cutting, near Milborne Port, Somerset.
L. Richardson Collection, purchased 1931.
Zd 4738, 4739

Morrisiceras morrisi (Oppel)
Arkell 1954, p. 121.
Fuller's Earth Rock, *morrisi* Zone.
Laycock railway cutting, near Milborne Port, Somerset.
Survey Collection (J. Rhodes) 1885.
JR 580

Morrisiceras morrisi (Oppel)
Arkell 1954, p. 121.
Fuller's Earth Rock, *morrisi* Zone.
Quarry to the east of Milborne Port, Somerset.
L. Richardson Collection, purchased 1931.
Zd 4736

Morrisiceras morrisi (Oppel)
Arkell 1954, p. 121.
Fuller's Earth Rock, *morrisi* Zone.
Dunkerton, Somerset.
Geological Society Collection (S. P. Pratt 1841), presented 1911.
GSa 4699

Morrisiceras sphaera S. S. Buckman
Arkell 1954, p. 122.
Fuller's Earth Rock, *morrisi* Zone.
Dunkerton, Somerset.
Geological Society Collection (S. P. Pratt 1841), presented 1911.
GSa 4700

Macrocephalites morrisi (Oppel)
S. S. Buckman 1893b, p. 43.
S. S. Buckman 1894, p. 440.
Morrisiceras sphaera S. S. Buckman HOLOTYPE
S. S. Buckman 1920, plate CLXVII.
S. S. Buckman 1921, p. 47.
Roman 1938, p. 204.
Arkell 1954, text-fig. 39; pp. 121-122.
Arkell 1957, fig. 352, 10; p. L293.
Stefanov 1963, pp. 187-188 [number misquoted as GSM 25617].
Torrens 1970, p. 145.
Hahn 1971, pp. 86-88.
Fuller's Earth Rock, Milborne Beds, *morrisi* Zone.
Milborne Wick, Somerset.
S. S. Buckman Collection, ex J. Buckman Collection, purchased 1922.
GSM 32018

Morrisiceras sphaera S. S. Buckman
Arkell 1954, p. 122.
Torrens 1970, pp. 143, 145.
Fuller's Earth Rock.
Bradford-on-Avon, Wiltshire.
Museum Collection.
GSM 25622

Morriceras irregulare Spath HOLOTYPE
Spath 1932, text-fig. 2; p. 15.
Morrisiceras fornicatum (S. S. Buckman)
Arkell & Donovan 1951, p. 242.
Arkell 1954, plate 14, fig. 11; pp. 122-123.
Great Oolite.
Pinfarthings, SW side of Minchinhampton, Gloucestershire.
Mrs Golightly Collection, presented per C. E. N. Bromehead 1924.
GSM 44060

Morrisites fornicatus S. S. Buckman HOLOTYPE
S. S. Buckman 1921, p. 48.
S. S. Buckman 1923, plate CCCLXXVIII.
Morrisiceras fornicatum (S. S. Buckman) HOLOTYPE
Arkell 1954, plate 14, fig. 12; pp. 122-123.
Torrens 1969, p. 71.
Fuller's Earth Rock.
Near Sherborne, Dorset.
S. S. Buckman Collection, ex J. Buckman Collection, purchased 1924.
GSM 47174

Morrisiceras fornicatum (S. S. Buckman)
Arkell 1954, p. 123.
Fuller's Earth Rock.
Quarry by drive-side, ¾ mile (1200m) E by S of Milborne Port church, Somerset.
L. Richardson Collection, purchased 1931.
Zd 4735

Lycetticeras comma (S. S. Buckman)
Arkell 1954, plate 15, fig. 8, pp. 124-125.
Fuller's Earth Rock.
Radstock (?Dunkerton), Avon [Somerset].
Museum Collection.
GSM 49573

Lycetticeras sknipum (S. S. Buckman)
Arkell 1954, plate 15, fig. 7, p. 127.
Fuller's Earth Rock.
Wellow Road, Bath, Avon, [Somerset.]
Geological Society Collection (S. P. Pratt 1841), presented 1911.
GSa 4705

Lycetticeras sknipum (S. S. Buckman)
Arkell 1954, p. 127.
Great Oolite.
Minchinhampton, Gloucestershire.
Museum Collection.
GSM 25618

Lycetticeras aff. **bulbosum** Arkell
Arkell 1954, text-fig. 46, p. 128.
Fuller's Earth Rock.
Dunkerton, Avon [Somerset].
Geological Society Collection (S. P. Pratt 1841), presented 1911.
GSa 4701

Procerites sp.
Muir-Wood 1936, p. 34.
Procerites wattonensis Arkell HOLOTYPE
Arkell 1958, plate 27, fig. 2, text-fig. 69, no. 9; p. 196.
Fuller's Earth, *wattonensis* Beds, *retrocostatum* Zone.
Base of cliff at Fault Corner, Eype, Dorset.
J. S. Turner Collection, presented 1934.
GSM 57743

Zigzagites imitator S. S. Buckman HOLOTYPE
S. S. Buckman 1922a, plate CCCI.
Arkell 1933, p. 293.
Arkell, Richardson, and Pringle 1933, p. 345.
Wagnericeras
Arkell 1953, p. 37.
Procerites imitator (S. S. Buckman) HOLOTYPE
Arkell 1958, pl. 26, fig. 2; text-fig. 69, no. 2; pp. 192-193, 235.
Sturani 1966, p. 43.
Torrens 1969, p. 73.
Hahn 1969, pp. 55-57.
Krystyn 1972, pp. 274-275.
Fuller's Earth, base of Hampen Marly Veds.
Railway cutting north of Troy Farm, Fritwell, Oxfordshire.
Survey Collection (J. Pringle) 1969.
GSM 30328 [formerly Pl 844]

Wagnericeras fortecostatum (de Grossouvre)
Arkell 1958, pl. 29, fig. 2; pp. 204-205, 235.
Fuller's Earth Rock.
Lansdown, Bath, Avon [Somerset].
Survey Collection (H. B. Woodward) 1886.
GSM 95037 [formerly 3751 HBW]

Wagnericeras fortecostatum (de Grossouvre)
Arkell 1958, p. 205.
Fuller's Earth Rock.
West Cranmore, Somerset.
Survey Collection (W. A. E. Ussher) 1868.
GSM 95036

Ammonites arbustigerus d'Orbigny
Morris and Lycett 1851, plate 2, fig. 4; p. 12.
Suspensites suspensus S. S. Buckman HOLOTYPE
S. S. Buckman 1922a, plate CCCXLVI.
Arkell 1933, p. 275.
Wagnericeras suspensum
(S. S. Buckman) HOLOTYPE
Cox and Arkell 1950, p. 94.
Wagnericeras (Suspensites) suspensum
(S. S. Buckman) HOLOTYPE
Arkell 1958, plate 29, fig. 8; p. 209.
Wagnericeras suspensum
(S. S. Buckman) HOLOTYPE
Wetzel 1966, p. 86.
Hahn 1969, pp. 66-68.
Torrens 1969, p. 70.
Krystyn 1972, p. 280.
Great Oolite.
Minchinhampton, Gloucestershire.
J. Lycett Collection, purchased 1867.
GSM 25609

Choffatia (Homoeoplanulites) homoeomorpha
S. S. Buckman
Arkell 1958, p. 227.
Fuller's Earth Rock.
Midford, Somerset.
Rev. H. H. Winwood Collection, presented 1894.
GSM 69934

Siemiradzkia aurigera (Oppel)
Arkell 1958, plate 33, fig. 8.
Fuller's Earth.
Borehole at Wincanton, Somerset.
Survey Collection (W. N. Edwards) 1925.
GSM 109380

Siemiradzkia? pseudoannularis (Lissajous)
Arkell 1958, plate 32, fig. 4; p. 230.
Lower Fuller's Earth.
Jack's Hill quarry, SE of Beaminster, Dorset.
Survey Collection (S. W. Hester) 1936.
GSM 109381 [formerly Ht 2170]

Siemiradzkia? pseudoannularis (Lissajous)
Arkell 1958, p. 230.
Lower Fuller's Earth.
Jack's Hill quarry, SE of Beaminster, Dorset.
Survey Collection (S. W. Hester) 1936.
Ht 2162, 2169

?Siemiradzkia pseudorjazanensis (Lissajous) worn nucleus
Arkell 1958, p. 228.
Field brash on Kemble Beds.
1380 yards (1256m) N 54°E of Westwell church, Oxfordshire.
Survey Collection (G. Bisson) 1952.
BN 654

Berbericeras schwandorfense Arkell
Arkell 1958, p. 231.
Fuller's Earth Rock.
Lane cutting, Maperton, Somerset.
L. Richardson Collection, presented 1933.
GSM 52181

Nautilus baberi Morris & Lycett HOLOTYPE
Morris & Lycett 1851, plate 1 figs. 1, 1A; p. 10.
Procymatoceras baberi (Morris & Lycett) HOLOTYPE
Cox & Arkell 1950, p. 90.
Great Oolite.
Minchinhampton, Gloucestershire.
J. Lycett Collection, purchased 1867.
GSM 59502

Ammonites subradiatus J. de C. Sowerby
?J. Buckman 1858, pp. 104, 122.
Benedictites hochstetteri (Oppel)
S. S. Buckman 1924, plate DXXIII.
Clydoniceras hochstetteri Oppel
Douvillé 1943, text-fig. 13; p. 17.
Clydoniceras discus (J. Sowerby) var. **hochstetteri** (Oppel)
Arkell 1951a, p. 34.
Lower Cornbrash, *discus* Zone.
Fairford, Gloucestershire.
S. S. Buckman Collection, ex J. Buckman Collection, purchased 1926.
GSM 47549

Clydoniceras discus (J. Sowerby)
S. S. Buckman 1927, plate DVI A.
Arkell 1951a, text-fig. 6, No.1B.
Lower Cornbrash, *discus* Zone.
Quarry north of the Bicester-Aylesbury Road, Blackthorne Hill, Bicester, Oxfordshire.
S. S. Buckman Collection, purchased 1928.
GSM 49289

Clydoniceras discus (J. Sowerby)
?Blake 1905, text-fig. 5c; p. 55.
Lower Cornbrash, *discus* Zone.
Bedford.
G. C. Crick Collection, presented 1881.
GSM 8649

Clydoniceras discus discus (J. Sowerby)
Arkell 1951a, plate 2, fig. 1; p. 35-36.
Lower Cornbrash, *discus* Zone.
Bedford.
G. C. Crick Collection, presented 1881.
GSM 25621

Delecticeras delectum Arkell HOLOTYPE
Arkell 1951a, plate 4, fig. 12; text-fig. 8; p. 45.
Arkell 1957, fig. 346, 3; p. L291.
Clydoniceras (Delecticeras) delectum (Arkell)
HOLOTYPE
Westermann 1958, p. 60.
Lower Cornbrash, *discus* Zone.
Bedford.
G. C. Crick Collection, presented ?1881.
GSM 62626

Clydoniceras hochstetteri (Oppel)
Blake 1905, plate 6, fig. 2; pp. 55-56.
Clydoniceras discus (J. Sowerby) **hochstetteri** (Oppel)
Cox & Arkell 1950, p. 92.
Lower Cornbrash, *discus* Zone.
Brize Norton, Oxfordshire.
Survey Collection (R. Gibbs) 1859.
GSM 8647 [formerly G 433]

Clydoniceras discus (J. Sowerby)
Arkell 1951a, plate 3, figs. 9 A, B.
Lower Cornbrash, *discus* Zone.
Islip Furnaces, Thrapston, Northamptonshire.
L. Richardson Collection, purchased 1931.
Zd 4561

Clydoniceras discus (J. Sowerby)
?Blake 1905, text-fig. 5D.
Clydoniceras thrapstonense Arkell
Arkell 1951a, p. 41.
Lower Cornbrash, *discus* Zone.
Cirencester, Gloucestershire.
Museum Collection.
GSM 8648

Perisphinctes subbakeriae (d'Orbigny)
Blake 1905, plate 5, fig. 2; pp. 49-51.
Homoeoplanulites homoeomorphus
S. S. Buckman HOLOTYPE
S. S. Buckman 1922a, plate CCCXXVII.
Choffatia 'homoeomorpha'
(S. S. Buckman) HOLOTYPE
Spath 1931, p. 325.
Choffatia (Homoeoplanulites) homoeomorpha
(S. S. Buckman) HOLOTYPE
Cox & Arkell 1950, p. 94.
Choffatia homoeomorpha (S. S. Buckman) HOLOTYPE
Arkell 1954, p. 119.
Choffatia (Homoeoplanulites)
homoeomorpha (S. S. Buckman) HOLOTYPE
Arkell 1957, fig. 405, 9; p. L317.
Arkell 1958, plate 30, fig. 4; pp. 225-227, 235.
Hahn 1969, pp. 71-72.
Homoeoplanulites (m. **Homoeoplanulites)**
homoeomorphus (S. S. Buckman) HOLOTYPE
Mangold 1970a, fig. 29, pp. 64-65.
Choffatia (Homoeoplanulites) homoeomorpha
(S. S. Buckman) HOLOTYPE
Krystyn 1972, pp. 283-284.
Stalbridge Western, near Sturminster, Dorset.
Museum Collection.
GSM 8654

Choffatia subbakeriae (d'Orbigny)
Arkell 1954, p. 119.
Arkell 1958, p. 218.
Lower Cornbrash, *discus* Zone.
Cutting No. 2, Great Western Railway relief line, Frome, Somerset.
Museum Collection.
Ht 853, 854

Choffatia subbakeriae (d'Orbigny)
Arkell 1954, p. 1.9.
Arkell 1958, plate 32, fig. 9; pp. 217-218.
Lower Cornbrash, *discus* Zone.
Long Handborough quarry, Woodstock, Oxfordshire.
Survey Collection (T. I. Pocock) 1904.
GSM 83149 [formerly 1236 HBW]

Choffatia subbakeriae (d'Orbigny)
Arkell 1958, p. 218.
Lower Cornbrash, *discus* Zone.
Berkley, near Frome, Somerset.
Survey Collection (H. B. Woodward) 1885.
GSM 95039

Choffatia (Homoeoplanulites) homoeomorpha
(S. S. Buckman)
Arkell 1954, p. 119.
Arkell 1958, p. 227.
Lower Cornbrash, *discus* Zone.
Cutting No. 3, Great Western Railway relief line, Frome, Somerset.
Survey Collection (F. B. A. Welch) 1931.
BW 148, 150

Choffatia sp. nov. No. 1.
Arkell 1954, p. 119.
Choffatia arisphinctoides Arkell HOLOTYPE
Arkell 1958, plate 32, fig. 3; pp. 218-219.
Homoeoplanulites (M. **Parachoffatia) arisphinctoides**
(Arkell) HOLOTYPE
Mangold 1970a, pp. 79-80.
Lower Cornbrash, *discus* Zone.
Cutting No. 2, Great Western Railway relief line, Frome, Somerset.
Survey Collection (S. W. Hester) 1931.
Ht 855

Choffatia sp. nov. No. 1
Arkell 1954, p. 119.
Choffatia arisphinctoides Arkell
Arkell 1958, p. 219.
Lower Cornbrash, *discus* Zone.
Berkley, near Frome, Somerset.
Survey Collection (H. B. Woodward) 1931.
GSM 95035

Loboplanulites longilobatus S. S. Buckman
HOLOTYPE
S. S. Buckman 1925, plate DXCVI.
Choffatia (Loboplanulites) longilobata
(S. S. Buckman) HOLOTYPE
Arkell 1958, text-figs. 79 no. 5, 81; pp. 222-223.
Subgrossouvria longilobata (S. S. Buckman)
HOLOTYPE
Elmi 1962, p. 206.
Procerites (Parachoffatia)
Mangold 1970, p. 73.
Long Hanborough northern quarry, Woodstock, Oxfordshire.
Lower Cornbrash, *discus* Zone.
Survey Collection (S. W. Hester) 1924.
GSM 37364 [formerly SH 4732]

Choffatia sp. nov. aff. **recuperoi** (Gemmellaro)
Cox & Arkell 1950, p. 94.
Choffatia (Loboplanulites) cerealis Arkell PARATYPE
Arkell 1958, plate 31, fig. 5; text-fig. 79 no. 3; pp. 206, 219-222, 235.
Lower Cornbrash, *discus* Zone.
Home Park, Sudbrooke, Lincolnshire.
Survey Collection (J. Rhodes and A. Macconochie) 1883.
GSM 95038 [formerly R 3822]

Choffatia (Loboplanulites) cerealis Arkell
Arkell 1958, p. 222.
Lower Cornbrash, *discus* Zone.
Radipole, Weymouth, Dorset.
Survey Collection (H. B. Woodward) 1884.
GSM 95034 [formerly 1381 HBW]

Table 3 Zones and subzones of the Upper Jurassic (after Wimbledon and Cope, 1978; Cope 1967; Ziegler 1962; Callomon 1955 and 1960.)

	Zone	Subzone
Portlandian	*Subcraspedites (Volgidiscus) lamplughi*	
	Subcraspedites (Subcraspedites) preplicomphalus	
	Subcraspedites (Subcraspedites) primitivus	
	Paracraspedites oppressus	
	Titanites anguiformis	
	Galbanites (Kerberites) kerberus	
	Galbanites (Galbanites) okusensis	
	Glaucolithites glaucolithus	
	Progalbanites albani	
Kimmeridgian	*Pavlovia rotunda*	
	Pavlovia pallasioides	
	Pectinatites (Pectinatites) pectinatus	
	Pectinatites (Arkellites) hudlestoni	
	Pectinatites (Virgatosphinctoides) wheatleyensis	
	Pectinatites (Virgatosphinctoides) scitulus	
	Pectinatites (Virgatosphinctoides) elegans	
	Aulacostephanus autissiodorensis	
	Aulacostephanus eudoxus	
	Aulacostephanus mutabilis	
	Rasenia cymodoce	
	Pictonia baylei	
Oxfordian	*Ringsteadia pseudocordata*	
	Decipia decipiens	
	Perisphinctes cautisnigrae	
	Perisphinctes (Arisphinctes) plicatilis	*Perisphinctes (Perisphinctes) parandieri*
		Perisphinctes (Perisphinctes) antecedens
		Cardioceras (Vertebriceras) vertebrale
	Cardioceras (Cardioceras) cordatum	*Cardioceras (Cardioceras) cordatum*
		Cardioceras (Cardioceras) costicardia
		Cardioceras (Scarburgiceras) bukowskii
	Quenstedtoceras (Quenstedtoceras) mariae	*Cardioceras (Scarburgiceras) praecordatum*
		Cardioceras (Scarburgiceras) scarburgense
Callovian	*Quenstedtoceras (Lamberticeras) lamberti*	
	Peltoceras (Peltoceras) athleta	
	Erymnoceras coronatum	*Kosmoceras (Zugokosmokeras) grossouvrei*
		Kosmoceras (Zugokosmokeras) obductum
	Kosmoceras (Gulielmites) jason	*Kosmoceras (Gulielmites) jason*
		Kosmoceras (Gulielmites) medea
	Sigaloceras (Sigaloceras) calloviense	*Sigaloceras (Catasigaloceras) enodatum*
		Sigaloceras (Sigaloceras) calloviense
		Proplanulites koenigi
	Macrocephalites (Macrocephalites) macrocephalus	*Macrocephalites (Kamptokephalites) kamptus*
		Macrocephalites (Macrocephalites) macrocephalus

Choffatia sp. nov. No. 2
Arkell 1954, p. 119.
Choffatia (Loboplanulites) kranaiformis Arkell HOLOTYPE
Arkell 1958, text-figs. 79 no. 1, and 82, pp. 224-225.
Choffatia (M. **Subgrossouvria) kranaiformis** (Arkell) HOLOTYPE
Mangold 1970a, p. 159.
Choffatia (Choffatia) kranaiformis (Arkell) HOLOTYPE
Krystyn 1972, pp. 282-283.
Lower Cornbrash, *discus* Zone.
Cutting No. 3, Great Western Railway relief line, Frome, Somerset.
Survey Collection (F. B. A. Welch) 1931.
BW 144

Choffatia sp. nov. aff. **recuperoi** (Gemmellaro)
Cox & Arkell 1950, p. 94.
Choffatia sp. nov. No. 2.
Arkell 1954, p. 119.
Choffatia (Loboplanulites) kranaiformis Arkell
Arkell 1958, p. 225.
Lower Cornbrash, *discus* Zone.
Cutting No. 3, Great Western Railway relief line, Frome, Somerset.
Survey Collection (F. B. A. Welch) 1931.
GSM BW 147

CALLOVIAN STAGE

Macrocephalites herveyi (J. Sowerby)
Blake 1905, plate 3; fig. 7; plate 4, fig. 2; p. 46.
Kamptokephalites kamptus S. S. Buckman HOLOTYPE
S. S. Buckman 1922a, plate CCCXLVII.
Macrocephalites (Kamptokephalites) herveyi (J. Sowerby)
Cox and Arkell 1950, p. 93.
Kamptokephalites kamptus S. S. Buckman HOLOTYPE
Basse and Perrodon 1951, p. 37.
Jeannet 1954, pp. 256-258.
Macrocephalites (Kamptokephalites) kamptus (S. S. Buckman) HOLOTYPE
Callomon 1955, p. 241.
Arkell 1957, fig. 352, 3, p. L294.
Upper Cornbrash, *macrocephalus* Zone.
Near Peterborough, Cambridgeshire.
D. Porter Collection, purchased 1869.
GSM 8650

Kamptokephalites aff. **dimerus** (Waagen)
Spath 1928, p. 197.
Upper Cornbrash, *macrocephalus* Zone.
Northamptonshire.
L. F. Spath Collection, purchased 1943.
GSM 72181

Macrocephalites macrocephalus (Schlotheim)
Blake 1905, plate 3, fig. 4; p. 43.
Macrocephalites (Kamptokephalites) terebratus (Phillips)
Cox and Arkell 1950, p. 94.
Upper Cornbrash, *macrocephalus* Zone.
Scarborough, Yorkshire.
J. Lycett Collection, purchased 1867.
GSM 8653

Macrocephalites typicus Blake PARATYPE
Blake 1905, fig. 4; p. 40 (No. 27 in table I); pp. 42-43
Dolikephalites dolius S. S. Buckman HOLOTYPE
S. S. Buckman 1923, plate CCCLXXII.
Dolikephalites dolus [sic] S. S. Buckman HOLOTYPE
Roman 1938, p. 212.
Macrocephalites (Dolikephalites) typicus Blake
PARATYPE
Cox and Arkell 1950, p. 93.
Dolikephalites dolius S. S. Buckman HOLOTYPE
Basse and Perrodon 1951, pp. 41-42.
Macrocephalites (Dolikephalites) typicus Blake PARATYPE
Callomon 1955, p. 240.
Arkell 1957, fig. 352, 2; p. L294.
Upper Cornbrash, *macrocephalus* Zone.
Near Peterborough, Northamptonshire.
D. Porter Collection, purchased 1869.
GSM 8651

Macrocephalites typicus Blake
Blake 1905, plate 3, fig. 3; p. 42.
Macrocephalites (Dolikephalites) typicus Blake
Cox & Arkell 1950, p. 93.
Upper Cornbrash, *macrocephalus* Zone.
Scarborough, Yorkshire.
J. Lycett Collection, purchased 1867.
GSM 8652

Macrocephalites (Dolikephalites) typicus Blake
Callomon 1955, p. 242.
Upper Cornbrash, *macrocephalus* Zone.
1100 yards (1001m) WNW of Titchmarsh, Northamptonshire.
Survey Collection (J. H. Taylor) 1942.
JHT 256

Macrocephalites (Kamptokephalites) sp. aff. **herveyi** (J. Sowerby)
Callomon 1955, p. 241.
Upper Cornbrash, *macrocephalus* Zone.
Near Peterborough, Northamptonshire.
D. Porter Collection, purchased 1869.
GSM 25624

Macrocephalites sp.
Callomon 1955, p. 249.
Upper Cornbrash, *macrocephalus* Zone.
Tip at Guilford Colliery, Kent.
Survey Collection (W. Manson) 1913.
WM 433, 435 [misprinted as WM 438]

Macrocephalites s.s.
Callomon 1971, p. 123.
Upper Cornbrash, *macrocephalus* Zone, *macrocephalus* Subzone.
Old quarry, Charlton, Wiltshire.
Survey Collection (R. D. Clark and D. E. Butler) 1969.
FJ 11

Macrocephalites macrocephalus Zittel **non** Schlotheim
Callomon 1971, p. 126.
Upper Cornbrash, *macrocephalus* Zone.
Locality unknown, ?South of England.
Museum Collection.
GSM 25632

Ammonites (Macrocephalites) macrocephalus Schlotheim
Newton and Teall 1897, plate 39, fig. 2.
macrocephalus Zone.
Cape Flora, Franz Josef Land.
Presented by the Jackson-Harmsworth Expedition, 1899.
FOR 927

Ammonites (Macrocephalites) macrocephalus Schlotheim
Newton and Teal 1897, plate 39, fig. 1.
macrocephalus Zone.
Talus, back of Elmwood, Northbrook Island, Franz Josef Land.
Presented by the Jackson-Harmsworth Expedition, 1899.
FOR 1050

Ammonites (Macrocephalites) macrocephalus Schlotheim var.
Newton and Teall 1897, plate 39, fig. 3.
macrocephalus Zone.
Talus, back of Elmwood, Northbrook Island, Franz Josef Land.
Presented by the Jackson-Harmsworth Expedition, 1899.
FOR 908

Ammonites (Macrocephalites) tchefkini? d'Orbigny
Newton and Teall 1897, plate 39, fig. 4; pp. 496-497.
Lower Callovian.
Western end of Cape Flora, Franz Josef Land.
Presented by the Jackson-Harmsworth Expedition, 1899.
FOR 965

Ammonites (Macrocephalites) tchefkini? d'Orbigny
Newton and Teall 1897, plate 39, fig. 6; pp. 496-497.
Lower Callovian.
Rondiceras tschefkini (d'Orbigny)
Meledina 1977, p. 103.
Western end of Cape Flora, Franz Josef Land.
Presented by the Jackson-Harmsworth Expedition, 1899.
FOR 954

Ammonites (Cadoceras) modiolaris Llwyd
Newton and Teall 1897, plate 39, figs. 7, 8; p. 497.
Lower Callovian.
Rondiceras tschefkini (d'Orbigny)
Meledina 1977, p. 103.
Talus, back of Elmwood, Northbrook Island, Franz Josef Land.
Presented by the Jackson-Harmsworth Expedition, 1899.
FOR 937

Ammonites (Cadoceras) modiolaris Llwyd
Newton and Teall 1897, plate 39, fig. 9; p. 497.
Lower Callovian
Rondiceras tschefkini (d'Orbigny)
Meledina 1977, p. 103.
Cape Flora, Franz Josef Land
Presented by the Jackson-Harmsworth Expedition, 1899.
FOR 901

Ammonites (Cadoceras) modiolaris Llwyd flattened var.
Newton and Teall 1897, plate 39, fig. 10; p. 497.
Pseudocadoceras sp.
Spath 1932, p. 62.
Lower Callovian
Western end of Cape Flora, Franz Josef Land.
Presented by the Jackson-Harmsworth Expedition, 1899.
FOR 964

Ammonites (Macrocephalites) ishmae Keyserling **arcticus** Newton and Teall HOLOTYPE of ssp.
Newton and Teall 1897, plate 40 fig. 1; pp. 500-501.
Lower Callovian.
Windy Gully, east of Elmwood, Northbrook Island, Franz Josef Land.
Presented by the Jackson-Harmsworth Expedition, 1899.
FOR 939

Ammonites (Macrocephalites) ishmae Keyserling
Newton and Teall 1897, plate 40, fig. 2; pp. 500-501.
Lower Callovian.
Windy Gully, east of Elmwood, Northbrook Island, Franz Josef Land.
Presented by the Jackson-Harmsworth Expedition, 1899.
FOR 940

Ammonites (Macrocephalites) ishmae Keyserling
Newton and Teall 1897, plate 40, fig. 3; pp. 500-501.
Lower Callovian.
Windy Gully east of Elmwood, Northbrook Island, Franz Josef Land.
Presented by the Jackson-Harmsworth Expedition 1899.
FOR 941

Cadoceras sublaeve (J. Sowerby) **communis** Spath
Spath 1932, p. 60.
Kellaways Beds, *calloviense* Zone.
Chippenham, Wiltshire.
L. F. Spath Collection, purchased 1943.
GSM 72199

Cadoceras tolype S. S. Buckman HOLOTYPE
S. S. Buckman 1923, plate CDVI.
Spath 1932, p. 67.
Cadoceras tolype S. S. Buckman HOLOTYPE
Meledina 1977, p. 51.
Kellaways Clay, *calloviense* Zone.
Probably originally from Chippenham, Wiltshire.
S. S. Buckman Collection, purchased 1924.
GSM 47193

Chamoussetia lenticularis (Phillips)
S. S. Buckman 1924, plate CDLXII.
Kellaways Clay, *calloviense* Zone, *koenigi* Subzone.
Trowbridge, Wiltshire.
Museum Collection.
GSM 30393

Toricellites approximatus S. S. Buckman HOLOTYPE
S. S. Buckman 1922a, plate CCCXXXVI.
Gowericeras sp.
Spath 1932, p. 90.
Kepplerites (Toricellites) approximatus
(S. S. Buckman) HOLOTYPE
Arkell 1957, fig. 362, 1; p. L298.
Tintant 1963, pp. 72, 168-169, 179-181.
Gowericeras approximatus (S. S. Buckman)
HOLOTYPE
Meledina 1977, p. 175.
Kellaways Clay, *calloviense* Zone, *koenigi* Subzone.
Rampisham, Dorset.
S. S. Buckman Collection, ex D. S. Darell Collection, purchased 1902.
GSM 7672

Kepplerites (Toricellites) approximatus
(S. S. Buckman)
Tintant 1963, p. 180.
Kellaways Clay, *calloviense* Zone.
Rampisham, Dorset.
S. S. Buckman Collection, purchased 1902.
GSM 8239

Kepplerites (Kepplerites) curtilobus (S. S. Buckman)
Tintant 1963, p. 98.
Kellaways Beds, *calloviense* Zone.
Scarborough, Yorkshire.
J. S. Bowerbank Collection, purchased 1864.
GSM 25693

Kepplerites (Kepplerites) curtilobus (S. S. Buckman)
Tintant 1963, p. 98.
Kellaways Beds, *calloviense* Zone.
Scarborough, Yorkshire.
J. Lycett Collection, purchased 1864 or 1867.
GSM 25694

Galilaeites curtilobus S. S. Buckman HOLOTYPE
S. S. Buckman 1922a, plate CCXCIV.
Arkell 1933, p. 347.
Kepplerites goweri (J. Sowerby)
Ilovaiskiy and Florenskiy 1941, pp. 158-160.
Kepplerites (Kepplerites) curtilobus
(S. S. Buckman) HOLOTYPE
Tintant 1963, pp. 72, 97-104.
Kellaways Rock, *calloviense* Zone.
Kellaways, Wiltshire.
Museum Collection.
GSM 25691

Kepplerites (Kepplerites) curtilobus (S. S. Buckman)
Tintant 1963, p. 98.
Kellaways Clay, *calloviense* Zone.
South Cerney, Gloucestershire.
S. S. Buckman Collection, ex J. Buckman Collection, purchased 1902.
GSM 7673

Kepplerites (Kepplerites) curtilobus (S. S. Buckman)
Tintant 1963, p. 98.
Kellaways Clay, *calloviense* Zone.
Kellaways, Wiltshire.
Museum Collection.
GSM 25690

Kepplerites (Kepplerites) curtilobus (S. S. Buckman)
Tintant 1963, p. 98.
Kellaways Clay, *calloviense* Zone.
Kellaways, Wiltshire.
W. Cunnington Collection, purchased 1875.
GSM 25658

Kepplerites (Kepplerites) curtilobus (S. S. Buckman)
Tintant 1963, p. 98.
Kellaways Beds, *calloviense* Zone.
Railway cutting, South Cerney, Gloucestershire.
Survey Collection, (J. Rhodes) 1887.
JR (red) 1712 [symbol omitted by Tintant]

Galilaeanus crucifer S. S. Buckman HOLOTYPE
S. S. Buckman 1922a, plate CCXCIII.
Kepplerites goweri (J. Sowerby)
Ilovaiskiy and Florenskiy 1941, pp. 158-160.
Kepplerites (Kepplerites) curtilobus (S. S. Buckman)
Tintant 1963, pp. 98, 102.
Kellaways Rock, *calloviense* Zone.
Kellaways, Wiltshire.
Earl of Enniskillen Collection, presented (date unknown).
GSM 25692

Kepplerites (Kepplerites) curtilobus (S. S. Buckman)
Tintant 1963, p. 98.
Kellaways Rock, *calloviense* Zone.
?Kellaways, Wiltshire.
Geological Society Collection, presented 1911.
GSa 3769

Kepplerites (Toricellites) distans Tintant
Y2099
[Tintant 1963 quoted this number in error on his plate 17, figure 6, cited p. 182; the specimen figured is the collections of the British Museum (Natural History), number C1071]

Kepplerites (Toricellites) distans Tintant
Tintant 1963, p. 182.
Kellaways Rock, *calloviense* Zone.
Gristhorpe, near Scarborough, Yorkshire.
J. Lycett Collection, purchased 1867.
GSM 25667, 25668, 25669

Gowericeras metorchum S. S. Buckman HOLOTYPE
S. S. Buckman 1921, plate CCLIV.
Gowericeras gowerianus (J. de C. Sowerby)
metorchum S. S. Buckman HOLOTYPE
Spath 1932, p. 90.
Gowericeras metorchum S. S. Buckman HOLOTYPE
Roman 1938, p. 257.
Kepplerites goweri (J. Sowerby)
Ilovaiskiy and Florenskiy 1941, p. 158.
Kepplerites (Gowericeras) gowerianus
(J. de C. Sowerby)
Tintant 1963, pp. 70, 110.
Gowericeras metorchum S. S. Buckman HOLOTYPE
Meledina 1977, p. 175.
Kellaways Clay, *calloviense* Zone, *koenigi* Subzone.
Chippenham, Wiltshire.
Museum Collection.
GSM 30456

Kepplerites (Gowericeras) gowerianus (J. de C. Sowerby)
Tintant 1963, p. 109.
Kellaways Beds, *calloviense* Zone.
Near Chippenham, Wiltshire.
Geological Society Collection (ex S. P. Pratt 1841 or 1843), presented 1911.
GSa 3697

Kepplerites (Gowericeras) gowerianus (J. de C. Sowerby)
Tintant 1963, p. 109.
Kellaways Beds, *calloviense* Zone.
Chippenham, Wiltshire.
J. Lycett Collection, purchased 1867.
GSM 54108

Kepplerites (Gowericeras) gowerianus (J. de C. Sowerby)
Tintant 1963, p. 109.
Kellaways Beds, *calloviense* Zone, *koenigi* Subzone.
Rampisham, Dorset.
S. S. Buckman Collection.
GSM 7674 [misquoted as 7647 by Tintant]

Gowericeras ventrale S. S. Buckman HOLOTYPE
S. S. Buckman 1922a, plate CCLXXXVIII.
Spath 1932, p. 89.
Kepplerites (Gowericeras) gowerianus (J. de C. Sowerby)
Tintant 1963, p. 110.
Gowericeras ventrale S. S. Buckman HOLOTYPE
Meledina 1977, p. 175.
Kellaways Clay, *calloviense* Zone.
Wiltshire (presumed to be Chippenham).
Museum Collection.
GSM 30460

Ammonites gowerianus J. de C. Sowerby
Woodward 1895, p. 30.
Galilaeiceras trichophorum S. S. Buckman HOLOTYPE
S. S. Buckman 1922a, plate CCXCI.
'Galilaeiceras' trichophorum S. S. Buckman HOLOTYPE
Spath 1932, p. 95.
Kepplerites (Kepplerites) trichophorus S. S. Buckman HOLOTYPE
Tintant 1963, pp. 90-96.
Kellaways Rock, *calloviense* Zone.
Little Somerford, Wiltshire.
Museum Collection.
GSM 4745

Gowericeras planus S. S. Buckman HOLOTYPE
S. S. Buckman 1922a, plates CCLXXXVII, CCLXXXVII*.
Arkell 1933, p. 369.
Kepplerites (Kepplerites) trichophorus (S. S. Buckman)
Tintant 1963, p. 91.
Roof-bed of the Brora Coal, *calloviense* Zone.
Brora, Sutherland.
Geological Society Collection, presented 1911.
Geol. Soc. Coll. 7188

Pleurocephalites folliformis S. S. Buckman HOLOTYPE
S. S. Buckman 1922a, plate CCCXLVIII.
Spath 1928, pp. 170-171.
Spath 1932, p. 72.
Kellaways Clay, *calloviense* Zone.
Chippenham, Wiltshire.
Museum Collection.
GSM 30567

Pleurocephalites liberalis S. S. Buckman HOLOTYPE
S. S. Buckman 1924, text-fig. 6, p. 23.
S. S. Buckman 1925, plate DLVIII.
Kellaways Clay, *calloviense* Zone.
Chippenham, Wiltshire.
Museum Collection.
GSM 30565

Macrocephalites (Kamptokephalites) aff. **herveyi** (J. Sowerby)
Callomon 1955, pp. 241, 247.
Kellaways Clay, *calloviense* Zone.
Cutting no.2, Great Western Railway relief line, Frome, Somerset.
Survey Collection (F. B. A. Welch) 1932.
BW 244

Macrocephalites (Kamptokephalites) aff. **herveyi** (J. Sowerby)
Callomon 1955, pp. 241, 247.
Kellaways Clay, *calloviense* Zone.
Cutting no.2, Great Western Railway relief line, Frome, Somerset.
Presented by a Mr Macdonald 1932.
BW 246

Kellawaysites multicostatus (Petitclerc)
S. S. Buckman 1925, plate DLXXXVII.
Arkell 1933, p. 347.
Kellaways Rock, *calloviense* Zone.
Chippenham, Wiltshire.
Museum Collection.
GSM 25683

Proplanulites fracidus S. S. Buckman HOLOTYPE
S. S. Buckman 1921, p. 40.
S. S. Buckman 1924, plate DVII.
Arkell 1933, p. 347.
Kellaways Rock, *calloviense* Zone, *koenigi* Subzone.
Chippenham, Wiltshire.
Museum Collection.
GSM 26082

Proplanulites ?fracidus S. S. Buckman
S. S. Buckman 1921, p. 40.
Kellaways Rock, *calloviense* Zone, *koenigi* Subzone.
Chippenham, Wiltshire.
Museum Collection.
GSM 30530

Proplanulites arciruga Teisseyre
S. S. Buckman 1921, p. 38.
S. S. Buckman 1922a, plate CCCXXXI.
Kellaways Rock, *calloviense* Zone.
Gristhorpe, near Scarborough, Yorkshire.
W. H. Hudleston Collection, presented by Miss C. A. Raisin 1920.
GSM 30777

Proplanulites aff. **arciruga** Teisseyre
S. S. Buckman 1921, p. 34.
Kellaways Clay, *calloviense* Zone.
Christian Malford, Wiltshire?
W. Cunnington Collection, purchased 1875.
GSM 30534

Proplanulites capistratus S. S. Buckman HOLOTYPE
S. S. Buckman 1921, plate CCXIII; p. 37.
Kellaways Clay, *calloviense* Zone, *koenigi* Subzone.
Chippenham, Wiltshire.
Museum Collection.
GSM 30532

Proplanulites capistratus S. S. Buckman PARATYPE
S. S. Buckman 1921, p. 37.
Kellaways Rock, *calloviense* Zone, *koenigi* Subzone.
Gristhorpe, near Scarborough, Yorkshire.
W. H. Hudleston Collection, presented by Miss C. A. Raisin 1920.
GSM 30778

Proplanulites auriculatus S. S. Buckman HOLOTYPE
S. S. Buckman 1921, p. 37.
Kellaways Clay, *calloviense* Zone, *koenigi* Subzone.
Chippenham, Wiltshire.
Museum Collection.
GSM 30526
[figured here plate 2, fig. 6]

Proplanulites auriculatus S. S. Buckman PARATYPE
S. S. Buckman 1921, p. 37.
Kellaways Clay, *calloviense* Zone, *koenigi* Subzone.
Chippenham, Wiltshire.
Museum Collection.
GSM 30528

Proplanulites capularis S. S. Buckman HOLOTYPE
S. S. Buckman 1921, p. 41.
Kellaways Rock (top), *calloviense* Zone, *koenigi* Subzone.
Chippenham, Wiltshire.
Museum Collection.
GSM 26081
[figured here plate 2 fig. 2]

Proplanulites ?capularis S. S. Buckman
S. S. Buckman 1921, p. 41.
Kellaways Rock, *calloviense* Zone.
Kellaways, Wiltshire.
Museum Collection.
GSM 26096

Proplanulites excentricus S. S. Buckman
S. S. Buckman 1921, p. 39.
Kellaways Rock, *calloviense* Zone, *koenigi* Subzone.
Kellaways, Wiltshire.
Museum Collection.
GSM 26094

Proplanulites excentricus S. S. Buckman
S. S. Buckman 1921, p. 39.
Kellaways Rock, *calloviense* Zone.
Gristhorpe, near Scarborough, Yorkshire.
W. H. Hudleston Collection, presented by Miss C. A. Raisin 1920.
GSM 30779

Proplanulites ferruginosus S. S. Buckman HOLOTYPE
S. S. Buckman 1921, p. 34.
Kellaways Rock, *calloviense* Zone, *koenigi* Subzone.
Scarborough, Yorkshire.
J. S. Bowerbank Collection, purchased 1864.
GSM 26105
[Figured here plate 2 fig. 8.]

Proplanulites fulvus S. S. Buckman HOLOTYPE
S. S. Buckman 1921, p. 39.
Kellaways Rock, *calloviense* Zone, *koenigi* Subzone.
Kellaways, Wiltshire.
Museum Collection.
GSM 26097
[Figured here plate 2, fig. 5.]

Proplanulites fulvus S. S. Buckman
S. S. Buckman 1921, p. 39.
Kellaways Rock, *calloviense* Zone, *koenigi* Subzone.
Chippenham, Wiltshire.
Museum Collection.
GSM 26083

Proplanulites involutus S. S. Buckman HOLOTYPE
S. S. Buckman 1921, p. 36.
Kellaways Clay, *calloviense* Zone.
Chippenham, Wiltshire.
Museum Collection.
GSM 30531
[Figured here plate 2 fig. 7.]

Proplanulites involutus S. S. Buckman
S. S. Buckman 1921, p. 36.
Kellaways Clay, *calloviense* Zone.
(Chippenham?) Wiltshire.
J. S. Bowerbank Collection, purchased 1864.
GSM 30538

Proplanulites involutus S. S. Buckman
S. S. Buckman 1921, p. 36.
Kellaways Clay, *calloviense* Zone.
Rampisham, Dorset.
S. S. Buckman Collection, purchased 1902.
GSM 7692

Proplanulites involutus S. S. Buckman
S. S. Buckman 1921, p. 36.
Kellaways Clay, *calloviense* Zone.
Chippenham, Wiltshire.
Museum Collection.
GSM 30527

Proplanulites koenigi (J. Sowerby)
S. S. Buckman 1921, p. 36.
S. S. Buckman 1922, plate CCLXXXI.
Kellaways Clay, *calloviense* Zone, *koenigi* Subzone.
Rampisham, Dorset.
S. S. Buckman Collection, ex D. S. Darell Collection, purchased 1902.
GSM 7688

Proplanulites koenigi (J. Sowerby)
S. S. Buckman 1921, p. 36.
Kellaways Clay, *calloviense* Zone, *koenigi* Subzone.
Chippenham, Wiltshire.
W. H. Hudleston Collection, presented by Miss C. A. Raisin 1920.
GSM 30774

Proplanulites koenigi (J. Sowerby)
S. S. Buckman 1921, p. 36.
Kellaways Clay, *calloviense* Zone, *koenigi* Subzone.
Weymouth, Dorset.
Museum Collection.
GSM 30537

Proplanulites basileus S. S. Buckman HOLOTYPE
S. S. Buckman 1921, plate CCLII; p. 34.
Kellaways Clay, *calloviense* Zone.
Chippenham, Wiltshire.
Museum Collection.
GSM 30741

Proplanulites laboratus S. S. Buckman HOLOTYPE
S. S. Buckman 1921, p. 36.
S. S. Buckman 1926, plate DCXLV.
Kellaways Clay, *calloviense* Zone.
Rampisham, Dorset.
S. S. Buckman Collection, ex D. S. Darell Collection, purchased 1902.
GSM 7685

Proplanulites laevigatus S. S. Buckman HOLOTYPE
S. S. Buckman 1921, plate CCXXXII; p. 34.
Kellaways Clay, *calloviense* Zone.
Rampisham, Dorset.
S. S. Buckman Collection, ex D. S. Darell Collection, purchased 1902.
GSM 30686 [formerly GSM 7692]

Proplanulites lobatus S. S. Buckman HOLOTYPE
S. S. Buckman 1922, plate CCCXXX.
Indosphinctes (Elatmites) lobatus (S. S. Buckman) HOLOTYPE
Mangold 1970, text-fig. 83; pp. 114-116.
Kellaways Clay, *calloviense* Zone.
Rampisham, Dorset.
S. S. Buckman Collection, ex D. S. Darell Collection, purchased 1902.
GSM 7682

Proplanulites latus S. S. Buckman HOLOTYPE
S. S. Buckman 1921, pp. 35-36.
Kellaways Rock, *calloviense* Zone.
Scarborough, Yorkshire.
J. S. Bowerbank Collection, purchased 1864.
GSM 26106
[Figured here plate 1, fig. 7.]

Proplanulites lentus S. S. Buckman HOLOTYPE
S. S. Buckman 1921, p. 36.
Kellaways Rock, *calloviense* Zone.
Kellaways, Wiltshire.
Earl of Enniskillen Collection, presented, date unknown.
GSM 26092
[Figured here plate 1, fig. 4.]

Proplanulites lyprus S. S. Buckman HOLOTYPE
S. S. Buckman 1921, p. 38.
Kellaways Rocks, *calloviense* Zone.
Kellaways, Wiltshire.
Museum Collection.
GSM 26080
[Figured here plate 1, fig. 9.]

Proplanulites lyprus S. S. Buckman
S. S. Buckman 1921, p. 38.
Kellaways Rock, *calloviense* Zone.
Wiltshire.
J. Lycett Collection, purchased 1867.
GSM 26103

Proplanulites majesticus S. S. Buckman HOLOTYPE
S. S. Buckman 1921, plate CCXXVI; p. 34.
Kellaways Clay, *calloviense* Zone.
Chippenham, Wiltshire.
Museum Collection.
GSM 30533

Proplanulites occultus S. S. Buckman HOLOTYPE
S. S. Buckman 1921, p. 35.
Cave 1977, p. 219.
Kellaways Clay, *calloviense* Zone.
Rodbourne, near Malmesbury, Wiltshire.
W. H. Hudleston Collection, presented by Miss C. A. Raisin 1920.
GSM 30775
[Figured here plate 1 fig. 8.]

Proplanulites oidaleus S. S. Buckman HOLOTYPE
S. S. Buckman 1921, p. 38.
Kellaways Rock, *calloviense* Zone.
Kellaways, Wiltshire.
Museum Collection.
GSM 26093
[Figured here plate 1, fig. 3.]

Proplanulites oidaleus S. S. Buckman
S. S. Buckman 1921, p. 38.
Kellaways Rock, *calloviense* Zone.
Chippenham, Wiltshire.
Museum Collection.
GSM 26084

Proplanulites oidaleus S. S. Buckman
S. S. Buckman 1921, p. 38.
Kellaways Rock, *calloviense* Zone.
Kellaways, Wiltshire.
Museum Collection.
GSM 26102

Proplanulites opimus S. S. Buckman HOLOTYPE
S. S. Buckman 1921, p. 35.
Kellaways Rock, *calloviense* Zone.
Chippenham, Wiltshire.
Museum Collection.
GSM 26085
[Figured here plate 1, fig. 1.]

Proplanulites opimus S. S. Buckman
S. S. Buckman 1921, p. 35.
Kellaways Rock, *calloviense* Zone.
Kellaways, Wiltshire..
Museum Collection.
GSM 26095

Proplanulites partitus S. S. Buckman HOLOTYPE
S. S. Buckman 1921, p. 39.
Kellaways Rock, *calloviense* Zone.
Kellaways, Wiltshire.
Museum Collection.
GSM 26099
[Figured here plate 1, fig. 6.]

Proplanulites petrosus S. S. Buckman HOLOTYPE
S. S. Buckman 1921, p. 38.
Kellaways Rock, *calloviense* Zone.
Kellaways, Wiltshire.
Museum Collection.
GSM 26091
[Figured here plate 1, fig. 11.]

Proplanulites rudis S. S. Buckman HOLOTYPE
S. S. Buckman 1921, p. 37.
Kellaways Clay, *calloviense* Zone.
Chippenham, Wiltshire.
Museum Collection.
GSM 30525
[Figured here plate 2, fig. 1.]

Proplanulites ?rudis S. S. Buckman
S. S. Buckman 1921, p. 37.
Kellaways Clay, *calloviense* Zone.
Loudon, Chippenham, Wiltshire.
W. H. Hudleston Collection, presented by Miss C. A. Raisin 1920.
GSM 30776

Proplanulites ?rudis S. S. Buckman
S. S. Buckman 1921, p. 37.
Kellaways Clay, *calloviense* Zone.
Wiltshire.
J. S. Bowerbank Collection, purchased 1864.
GSM 30539

Proplanulites polonicus S. S. Buckman PARATYPE
S. S. Buckman 1921, p. 35.
Kellaways Clay, *calloviense* Zone.
Rampisham, Dorset.
S. S. Buckman Collection, purchased 1902.
GSM 7693

Proplanulites rufus S. S. Buckman HOLOTYPE
S. S. Buckman 1921, p. 39.
Kellaways Rock, *calloviense* Zone.
Scarborough, Yorkshire.
Museum Collection.
GSM 26104
[Figured here, plate 2, fig. 3.]

Proplanulites stiphrus S. S. Buckman HOLOTYPE
S. S. Buckman 1921, p. 38.
Kellaways Rock, *calloviense* Zone.
Kellaways, Wiltshire.
Museum Collection.
GSM 26088
[Figured here plate 2, fig. 4.]

Proplanulites stiphrus S. S. Buckman
S. S. Buckman 1921, p. 38.
Kellaways Rock, *calloviense* Zone.
Chippenham, Wiltshire.
Museum Collection.
GSM 26086

Proplanulites tridens S. S. Buckman HOLOTYPE
S. S. Buckman 1921, p. 38.
Kellaways Rock, *calloviense* Zone.
Kellaways, Wiltshire.
Museum Collection.
GSM 26090
[Figured here plate 1, fig. 5.]

Proplanulites ?fulvus S. S. Buckman
S. S. Buckman 1921, p. 40.
Kellaways Rock, *calloviense* Zone.
Kellaways, Wiltshire.
Museum Collection.
GSM 26087, 26101

Proplanulites subcuneiformis S. S. Buckman
S. S. Buckman 1921, p. 37.
Kellaways Clay, *calloviense* Zone.
Chippenham, Wiltshire.
Museum Collection.
GSM 30529

Proplanulites subcuneiformis S. S. Buckman
S. S. Buckman 1921, p. 37.
Kellaways Clay, *calloviense* Zone.
Christian Malford?, Wiltshire.
W. Cunnington Collection, purchased 1875.
GSM 30536

Proplanulites sp.
S. S. Buckman 1921, p. 35.
Kellaways Rock, *calloviense* Zone.
Chippenham, Wiltshire.
Museum Collection.
GSM 26089 [quoted in error as 26098], 26100

Proplanulites sp.
Spath 1931, p. 312.
Kellaways Rock, *calloviense* Zone.
Wiltshire.
L. F. Spath Collection purchased 1943.
GSM 72182

Ammonites bakeriae J. de C. Sowerby
Woodward 1895, p. 30.
Crassiplanulites crassiruga S. S. Buckman HOLOTYPE
S. S. Buckman 1921, plate CCLIII; p. 42.
Kellaways Rock, *calloviense* Zone.
North of turning to King's Mead Mill, Little Somerford, Wiltshire.
T. Holloway Collection, presented 1893.
GSM 4744

Crassiplanulites crassicosta S. S. Buckman HOLOTYPE
S. S. Buckman 1921, plates CCXXVII A, B; p. 42.
'Crassiplanulites' crassicosta S. S. Buckman HOLOTYPE
Spath 1931, p. 314.
Crassiplanulites crassicosta S. S. Buckman HOLOTYPE
Roman 1938, p. 265.
Luppov and Drushchits 1958, plate 36, fig. 9.
Kellaways Rock, *calloviense* Zone.
Kellaways, Wiltshire.
Museum Collection.
GSM 25649

Macrocephaliceras macrocephalum (Schlotheim)
S. S. Buckman 1922a, plate CCCXIII.
'Macrocephaliceras'
Spath 1928, p. 170.
Macrocephalites cf. **macrocephalus** (Schlotheim)
Callomon 1955, p. 248.
Kellaways Clay, ?*calloviense* Zone.
NE end of Backwater, Radipole, Dorset.
S. S. Buckman Collection, purchased 1924.
GSM 47128

Kosmoceras (Kosmoceras) planicerclus (S. S. Buckman)
Tintant 1963, plate 33 fig. 1; pp. 287-289.
Kellaways Beds, *calloviense* Zone, *enodatum* Subzone.
Station quarry, South Cave, Yorkshire.
C. W. Wright Collection, presented 1948.
Zk 1444

Kosmoceras (Kosmoceras) planicerclus (S. S. Buckman)
Tintant 1963, plate 33, fig. 2; pp. 287-289.
Kellaways Rock, *calloviense* Zone, *enodatum* Subzone.
Station quarry, South Cave, Yorkshire.
C. W. Wright Collection, presented 1948.
Zk 1438

Kosmoceras (Kosmoceras) planicerclus (S. S. Buckman)
Tintant 1963, plate 33, fig. 3; pp. 287-289.
Kellaways Rock, *calloviense* Zone, *enodatum* Subzone.
Station quarry, South Cave, Yorkshire.
C. W. Wright Collection, presented 1948.
Zk 1446

Kosmoceras (Catasigaloceras) planicerclus (S. S. Buckman)
Callomon 1955, plate 2, fig. 5; p. 227.
Kosmoceras (Zugokosmoceras) enodatum Nikitin
Tintant 1963, p. 235.
Kellaways Rock, *calloviense* Zone, *enodatum* Subzone.
Station quarry, South Cave, Yorkshire.
C. W. Wright Collection, presented 1948.
Zk 1449

Kosmoceras (Zugokosmoceras) enodatum Nikitin
Tintant 1963, p. 235.
Kellaways Rock, *calloviense* Zone, *enodatum* Subzone.
Station quarry, South Cave, Yorkshire.
C. W. Wright Collection, presented 1948.
Zk 1448

Kosmoceras (Zugokosmoceras) enodatum Nikitin
Tintant 1963, plate 24, fig. 5; p. 235.
Kellaways Rock, *calloviense* Zone, *enodatum* Subzone.
Station quarry, South Cave, Yorkshire.
C. W. Wright Collection, presented 1948.
Zk 1441 [quoted as ZK 1448]

Kosmoceras (Gulielmites) medea Callomon
Callomon 1955, plate 3, fig. 3;
Tintant 1963, p. 244.
Kellaways Rock, *calloviense* Zone, *enodatum* Subzone.
Guilford Colliery (depth 1204-1234 feet/366.86-376.00m), Kent.
Survey Collection (W. Manson) 1913.
WM 289

Kosmoceras (Gulielmites) medea Callomon
Callomon 1955, plate 2, fig. 4.
Tintant 1963, p. 244.
Kellaways Rock, *calloviense* Zone, *enodatum* Subzone.
Guilford Colliery (depth 1204-1234 feet/366.86-376.00m), Kent.
Survey Collection (W. Manson) 1913.
WM 180

Gulielmites conlaxatum S. S. Buckman HOLOTYPE
S. S. Buckman 1923, plate CDXVIII.
Kosmoceras (Zugokosmoceras) jason (Reinecke)
Tintant 1963, pp. 228, 249, 261.
Lower Oxford Clay, *jason* Zone.
Backwater, Radipole, Weymouth, Dorset.
Museum Collection.
GSM 30505

Kosmoceras (Gulielmiceras) sp. cf. **pauper** Spath
Spath 1932, p. 97.
Kellaways Rock, *jason* Zone.
South Cave, Yorkshire.
L. F. Spath Collection, purchased 1943.
GSM 72201

Kosmoceras (Gulielmites) jason (Reinecke)
Callomon 1955, plate 3, fig. 2.
Tintant 1963, p. 262.
Kellaways Rock, *jason* Zone.
Locality unknown, probably Wiltshire.
W. Cunnington Collection, purchased 1875.
GSM 26072

Geopeltis brevipinnis (Owen)
Carreck 1960, p. 346.
Lower Oxford Clay, *coronatum* Zone.
Crook Hill brickworks, Chickerell, near Weymouth, Dorset.
F. H. Moore Collection, presented 1959.
GSM 98378, 98379

Anakosmokeras effulgens S. S. Buckman HOLOTYPE
S. S. Buckman 1925, plates DXCVIIA, B.
Kosmoceras effulgens (S. S. Buckman) HOLOTYPE
Arkell 1933, p. 349.
Kosmoceras (Gulielmites) effulgens (S. S. Buckman) HOLOTYPE
Callomon 1955, p. 229.
Lower Oxford Clay.
Well at Gosford Hill farm, Kidlington, Oxfordshire.
Survey Collection (J. Pringle) 1926.
GSM 37499 [formerly He 340]

Ammonites fluctuosus Pratt HOLOTYPE?
?Pratt 1841, plate 6, fig. 1; p. 164.
Binatisphinctes fluctuosus (Pratt)
S. S. Buckman 1925, plate DCXV.
Lower Oxford Clay, *?coronatum* Zone.
Christian Malford, Wiltshire.
S. P. Pratt Collection, presented 1851.
GSM 30353

Ammonites sedgwickii Pratt HOLOTYPE?
?Pratt 1841, plate 5, fig. 1; pp. 163, 165.
Gulielmites sedgwickii (Pratt)
S. S. Buckman 1925, plate DXCVIII.
Lower Oxford Clay, *coronatum* Zone, *obductum* Subzone.
Christian Malford, Wiltshire.
S. P. Pratt Collection, presented 1851.
GSM 30518

Ammonites stutchburii Pratt
Pratt 1841, p. 163, plate 4, fig. 3?
Lower Oxford Clay, *coronatum* Zone.
Great Western Railway, Christian Malford, Wiltshire.
S. P. Pratt Collection, presented 1851.
GSM 30519

Lunuloceras lonsdalii (Pratt)
S. S. Buckman 1927, plate DII A.
Lower Oxford Clay, *coronatum* Zone.
Christian Malford, Wiltshire.
S. P. Pratt Collection, presented 1851.
GSM 30562

Pseudocadoceras? concinnum S. S. Buckman HOLOTYPE
S. S. Buckman 1927, plate DCCXXXV.
Cadoceras (Pseudocadoceras) concinnum (S. S. Buckman) HOLOTYPE
Callomon 1955, p. 232.
Lower Oxford Clay, *coronatum* Zone.
Christian Malford, Wiltshire.
Museum Collection.
GSM 30427

Pseudocadoceras? laminatum S. S. Buckman HOLOTYPE
S. S. Buckman 1927, plate DCCXXVII.
Cadoceras (Pseudocadoceras) laminatum (S. S. Buckman) HOLOTYPE
Callomon 1955, p. 232.
Lower Oxford Clay, *coronatum* Zone.
Museum Collection.
GSM 30430

Reineckeia (Reineckeites) duplex S. S. Buckman
Callomon 1955, p. 234.
Lower Oxford Clay, *coronatum* Zone.
Near Weymouth, Dorset.
L. F. Spath Collection, purchased 1945.
GSM 72894

Hoplikosmokeras spiculatum S. S. Buckman HOLOTYPE
S. S. Buckman 1925, plate DLXV.
Lower Oxford Clay, *coronatum* Zone.
Calvert Brickyard, Buckinghamshire.
S. S. Buckman Collection, purchased 1926.
GSM 47569

Spinikosmokeras acutistriatum S. S. Buckman ex Robson MS.
S. S. Buckman 1924, plate CDLXXXVI B.
Lower Oxford Clay, *coronatum* Zone.
Christian Malford, Wiltshire.
W. Cunnington Collection, purchased 1875.
GSM 30487

Katakosmokeras degradatum S. S. Buckman HOLOTYPE
S. S. Buckman 1925, plate DXLVIII.
Kosmoceras degradatum (S. S. Buckman) HOLOTYPE
Arkell 1933, p. 371.
Kosmoceras (Lobokosmokeras) degradatum (S. S. Buckman) HOLOTYPE
Turner 1966, p. 247.
Lower Oxford Clay, *coronatum* Zone.
Loch Staffin, Skye.
Museum Collection.
GSM 30540

Hoplikosmokeras fibuliferum S. S. Buckman HOLOTYPE
S. S. Buckman 1924, plate CDLXXXIX.
Kosmoceras (Kosmoceras) fibuliferum fibuliferum (S. S. Buckman) HOLOTYPE
Tintant 1963, pp. 333–339, 341.
Lower Oxford Clay, *coronatum* Zone.
Christian Malford, Wiltshire.
Museum Collection.
GSM 30498

Hoplikosmokeras hoplistes S. S. Buckman HOLOTYPE
S. S. Buckman 1924, plate CDLXXXVIII.
Arkell 1957, fig. 364, 7; p. L301.
Lower Oxford Clay, *coronatum* Zone.
Christian Malford, Wiltshire.
W. Cunnington Collection, purchased 1879.
GSM 30490

Ammonites gulielmi J. Sowerby
Pratt 1841, p. 164.
Hoplikosmokeras phaeinum S. S. Buckman HOLOTYPE
S. S. Buckman 1924, plate CDXC.
Lower Oxford Clay, *coronatum* Zone.
Christian Malford, Wiltshire.
S. P. Pratt Collection, presented 1851.
GSM 30514

Spinikosmokeras acutistriatum S. S. Buckman ex Robson MS.
S. S. Buckman 1925, plate CDLXXXVI C.
Lower Oxford Clay, Acutistriatum Band, *athleta* Zone.
Calvert brickyard, Buckinghamshire.
S. S. Buckman Collection, purchased 1926.
GSM 47532

Hectioceras (Brightia) glyptum (S. S. Buckman)
Arkell 1939, p. 144.
Lower Oxford Clay, *athleta* Zone.
Two miles (3.22km) west of Quainton, Buckinghamshire.
Musuem Collection.
GSM 30461-30467

Bikosmokeras geminatum S. S. Buckman HOLOTYPE
S. S. Buckman 1926, plate DCXXV.
Lower Oxford Clay, *athleta* Zone.
Wolvercote Brickyard, Upper Wolvercote, Oxfordshire.
Survey Collection (S. W. Hester) 1924.
GSM 37480 [formerly SH 4752]

Lobokosmokeras proniae (Teisseyre)
S. S. Buckman 1923, plate CDXXXVI.
Lower Oxford Clay, *athleta* Zone.
Summertown Brickyard, Oxford.
S. S. Buckman Collection, purchased 1925.
GSM 37295

Ammonites duncani J. Sowerby
Woodward 1895, text-fig. 9; p. 12.
Lower Oxford Clay, *athleta* Zone.
Whittlesey, Cambridgeshire.
D. Porter Collection, purchased 1869.
GSM 30402

Peltoceras athleta (Phillips)
Spath 1931, plate 110, fig. 7; p. 564.
Lower Oxford Clay, *athleta* Zone.
Weymouth, Dorset.
L. F. Spath Collection, purchased 1943.
GSM 72186

Horioceras baugieri (d'Orbigny)
Spath 1933, p. 859.
Lower Oxford Clay, *lamberti* Zone.
Tidmoor Point, Weymouth, Dorset.
L. F. Spath Collection, purchased 1943.
GSM 72191

Putealiceras puteale (Leckenby)
Spath 1933, p. 858.
Lower Oxford Clay, *lamberti* Zone.
Tidmoor Point, Weymouth, Dorset.
L. F. Spath Collection, purchased 1943.
GSM 72193

Trinisphinctes trinus S. S. Buckman HOLOTYPE
S. S. Buckman 1922a, plate CCCXXXII.
Grossouvria trina (S. S. Buckman) HOLOTYPE
Arkell 1939b, p. 179.
Lower Oxford Clay, *athleta* or *lamberti* Zone.
Fleet Bridge, Weymouth, Dorset.
E. T. Newton Collection, presented 1898.
GSM 6509

Euaspidoceras armatum (Loriol)
Spath 1933, p. 859.
Lower Oxford Clay, *lamberti* Zone.
Tidmoor Point, Weymouth, Dorset.
L. F. Spath Collection, purchased 1943.
GSM 72196

Bonariella bicostata (Stahl)
Spath 1933, p. 858.
Lower Oxford Clay, *lamberti* Zone.
Tidmoor Point, Weymouth, Dorset.
L. F. Spath Collection, purchased 1943.
GSM 72192

Hecticoceras (Putealiceras) rossiense (Teisseyre)
Arkell 1939b, p. 165.
Hackness Rock, *lamberti* Zone.
Scarborough, Yorkshire.
J. Lycett Collection, purchased 1869.
GSM 26178

Peltoceras metamorphicum Spath
Spath 1931, p. 565.
Lower Oxford Clay, *lamberti* Zone.
Tidmoor Point, Weymouth, Dorset.
L. F. Spath Collection, purchased 1943.
GSM 72189

Rursiceras torosum (Oppel)
Spath 1933, p. 859.
Lower Oxford Clay, *lamberti* Zone.
Tidmoor Point, Weymouth, Dorset.
L. F. Spath Collection, purchased 1943.
GSM 72197, 72198

Properisphinctes aff. **bernensis** (Loriol)
Spath 1933, p. 859.
Lower Oxford Clay, *lamberti* Zone.
Tidmoor Point, Weymouth, Dorset.
L. F. Spath Collection, purchased 1943.
GSM 72195

Ammonites lamberti J. Sowerby
Newton and Teall 1898, plate 29, fig. 2; p. 649.
Quenstedtoceras lamberti (J. Sowerby)
Spath 1932, p. 140.
lamberti Zone, directly below basalt.
Elmwood, Northbrook Island, Franz Josef Land.
Presented by the Jackson-Harmsworth Expedition, 1899.
FOR 1073

OXFORDIAN STAGE

Cardioceras (Scarburgiceras) praecordatum Douvillé **praemartini** Spath
Spath 1939, plate 6, fig. 8; p. 92.
Oxford Clay, *mariae* Zone, *praecordatum* Subzone.
London Brick Co. pit, Warboys, Cambridgeshire [Huntingdonshire].
Survey Collection (W. Dewar) 1937.
GSM 56539

Cardioceras (Scarburgiceras) praecordatum Douvillé **praemartini** Spath HOLOTYPE of ssp.
Spath 1939, plate 6, fig. 1; p. 92.
Oxford Clay, *mariae* Zone, *praecordatum* Subzone.
London Brick Co. pit, Warboys, Cambridgeshire [Huntingdonshire].
Survey Collection (W. Dewar) 1937.
GSM 56535

Cardioceras (Scarburgiceras) praecordatum praecordatum Douvillé trans. to **praemartini** Spath
Spath 1939, plate 7, fig. 2; p. 92.
Oxford Clay, *mariae* Zone, *praecordatum* Subzone.
Warboys, Cambridgeshire [Huntingdonshire].
L. F. Spath Collection, purchased 1943.
GSM 72238

Cardioceras (Scarburgiceras) praecordatum Douvillé **praemartini** Spath
Spath 1939, plate 7, fig. 1; p. 92.
Oxford Clay, *mariae* Zone, *praecordatum* Subzone.
London Brick Co. pit, Warboys, Cambridgeshire [Huntingdonshire].
Survey Collection (W. Dewar) 1937.
GSM 56541

Cardioceras (Scarburgiceras) praecordatum Douvillé **transitoria** Spath HOLOTYPE of ssp.
Spath 1939, plate 6, fig. 6; p. 93.
Oxford Clay, *mariae* Zone, *praecordatum* Subzone.
London Brick Co. pit, Warboys, Cambridgeshire [Huntingdonshire].
Survey Collection (W. Dewar) 1937.
GSM 56537

Cardioceras (Scarburgiceras) praecordatum Douvillé mut. β Spath HOLOTYPE of 'Mutation'
Spath 1939, plate 6, fig. 3; p. 93.
Oxford Clay, *mariae* Zone.
London Brick Co. pit, Warboys, Cambridgeshire [Huntingdonshire].
Survey Collection (W. Dewar) 1937.
GSM 56536

Cardioceras (Scarburgiceras) praecordatum Douvillé mut. β Spath
Spath 1939, plate 6, fig. 9; p. 93.
Oxford Clay, *mariae* Zone.
London Brick Co. pit, Warboys, Cambridgeshire [Huntingdonshire].
Survey Collection (W. Dewar) 1937.
GSM 56540

Cardioceras cordatum (J. Sowerby)
Davies 1907, p. 40.
Oxford Clay, *mariae* Zone.
Well, Studley, Oxfordshire.
A. M. Davies Collection, presented 1937.
GSM 59664

Cardioceras praecordatum Douvillé
Arkell 1947, p. 356.
Oxford Clay, *mariae* Zone, *praecordatum* Subzone.
Railway cutting, north end of tunnel, Ampthill, Bedfordshire.
Survey Collection (J. Rhodes) 1886.
JR 3304-3306, 3310, 3311

Cardioceras sp.
Kitchin & Pringle 1923, pp. 62, 64.
Oxford Clay, *mariae* Zone, *praecordatum* Subzone.
Bere Farm borehole, St. Margarets Cliff, Kent.
Survey Collection (J. Pringle) 1913.
GSM 108546 [formerly Pl 4891]

Cardioceras (Scarburgiceras) aff. **scarburgense** (Young & Bird)
Spath 1939, plate 6, fig. 11; p. 90.
Oxford Clay, *mariae* Zone, *scarburgense* Subzone.
Weymouth, Dorset.
L. F. Spath Collection, purchased 1943.
GSM 72237

Cardioceras (Scarburgiceras) scarburgense (Young & Bird) **crassa** Spath HOLOTYPE of ssp.
Spath 1939, plate 7, fig. 12; p. 90.
Oxford Clay, mariae Zone, *scarburgense* Subzone.
London Brick Co. pit, Warboys, Cambridgeshire [Huntingdonshire].
Survey Collection (W. Dewar) 1937.
GSM 56546

Cardioceras (Scarburgiceras) scarburgense (Young & Bird) **?crassa** Spath
Spath 1939, plate 7, fig. 10; fig. 90.
Oxford Clay, *mariae* Zone, *scarburgense* Subzone.
London Brick Co. pit, Warboys, Cambridgeshire [Huntingdonshire].
Survey Collection (W. Dewar) 1937.
GSM 56544

Cardioceras (Scarburgiceras) scarburgense (Young & Bird) **normandiana** Spath HOLOTYPE of ssp.
Spath 1939, plate 7, fig. 9; p. 90.
Oxford Clay, *mariae* Zone, *scarburgense* Subzone.
Warboys, Cambridgeshire [Huntingdonshire].
L. F. Spath Collection, purchased 1943.
GSM 72239

Peltoceras cf. **interscissum** Uhlig
S. S. Buckman 1920, p. 17.
Peltoceratoides torosus (Oppel)
S. S. Buckman 1925, plate DLXIII.
Arkell 1933, p. 371.
Arkell 1947a, p. 298.
Oxford Clay, *mariae* Zone.
Loch Staffin, Skye.
Museum Collection.
GSM 30449

Popanites scaphitoides (Coquand)
Spath 1939, p. 87.
Oxford Clay, *mariae* Zone.
London Brick Co. pit, Warboys, Cambridgeshire [Huntingdonshire].
Survey Collection (W. Dewar and W. G. E. Graham) 1937.
Dr 2729

Creniceras renggeri (Oppel)
Arkell 1933, plate 37, figs. 4, 4a.
Oxford Clay, *mariae* Zone.
Ludgershall, Buckinghamshire.
S. S. Buckman Collection, purchased 1912.
GSM 27791, 27792

Pavloviceras bathyomphalum S. S. Buckman
S. S. Buckman 1920, p. 18.
Oxford Clay, *mariae* Zone.
Cutting, Great Northern Railway, Walton, Cambridgeshire [Huntingdonshire],
Museum Collection.
GSM 30571

Pavloviceras omphaloides (J. Sowerby)
S. S. Buckman 1920, p. 18.
S. S. Buckman 1921, plate CXCV.
Oxford Clay, *mariae* Zone.
Backwater, Radipole, Dorset.
Museum Collection.
GSM 30569

Cardioceras (Scarburgiceras) aff. **alphacordatum** Spath
Arkell 1946, pp. 303-304.
Scarborough Ball Beds, *cordatum* Zone.
Scarborough, Yorkshire.
J. S. Bowerbank Collection, purchased 1864.
GSM 30647

Cardioceras martini Reeside **anglica** Spath, HOLOTYPE of ssp.
Spath 1939, plate 7, fig. 5; p. 94.
Cardioceras (Scarburgiceras) bukowskii Maire
Arkell 1946, p. 306.
Oxford Clay, *cordatum* Zone.
London Brick Co. pit, Warboys, Cambridgeshire [Huntingdonshire].
Survey Collection (W. Dewar) 1937.
GSM 56543

Cardioceras (Cardioceras) cordatum (J. Sowerby)
Arkell 1946, p. 314.
Coral Rag, ferruginous Lower Calcareous Grit, *cordatum* Zone.
Seend, Wiltshire.
Museum Collection.
GSM 30295

Cardioceras costellatum S. S. Buckman
S. S. Buckman 1925, plate DCXVI A.
Arkell 1936, p. 176.
Cardioceras (Subvertebriceras) costellatum S. S. Buckman HOLOTYPE
Arkell 1946, plate 69, fig. 19, text-fig. 112; p. 325.
Oxford Clay, *cordatum* Zone.
Horton Brickyard, Horton-cum-Studley, Oxfordshire.
S. S. Buckman Collection, purchased 1927.
GSM 47821

Cardioceras costellatum S. S. Buckman PARATYPE
S. S. Buckman 1925, plate DCXVII B.
Arkell 1936, p. 176.
Oxford Clay, *cordatum* Zone, *costicardia* Subzone.
Horton Brickyard, Horton-cum-Studley, Oxfordshire.
S. S. Buckman Collection, purchased 1927.
GSM 47822

Cardioceras costicardia S. S. Buckman HOLOTYPE
S. S. Buckman 1926, plate DCXXXIII.
Arkell 1936, p. 176.
Cardioceras (Cardioceras) costicardia S. S. Buckman HOLOTYPE
Arkell 1946, plate 69, fig. 17; pp. 319-321.
Oxford Clay, *cordatum* Zone, *costicardia* Subzone.
Horton Brickyard, Horton-cum-Studley, Oxfordshire.
S. S. Buckman Collection, purchased 1927
GSM 47833

Cardioceras sp.
Wilson 1936, p. 258.
Cardioceras (Cardioceras) costicardia S. S. Buckman
Arkell 1946, p. 321.
Oxford Clay-Calcareous Grit "Transition Series", *cordatum* Zone.
Railway cutting, Huttons Ambo, Yorkshire.
Survey Collection (H. Walters) 1871.
P 1456

Vertebriceras dorsale S. S. Buckman HOLOTYPE
S. S. Buckman 1920, p. 16.
S. S. Buckman 1921, plate CXCVIII.
Roman 1938, p. 229.
Cardioceras (Vertebriceras) dorsale (S. S. Buckman) HOLOTYPE
Arkell 1942, plate 54, fig. 3; p. 250.
Arkell 1957, fig. 378,1 c d; p. L306.
Corallian, Shell Bed, *cordatum* Zone.
Horspath Road Quarry, Cowley, Oxford.
S. S. Buckman Collection, purchased 1923.
GSM 32030

Cardioceras (Scarburgiceras) harmonicum Maire trans. to **subexcavatum** Maire
Arkell 1946, plate 71, fig. 3; p. 301.
Corallian, Ball Beds, *cordatum* Zone.
Scarborough, Yorkshire.
Museum Collection.
GSM 30650

Cardioceras (Scarburgiceras) harmonicum Maire
Arkell 1946, p. 301.
Corallian, Ball Beds, *cordatum* Zone.
Scarborough, Yorkshire.
J. S. Bowerbank Collection, purchased 1864.
GSM 30645

Miticardioceras mite S. S. Buckman HOLOTYPE
S. S. Buckman 1923, plate CCCLXXV.
Cardioceras (Cardioceras) mite (S. S. Buckman) HOLOTYPE
Arkell 1946, pp. lxxv, 315, 318, 395.
Oxford Clay, 'Worminghall Rock', *cordatum* Zone.
Well at Field Farm, Worminghall, Buckinghamshire.
S. S. Buckman Collection, purchased 1924.
GSM 47171

Plasmatoceras plastum S. S. Buckman HOLOTYPE
S. S. Buckman 1925, plate DCXVII; p. 66.
Cardioceras (Plasmatoceras) plastum (S. S. Buckman) HOLOTYPE
Arkell 1941-5, plate 69, fig. 21; pp. lxxvii, lxxxii, 308.
Oxford Clay, *cordatum* Zone.
Labelled as 'Bowood' [probably referring to collector John Spencer of Bowood; locality suggested by Arkell is Vastern, near Wootton Bassett, Wiltshire.]
Museum Collection.
GSM 30524

Cardioceras quadrarium S. S. Buckman HOLOTYPE
S. S. Buckman 1926, plate DCXC.
Arkell 1936b, p. 176.
Cardioceras (Vertebriceras) quadrarium (S. S. Buckman) HOLOTYPE
Arkell 1946, plate 70, fig. 13; pp. 328-331.
Oxford Clay, *cordatum* Zone.
Horton Brickyard, Horton-cum-Studley, Oxfordshire.
S. S. Buckman Collection, purchased 1928.
GSM 49286

Sagitticeras sagitta S. S. Buckman HOLOTYPE
S. S. Buckman 1920, p. 19.
S. S. Buckman 1921, plate CCLX.
Cardioceras (Sagitticeras) sagitta (S. S. Buckman) HOLOTYPE
Arkell 1946, plate 70, fig. 15; pp. 332-333.
Oxford Clay, *cordatum* Zone.
Backwater, Weymouth, Dorset.
Museum Collection.
GSM 30371

'Cardioceras' dieneri Neumann
S. S. Buckman 1925, p. 66.
Oxford Clay, *cordatum* Zone.
Brickfield, Purton, Wiltshire.
A. M. Davies Collection, presented 1937.
GSM 59667

Peltomorphites hoplophorus S. S. Buckman HOLOTYPE
S. S. Buckman 1925, plates DLXIV A, B.
Peltoceras (Peltomorphites) hoplophorum (S. S. Buckman) HOLOTYPE
Arkell 1944, pp. 294-295.
Peltomorphites hoplophorus S. S. Buckman HOLOTYPE
Stefanov 1963, p. 98.
Oxford Clay, Jordan Cliff Beds, *cordatum* Zone.
Old Coastguard Station, Jordan Cliff below Overcomb House, Preston, Dorset.
S. S. Buckman Collection, purchased 1926.
GSM 47568

Cardioceras suessiforme Spath HOLOTYPE
Spath 1939, plate 6, fig. 4; p. 94.
Cardioceras (Scarburgiceras) excavatoides Maire
Arkell 1946, p. 301.
Turner 1970, p. 374.
Oxford Clay, *cordatum* Zone
Loch Staffin, Skye.
L. F. Spath Collection, purchased 1943.
GSM 72236

Cardioceras suessiforme Spath PARATYPE
Spath 1939, plate 7, fig. 13; p. 94.
Cardioceras (Scarburgiceras) excavatoides Maire
Arkell 1946, p. 301.
Oxford Clay, *cordatum* Zone.
London Brick Co. pit, Warboys, Cambridgeshire [Huntingdonshire].
Survey Collection (W. Dewar) 1937.
GSM 56547

Cardioceras anacanthum S. S. Buckman HOLOTYPE
S. S. Buckman 1927, plate DCCIII.
Arkell 1936b, p. 177.
Goliathiceras (Pachycardioceras) anacanthum (S. S. Buckman) HOLOTYPE
Arkell 1947a, plate 71, fig. 6; p. 337.
Oxford Clay, *cordatum* Zone.
Jordan Cliff, Preston, near Weymouth, Dorset.
S. S. Buckman Collection, purchased 1928.
GSM 49294

Goliathiceras (Pachycardioceras) anacanthum (S. S. Buckman)
Arkell 1947a, p. 337.
Corallian, Ball Beds, *cordatum* Zone.
Scarborough, Yorkshire.
J. S. Bowerbank Collection, purchased 1864.
GSM 30644

Korythoceras korys S. S. Buckman PARATYPE
S. S. Buckman 1920, p. 17.
Goliathiceras (Korythoceras) korys (S. S. Buckman) PARATYPE
Arkell 1947a, p. 341.
Oxford Clay, *cordatum* Zone.
Loch Staffin, Skye.
Museum Collection.
GSM 30381

Korythoceras korys S. S. Buckman HOLOTYPE
S. S. Buckman 1920, p. 17.
S. S. Buckman 1922a, plate CCCLXI.
Arkell 1933, p. 371.
Goliathiceras (Korythoceras) korys (S. S. Buckman) HOLOTYPE
Arkell 1947a, text-fig. 122; pp. lxxxi, 341.
Arkell 1957, fig. 375, 2; p. L306.
Cardioceras (Korythoceras) korys (S. S. Buckman) HOLOTYPE
Turner 1966, p. 247.
Goliathiceras (Korythoceras) korys (S. S. Buckman) HOLOTYPE
Turner 1970, plate 2, figs. A-C (cast); pp. 373-374.
Oxford Clay, *cordatum* Zone.
Loch Staffin, Skye.
Museum Collection.
GSM 30380

Hortoniceras sidericum S. S. Buckman HOLOTYPE
S. S. Buckman 1922a, plate CCXCVI.
Goliathiceras ("Hortoniceras") sidericum (S. S. Buckman) HOLOTYPE
Arkell 1937c, p. 450.
Goliathiceras (Goliathiceras) sidericum (S. S. Buckman) HOLOTYPE
Arkell 1947a, plate 74, fig. 8; text-fig. 123 no. 2, pp. 342-343.
Upper Oxford Clay, *cordatum* Zone.
Horton Brickyard, Horton-cum-Studley, Oxfordshire.
S. S. Buckman Collection, purchased 1924.
GSM 47117

Goliathiceras (Pachycardioceras) globulus Arkell
Arkell 1947a, plate 72, fig. 12; pp. 340-341.
Corallian, Ball Beds, *cordatum* Zone.
Cayton Bay, near Scarborough, Yorkshire.
J. S. Bowerbank Collection, purchased 1864.
GSM 30649

Aspidoceras akantheen S. S. Buckman HOLOTYPE
S. S. Buckman 1928, plates DCCLXX A, B.
Aspidoceras (Euaspidoceras) akantheen S. S. Buckman HOLOTYPE
Arkell 1940, text-fig. 73; pp. 206-209.
Corallian, Berkshire Oolites, *cordatum* or *plicatilis* Zone.
Pressed Steel Works, Cowley, Oxford.
S. S. Buckman Collection, purchased 1928.
GSM 49344

Aspidoceras (Euaspidoceras) akantheen S. S. Buckman
Arkell 1940, plate 44, figs. 3 A,B; pp. 308-309.
Corallian, Preston Grit, *Trigonia hudlestoni* Beds, *cordatum* Zone.
Redcliff, Weymouth, Dorset.
Museum Collection.
GSM 30682

Aspidoceras (Euaspidoceras) nikitini Borissjak
Arkell 1944, plate 61, fig. 3; pp. 276-277.
Corallian, Lower Calcareous Grit, *cordatum* Zone.
Black Dog siding, Calne, Wiltshire.
Miss M. S. Johnston Collection, presented 1926.
GSM 47744

Aspidoceras vettersianum Neumann
S. S. Buckman 1927, plates DCCLX A, B.
Aspidoceras (Euaspidoceras) paucituberculatum Arkell
Arkell 1940, plate 46, fig. 3; pp. 211, 213-215.
Corallian, Shell Bed/Berkshire Oolites, *cordatum* or *plicatilis* Zone.
Pressed Steel Works, Cowley, Oxford.
S. S. Buckman Collection, purchased 1929.
GSM 49338

Cardioceras cariniferum S. S. Buckman HOLOTYPE
S. S. Buckman 1926, plate DCXXVII
Cardioceras (Sagitticeras) cariniferum S. S. Buckman HOLOTYPE
Arkell 1936a, pp. 165-166.
Arkell 1942, plate 54, fig. 1; text-fig. 88f; pp. 252-253.
Corallian, Shell Bed, *cordatum* Zone.
Magdalen Pit, Headington, Oxford.
S. S. Buckman Collection, purchased 1927.
GSM 47827

Vertebriceras quadratum (J. Sowerby)
S. S. Buckman 1925, plate DCXIX.
Cardioceras (Vertebriceras) quadratum (S. S. Buckman *non* J. Sowerby)
Arkell 1936b, pp. 164, 168.
Cardioceras (Vertebriceras) cowleyense Arkell HOLOTYPE
Arkell 1942, plate 54, fig. 4; pp. 246-247.
Corallian, Shell Bed, *cordatum* Zone.
Horspath Road Quarry, Cowley, Oxford.
S. S. Buckman Collection, purchased 1927.
GSM 47823

Anacardioceras delicatum S. S. Buckman HOLOTYPE
S. S. Buckman 1926, plate DCXXX.
Cardioceras (Scoticardioceras) excavatum (J. Sowerby)
Arkell 1941, pp. 220, 224-225.
Corallian, *cordatum* Zone.
Near the Industrial School, Cowley, Oxford.
S. S. Buckman Collection, purchased 1927.
GSM 47830

Sagitticeras moderatum S. S. Buckman HOLOTYPE
S. S. Buckman 1925, plate DC.
Cardioceras (Sagitticeras) moderatum (S. S. Buckman) HOLOTYPE
Arkell 1936b, p. 166.
Arkell 1942, text-fig. 89; pp. 251-252.
Corallian, Shell Bed, *cordatum* Zone.
Magdalen Pit, Headington, Oxford.
S. S. Buckman Collection, purchased 1927.
GSM 47778

Cardioceras suessi? Siemiradzki
S. S. Buckman 1925, p. 65.
Paracardioceras persecans S. S. Buckman HOLOTYPE
S. S. Buckman 1925, plate DLXXXVIII.
Cardioceras (Cardioceras) persecans (S. S. Buckman) HOLOTYPE
Arkell 1946, text-fig. 110; pp. 315-316, 318.
Corallian, Nothe Grit, *cordatum* Zone.
Ham Cliff, Osmington, near Weymouth, Dorset.
S. S. Buckman Collection, purchased 1927.
GSM 47770

Anacardioceras serrigerum S. S. Buckman HOLOTYPE
S. S. Buckman 1926, plates DCXCI A, B.
Cardioceras (Scoticardioceras) serrigerum (S. S. Buckman) HOLOTYPE
Arkell 1941, plate 50, fig. 2; text-fig. 79; p. 226.
Corallian, Berkshire Oolites, *cordatum* Zone.
Horspath Road Quarry, near the Industrial School, Cowley, Oxford.
S. S. Buckman Collection, purchased 1928.
GSM 49287

Goliathiceras ammonoides (Young & Bird)
S. S. Buckman 1919, plate CXXXII C.
Goliathiceras (Goliathiceras) ammonoides (Young & Bird)
Arkell 1942-1943, plates 56, fig. 3, 57 fig. 4; pp. 254-255.
Arkell 1957, fig. 373, 2; pp. L304-305.
Corallian, Lower Calcareous Grit, *cordatum* Zone.
Cowley, Oxford.
S. S. Buckman Collection, purchased 1922.
GSM 32003

Anacardioceras delicatulum S. S. Buckman HOLOTYPE
S. S. Buckman 1926, plate DCXXXV.
Cardioceras (Scoticardioceras) delicatulum (S. S. Buckman) HOLOTYPE
Arkell 1941, text-fig. 80; pp. 226-229.
Corallian, Berkshire Oolites, *cordatum* Zone.
Industrial Schools Quarry, Cowley, Oxford.
S. S. Buckman Collection, purchased 1927.
GSM 47834

Aspidoceras (Euaspidoceras) perarmatum (J. Sowerby)
Arkell 1940, plate 41, fig. 4; pp. 193, 197.
Corallian, Shell Bed, *cordatum* Zone.
Bullingdon, Oxford.
Earl of Enniskillen Collection presented (date unknown, probably 1853).
GSM 55524

Vertebriceras costulosum S. S. Buckman HOLOTYPE
S. S. Buckman 1926, plate DCXXXVI.
Cardioceras (Vertebriceras) costulosum (S. S. Buckman) HOLOTYPE
Arkell 1936b, p. 166.
Cardioceras (Subvertebriceras) costulosum (S. S. Buckman) HOLOTYPE
Arkell 1942, text-fig. 87; pp. 244-246.
Corallian, Shell Bed, *cordatum* Zone.
Magdalen College Pit, Headington, Oxford.
S. S. Buckman Collection, purchased 1927.
GSM 47835

Goliathiceras microtrypa S. S. Buckman HOLOTYPE
S. S. Buckman 1923, plate CCCLXXX.
Cardioceras (Goliathiceras) microtrypa (S. S. Buckman) HOLOTYPE
Arkell 1936b, pp. 165-166.
Goliathiceras microtrypa S. S. Buckman HOLOTYPE
Arkell 1943, plate 58, fig. 1; pp. 262-263.
Corallian, Shell Bed (derived, ex Littlemore Sands), *cordatum* Zone.
Magdalen College Pit, Headington, Oxford.
S. S. Buckman Collection, purchased 1924.
GSM 47175

Anacardioceras excavatum (J. Sowerby)
S. S. Buckman 1924, plate CDLXIII.
Cardioceras (Scoticardioceras) excavatum (J. Sowerby)
Arkell 1941, p. 220.
Corallian, Lower Calcareous Grit, *cordatum* Zone.
Cowley, Oxford
S. S. Buckman Collection, purchased 1925
GSM 37312

Cardioceras (Cawtoniceras) cawtonense (Blake & Hudleston)
Arkell 1942, p. 239.
Elsworth Rock, *plicatilis* Zone.
Elsworth, Cambridgeshire.
W. H. Hudleston Collection, presented by Miss C. A. Raisin 1920.
Y 1773

Cardioceras (Maltoniceras) brightoni Arkell HOLOTYPE
Arkell 1941, plate 52, fig. 16; pp. 233-234.
Corallian, Trigonia hudlestoni Beds, *plicatilis* Zone.
South Quarries, Highworth, Wiltshire.
Museum Collection.
GSM 30639

Ammonites cawtonensis Blake & Hudleston
Blake and Hudleston 1877, plate 13, fig. 2; pp. 370, 392, 430.
Cawtoniceras cawtonense (Blake & Hudleston) LECTOTYPE
S. S. Buckman 1923, plate CDLIV.
Cardioceras (Cawtoniceras) cawtonense (Blake & Hudleston) LECTOTYPE
Arkell 1941-1942, plate 52, fig. 13; pp. 238-239.
Arkell 1957, fig. 375, 9; p. L306.
Corallian, *plicatilis* Zone.
Sike Gate, Cawton, Yorkshire.
W. H. Hudleston Collection, presented by Miss C. A. Raisin 1920.
GSM 46265

Anacardioceras cordatiforme S. S. Buckman HOLOTYPE
S. S. Buckman 1923, plate CDXX.
Cardioceras (Cardioceras) cordatiforme (S. S. Buckman) HOLOTYPE
Arkell 1941, plate 48, fig. 5, p. 217.
Corallian, Berkshire Oolites, *plicatilis* Zone.
Industrial Schools Quarry, Cowley, Oxford.
S. S. Buckman Collection, purchased 1924.
GSM 47201

Cardioceras (Cardioceras) highmoori Arkell
Arkell 1941, plate 48, fig. 3; pp. 218-219.
Corallian, *plicatilis* Zone.
South Quarries, Highworth, Wiltshire.
Museum Collection.
GSM 30638

Anacardioceras secundarium S. S. Buckman HOLOTYPE
S. S. Buckman 1926, plate DCXXIX.
Cardioceras (Scoticardioceras) excavatum (J. Sowerby).
Arkell 1941, pp. 220, 222, 224-225.
Corallian, *plicatilis* Zone.
Industrial School, Cowley, Oxford.
S. S. Buckman Collection, purchased 1927.
GSM 47829

Chalcedoniceras chalcedonicum (Young & Bird)
S. S. Buckman 1922a, plate CCXCV A; p. 51.
Cardioceras sp. sensu lato
Arkell 1941, p. lxxv.
Corallian, Berkshire Oolites, *plicatilis* Zone.
Horspath, Oxford.
S. S. Buckman Collection, purchased 1924.
GSM 47116

Vertebriceras rachis S. S. Buckman HOLOTYPE
S. S. Buckman 1920, p. 16.
S. S. Buckman 1926, plate DCXLVIII.
Cardioceras (Vertebriceras) vertebrale (J. Sowerby)
Arkell 1936b, p. 168.
Arkell 1942, pp. 248-249.
Corallian, *plicatilis* Zone, *vertebrale* Subzone.
Horspath Road Quarry, Cowley, Oxford.
S. S. Buckman Collection, purchased 1927.
GSM 47842

Dichotomosphinctes holtonensis S. S. Buckman HOLOTYPE
S. S. Buckman 1927, plate DCCXVII A.
Arkell 1933, p. 571.
Arkell 1935, p. 16.
Perisphinctes (Perisphinctes) parandieri Loriol
Arkell 1939a, text-fig. 32; pp. 105-111.
Corallian, Wheatley Limestones, *plicatilis* Zone.
Lye Hill Quarry, Holton, Oxfordshire.
S. S. Buckman Collection, purchased 1928.
GSM 49308

Anacardioceras expositum S. S. Buckman HOLOTYPE
S. S. Buckman 1926, plate DCXXVIII A, B.
Cardioceras (Scoticardioceras) expositum (S. S. Buckman) HOLOTYPE
Arkell 1941, plate 50, fig. 4; pp. 225-226.
Corallian, Berkshire Oolites, *plicatilis* Zone.
Industrial Schools Quarry, Cowley, Oxford.
S. S. Buckman Collection, purchased 1927.
GSM 47828

Perisphinctes (Kranaosphinctes) decurrens (S. S. Buckman)
Callomon 1960, p. 195.
Corallian, Pusey Flags, *plicatilis* Zone.
Stanford Pit, Stanford-in-the Vale, Oxfordshire [Berkshire].
R.E.H. Reid Collection, presented 1957.
GSM 95043

Kranaosphinctes decurrens S. S. Buckman HOLOTYPE
S. S. Buckman 1923, plate CDXLIX.
Perisphinctes (Kranaosphinctes) decurrens (S. S. Buckman) HOLOTYPE
Arkell 1939a, plate 39, fig. 5; pp. 175-179.
Corallian, *plicatilis* Zone.
Holloway, Cowley, Oxford.
S. S. Buckman Collection, purchased 1925.
GSM 37300

Perisphinctes biplex (J. Sowerby)
S. S. Buckman 1922, plate CCLXXXII.
Perisphinctes (Perisphinctes) tumulosus S. S. Buckman
Arkell 1936b, p. 166.
Perisphinctes (Perisphinctes) chloroolilticus (Gumbel)
Arkell 1938, plate 18, fig. 7; pp. 96-99, 104.
Corallian, Shell Bed, *plicatilis* Zone.
Magdalen College Pit, Headington, Oxford.
S. S. Buckman Collection, purchased 1924.
GSM 47115

Perisphinctes (Discosphinctes) cautisrufae Arkell HOLOTYPE
Arkell 1936a, plate 10, fig. 1; text-fig. 13; pp. 35-38.
Arkell 1947b, plate 3, fig. 5.
Corallian, Red Beds, *plicatilis* Zone.
Redcliff (or Shortlake), Weymouth, Dorset.
Museum Collection.
GSM 30664

Arisphinctes ariprepes S. S. Buckman HOLOTYPE
S. S. Buckman 1924, plates DXI A, B.
S. S. Buckman 1925, plate DXI C.
Perisphinctes (Arisphinctes) cotovui Simionescu
Arkell 1935a, plate A fig. 4; p. xiii.
Arkell 1936b, p. 153.
Arkell 1939a, plate 24 fig. 5; pp. 127, 133.
Arkell 1940, p. lvi.
Arisphinctes ariprepes S. S. Buckman HOLOTYPE
Luppov and Drushchits 1958, plate 36, fig. 10.
Perisphinctes (Arisphinctes) cotovui Simionescu
Malinowska 1972a, fig. 4; pp. 177-180.
Corallian, Hard Bed above Littlemore Sands, *plicatilis* Zone.
Brittleton Barn Quarry, Horspath, Oxford.
S. S. Buckman Collection, purchased 1926.
GSM 47543

Cardioceras (Maltoniceras) bodeni Maire
Arkell 1941, p. 237.
Elsworth Rock, *plicatilis* Zone.
Elsworth, Cambridgeshire.
Survey Collection (R. Gibbs) 1864.
d 1086

Cardioceras (Maltoniceras) ? bodeni Maire
Arkell 1941, p. 237.
Elsworth Rock, *plicatilis* Zone.
Elsworth, Cambridgeshire.
W. H. Hudleston Collection, presented by Miss C. A. Raisin 1920.
Y 1775

Cardioceras (Subvertebriceras) densiplicatum Boden
Arkell 1942, p. 241.
Elsworth Rock, *plicatilis* Zone.
Elsworth, Cambridgeshire.
Survey Collection (R. Gibbs) 1864,
d 1087, 1099

Goliathiceras (Goliathiceras) gorgon Arkell HOLOTYPE
Arkell 1943, plate 59, fig. 1; p. 256.
Elsworth Rock, *plicatilis* Zone.
Elsworth, Cambridgeshire.
Survey Collection (R. Gibbs) 1864.
d 1066

Perisphinctes (Dichotomosphinctes) ouatius (S. S. Buckman)
Arkell 1938, p. 94.
Elsworth Rock, *plicatilis* Zone.
Elsworth, Cambridgeshire.
W. H. Hudleston Collection, presented by Miss C. A. Raisin 1920.
Y 1774

Otosphinctes ouatius S. S. Buckman HOLOTYPE
S. S. Buckman 1926, plate DCXLIX.
Arkell 1936a, pp.xliii-xliv.
Perisphinctes (Dichotomosphinctes) ouatius (S. S. Buckman) HOLOTYPE
Arkell 1938, plate 17, fig. 5; pp. 93-94.
Corallian, Berkshire Oolites, *plicatilis* Zone.
Industrial Schools Quarry, Cowley, Oxford.
S. S. Buckman Collection, purchased 1927.
GSM 47843

Perisphinctes (Dichotomosphinctes) ouatius (S. S. Buckman)
Arkell 1938, p. 94.
Elsworth Rock, *plicatilis* Zone.
200 yds (182m) south of school, Elsworth, Cambridgeshire.
Survey Collection (W. Dewar) 1932.
Dw 2262

Perisphinctes (Dichotomosphinctes) rotoides Ronchadzé
Arkell 1938, p. 93.
Elsworth Rock, *plicatilis* Zone.
200 yards (182m) south of school, Elsworth, Cambridgeshire.
Survey Collection (W. Dewar) 1932.
Dw 2276 A

Perisphinctes (Arisphinctes) kingstonensis Arkell
Arkell 1939a, plate 32, fig. 6.
Elsworth Rock, *plicatilis* Zone.
200 yards (182m) south of school, Elsworth, Cambridgeshire.
Survey Collection (W. Dewar) 1932.
Dw 2261

Perisphinctes (Arisphinctes) laevipickeringius (Young & Bird)
Arkell 1939a, plate 30, fig. 6; pp. 142-145.
Corallian, limestone band (equivalent of Elsworth Rock?), *plicatilis* Zone.
London Brick Co. pit, Warboys, Cambridgeshire [Huntingdonshire].
Survey Collection (E. E. L. Dixon) 1936-1937.
GSM 60812

Perisphinctes (Arisphinctes) laevipickeringius (Young & Bird)
Arkell 1939a, plate 33, fig. 6; pp. 142-145.
Corallian, limestone band (equivalent of Elsworth Rock?), *plicatilis* Zone.
London Brick Co. pit, Warboys, Cambridgeshire [Huntingdonshire].
Survey Collection (E. E. L. Dixon) 1937-1938.
GSM 60813

Perisphinctes wartae Bukowski
Salfeld 1914, p. 249.
Perisphinctes (Dichotomosphinctes) auriculatus Arkell
Arkell 1938, p. 78.
Corallian, Trigonia hudlestoni beds, *plicatilis* Zone.
South Quarries, Highworth, Wiltshire.
J. Lycett Collection, purchased 1867.
GSM 25497

Perisphinctes wartae Bukowski
Salfeld 1914, p. 249.
Corallian, Coral Rag, *plicatilis* Zone.
?Highworth, Wiltshire.
J. Lycett Collection, purchased 1867.
GSM 25483

Perisphinctes (Liosphinctes) apolipon (S. S. Buckman)
Callomon 1960, p. 194.
Corallian, *plicatilis* Zone, *antecedens* Subzone.
Lamb and Flag Quarry, Kingston Bagpuize, Oxfordshire [Berkshire].
Survey Collection (S. W. Hester) 1925.
SH 4779

Liosphinctes apolipon
S. S. Buckman HOLOTYPE
S. S. Buckman 1925, plate DLXVI.
Perisphinctes (Liosphinctes) apolipon
(S. S. Buckman) HOLOTYPE
Arkell 1936a, p. 166.
Arkell 1939a, plate 35, fig. 3; pp. 161-163.
Arkell 1957, fig. 409, 3; p. L322.
Corallian, Berkshire Oolites, "Brown Course", *plicatilis* Zone.
Industrial Schools Quarry, Cowley, Oxford.
S. S. Buckman Collection, purchased 1926.
GSM 47570

Dichotomosphinctes antecedens (Salfeld)
S. S. Buckman 1926, plate DCL.
Perisphinctes (Dichotomosphinctes) buckmani
Arkell HOLOTYPE
Arkell 1936b, p. 166.
Arkell 1938, plate 14, fig. 1; pp. 79-83.
Malinowska 1972a, fig. 9; pp. 186-187.
Sapunov 1973, pp. 112-113.
Corallian, Shell Bed, *plicatilis* Zone.
Magdalen College Pit, Headington, Oxford.
S. S. Buckman Collection, purchased 1927.
GSM 47844

Cymatosphinctes cymatophorus S. S. Buckman
HOLOTYPE
S. S. Buckman 1923, plates CDL A, B.
Perisphinctes (Cymatosphinctes) cymatophorus
(S. S. Buckman) HOLOTYPE
Arkell 1935b, plate A, fig. 2, p. xii.
Arkell 1936b, p. 168.
Perisphinctes (Kranaosphinctes) cymatophorus
(S. S. Buckman) HOLOTYPE
Arkell 1939a, plate 27, fig. 5; pp. 168-175.
Corallian, Shell Bed, *plicatilis* Zone.
Horspath Road Quarry, Cowley, Oxford.
S. S. Buckman Collection, purchased 1925.
GSM 37301

Perisphinctes cowleyensis S. S. Buckman HOLOTYPE
S. S. Buckman 1926, plates DCLXIIIA, B.
Arkell 1935b, pp. xv-xvi.
Perisphinctes (Arisphinctes) cowleyensis
S. S. Buckman HOLOTYPE
Arkell 1939a, plate 42, fig. 3; pp. 139-142.
Corallian, Berkshire Oolites, *plicatilis* Zone.
Excavations for house construction (in 1921), Hollow Way, Cowley, Oxford.
S. S. Buckman Collection, purchased
GSM 47850

Perisphinctes (Arisphinctes) ringsteadensis
Arkell PARATYPE
Arkell 1935b, plate 3, fig. 3; pp. 19-21.
Corallian, Trigonia hudlestoni Beds (Red Beds), *cautisnigrae* Zone.
West of Osmington, Dorset.
L. F. Spath Collection, purchased.
GSM 72209

Perisphinctes (Biplices?) sp.
Arkell 1935b, pp. 28-29.
Arkell 1936a, plate 7, fig. 4.
Corallian, Red Beds, *cautisnigrae* Zone.
Red Cliff, Weymouth, Dorset.
Museum Collection.
GSM 30626

Perisphinctes (Perisphinctes) cautisnigrae Arkell
Arkell 1935b, plate 1 fig. 2; plate 3, fig. 2; text-fig. 5; p. 15.
Corallian, Trigonia hudlestoni Beds (Red Beds), *cautisnigrae* Zone.
West of Osmington, Dorset.
L. F. Spath Collection, purchased 1943.
GSM 72208

Amoeboceras leucum Spath HOLOTYPE
Spath 1935, plate 5, fig. 3; p. 22.
Amoeboceras (Prionodoceras) leucum
Spath HOLOTYPE
Arkell 1948, p. 394.
Pleistocene drift derived from Ampthill Clay, *decipiens* Zone.
Cambridgeshire.
L. F. Spath Collection, purchased 1943.
GSM 72211

Cardioceras praebauhini Salfeld SYNTYPE
Salfeld 1915, plate 17, fig. 5; pp. 178-179.
Pleistocene drift, derived from Ampthill Clay, *decipiens* Zone.
[Locality given on label on specimen: well, 2 miles SSE of Biggleswade, Bedfordshire, but Salfeld quotes Ormsby St. Margaret, Norfolk.]
Survey Collection (J. H. Blake) c.1890.
GSM 26054 [formerly 238 JHB] [Specimen is partially decomposed]

Amoeboceras (Prionodoceras) prionodes
(S. S. Buckman)
Spath 1939, p. 89.
Ampthill Clay, *decipiens* Zone.
London Brick Co. pit, Warboys, Cambridgeshire [Huntingdonshire]
W. Dewar Collection, presented 1938.
Zf 51

Amoeboceras prionodes (S. S. Buckman)
Spath 1935, p. 22.
Pleistocene drift, derived from Ampthill Clay, *decipiens* Zone.
Bedfordshire.
L. F. Spath Collection, purchased 1943.
GSM 72205

Amoeboceras aff. **pseudocaelatum** Spath
Arkell 1935b, plate 3, fig. 11.
Ampthill Clay, *decipiens* Zone.
Long Stanton, Cambridgeshire.
Survey Collection (E. E. L. Dixon) 1932.
GSM 54906 [formerly ED 2274]

Amoeboceras aff. **pseudocaelatum** Spath
Arkell 1935b, plate 3, fig. 9.
Ampthill Clay, *decipiens* Zone.
Reservoir site, Long Stanton, Cambridgeshire.
Survey Collection (W. Dewar) 1932.
GSM 54904 [formerly Dw 2723]

Amoeboceras aff. **pseudocaelatum** Spath
Arkell 1935b, plate 3, fig. 12.
Ampthill Clay, *decipiens* Zone.
Reservoir site, Long Stanton, Cambridgeshire.
Survey Collection (E. E. L. Dixon) 1932.
GSM 54907 [formerly ED 2274]

Amoeboceras aff. **pseudocaelatum** Spath
Arkell 1935b, plate 3 fig. 10.
Ampthill Clay, *decipiens* Zone.
Reservoir site, Long Stanton, Cambridgeshire.
Survey Collection (E. E. L. Dixon) 1932.
GSM 54905 [formerly ED 2273]

Amoeboceras aff. **pseudocaelatum** Spath
Arkell 1935b, plate 3, fig. 6.
Ampthill Clay, *decipiens* Zone.
Reservoir site, Long Stanton, Cambridgeshire.
Survey Collection (W. Dewar) 1932.
GSM 54901 [formerly Dw 2725]

Amoeboceras aff. **pseudocaelatum** Spath
Arkell 1935b, plate 3, fig. 7.
Ampthill Clay, *decipiens* Zone.
Reservoir site, Long Stanton, Cambridgeshire.
Survey Collection (W. Dewar) 1932.
GSM 54902 [formerly Dw 2719]

Cardioceras serratum (J. Sowerby)
Salfeld 1915, plate 18, fig. 1; p. 173.
Prionoderas (Amoeboceras) serratum
(J. Sowerby) NEOTYPE
Arkell 1937a, p. 50.
Arkell 1937b, pp. 66-67.
Spath 1943, p. 114.
Amoeboceras serratum (J. Sowerby) NEOTYPE
Sykes and Surlyk 1976, p. 424.
Pleistocene drift, derived from Ampthill Clay.
Lowestoft, Suffolk.
Survey Collection (J. H. Blake) c.1890.
GSM 26059 [formerly JHB 289]

Cardioceras serratum (J. Sowerby)
Salfeld 1915, plate 18, fig. 2.
Pleistocene drift, derived from Ampthill Clay.
Lowestoft, Suffolk.
Survey Collection (J. H. Blake) c.1890.
GSM 26058 [formerly JHB 288]

Cardioceras serratum (J. Sowerby)
Salfeld 1915, p. 173.
Pleistocene drift, derived from Ampthill Clay,
decipiens Zone.
Waterworks, Yarmouth, Norfolk.
Survey Collection (J. H. Blake) c.1890.
GSM 26055 [formerly JHB 239]

Prionodoceras excentricum S. S. Buckman HOLOTYPE
S. S. Buckman 1924, plate CDLXIV.
Amoeboceras (Prionodoceras) glosensis (Bigot & Brasil)
Arkell 1937a, p. 50.
Pleistocene drift, derived from Ampthill Clay,
decipiens Zone.
Cutting, Great Northern Railway, Walton,
Cambridgeshire [Huntingdonshire].
T. Reynolds Collection, presented ?1851.
GSM 30392

Ammonites cordatus var. **excavatus** J. Sowerby
Woodward 1895, p. 56.
Prionodoceras truculentum S. S. Buckman HOLOTYPE
S. S. Buckman 1927, plate DCCIV.
Amoeboceras (Prionodoceras) truculentum
(S. S. Buckman) HOLOTYPE
Arkell 1937a, pp. 50-51.
Pleistocene drift, derived from Ampthill Clay.
Cutting, Great Northern Railway, Walton,
Cambridgeshire [Huntingdonshire].
Museum Collection.
GSM 30379

Amoeboceras (Prionodoceras) cf. **truculentum**
(S. S. Buckman)
Arkell 1937b, p. 66.
Ampthill Clay.
Reservoir site, Long Stanton, Cambridgeshire.
Survey Collection (W. Dewar) 1932.
Dw 2758, 2761

Perisphinctes (Dichotomosphinctes) osmingtonensis
Arkell
Arkell 1935b, pp. 34-35.
Perisphinctes (Arisphinctes) osmingtonensis Arkell
Arkell 1947a, pp. 354, 370.
Ampthill Clay, Boxworth Stone.
Boxworth, Cambridgeshire.
Survey Collection (C. B. Wedd) 1900.
103, 104 CBW

Cardioceras ovale (Quenstedt)
Salfeld 1915, p. 168.
Pleistocene drift, derived from Ampthill Clay.
Well 2 miles SSE of Biggleswade, Bedfordshire.
H. Home Collection, presented 1903.
GSM 26048

Amoeboceras alternoides (Nikitin)
Spath 1935, p. 22.
Pleistocene drift, derived from Ampthill Clay,
decipiens Zone.
Bedfordshire.
L. F. Spath Collection, purchased 1943.
GSM 72204

Cardioceras excavatum (J. Sowerby)
Davies 1917, p. 35.
Ampthill Clay, Brill Serpulite Bed, *decipiens* Zone.
Rid's Hill Brickyard, Brill, Buckinghamshire.
A. M. Davies Collection, presented 1937.
GSM 59667

Amoeboceras (Prionodoceras) glosensis (Bigot & Brasil)
Arkell 1937a, p. 51.
Pleistocene drift, derived from Ampthill Clay,
decipiens Zone.
Norfolk.
H. B. Woodward Collection, ex J. Gunn Collection,
presented 1896.
GSM 5629

Decipia lintonensis Arkell
Hancock 1954, p. 250.
Ampthill Clay.
Bathe Hill, Holywell-cum-Needingworth, St. Ives,
Cambridgeshire [Huntingdonshire].
Survey Collection (S. E. Hollingworth) 1937.
SEH 307

Decipia decipiens (J. Sowerby)
Arkell 1947a, pp. 356, 373.
Ampthill Clay, *decipiens* Zone.
Railway cutting, south end of tunnel, Ampthill, Bedfordshire.
Survey Collection (J. Rhodes) 1886.
JR 3313, 3335

Decipia sp.
Arkell 1935b, plate 3, fig. 1.
Arkell 1947a, plate 78, fig. 10; p. 373.
Ampthill Clay, *decipiens* Zone.
Reservoir site, Long Stanton, Cambridgeshire.
Survey Collection (W. Dewar) 1932.
GSM 54896 [formerly Dw 2697]

Decipia sp.
Arkell 1935b, plate 3, fig. 2.
Arkell 1947a, plate 78, fig. 12; p. 373.
Ampthill Clay, *decipiens* Zone.
Reservoir site, Long Stanton, Cambridgeshire.
Survey Collection (W. Dewar) 1932.
GSM 54897 [formerly DW 2696]

Decipia sp.
Arkell 1935b, plate 3, fig. 3.
Arkell 1947a, plate 78, fig. 11; p. 373.
Ampthill Clay, *decipiens* Zone.
Reservoir site, Long Stanton, Cambridgeshire.
Survey Collection (W. Dewar) 1932.
GSM 54898 [formerly Dw 2698]

Decipia sp.
Arkell 1935b, plate 3, fig. 4.
Arkell 1947a, plate 78, fig. 9; p. 373
Ampthill Clay, *decipiens* Zone.
Reservoir site, Long Stanton, Cambridgeshire.
Survey Collection (W. Dewar) 1932
GSM 54899 [formerly Dw 2664]

Decipia (Pomerania) dewari Arkell
Arkell 1947a, plate 78, fig. 5.
Ampthill Clay, *decipiens* Zone.
Reservoir site, Long Stanton, Cambridgeshire.
Survey Collection (W. Dewar) 1932.
Dw 2714

Amoeboceras ovale (Quenstedt)
Spath 1935, p. 22.
Corallian, ?*decipiens* Zone.
Swindon, Wiltshire.
L. F. Spath Collection, purchased 1943.
GSM 72207

Perisphinctes (Perisphinctes) variocostatus (Buckland)
Arkell 1947a, plate 76, fig. 2; pp. 363, 364.
Pleistocene Drift, derived from Ampthill Clay, *decipiens* Zone.
Harham, Suffolk.
Museum Collection.
GSM 8848

Perisphinctes sp.
Arkell 1935b, p. 67.
Perisphinctes (Ampthillia) ampthillensis Arkell
Arkell 1947a, p. 361.
Ampthill Clay.
Railway cutting, N end of tunnel, Ampthill, Bedfordshire.
Survey Collection (J. Rhodes) 1886.
JR 3314

Decipia (Pomerania) dewari Arkell HOLOTYPE
Arkell 1947a, plate 78, fig. 1; text-fig. 135, p. 375.
Ampthill Clay, *decipiens* Zone.
Reservoir site, Long Stanton, Cambridgeshire.
Survey Collection (W. Dewar) 1932.
Dw 2710

Decipia (Pomerania) dixoni Arkell HOLOTYPE
Arkell 1947a, plate 78, fig. 4; text-fig. 134; p. 374.
Ampthill Clay, *decipiens* Zone.
Reservoir site, Long Stanton, Cambridgeshire.
Survey Collection (W. Dewar) 1932.
Dw 2713

Decipia (Pomerania) cf. **robusta** (Dohm)
Arkell 1947a, plate 78, fig. 3; p. 376.
Ampthill Clay, *decipiens* Zone.
Reservoir site, Long Stanton, Cambridgeshire.
Survey Collection (W. Dewar) 1932.
Dw 2708

Decipia (Pomerania) cf. **robusta** (Dohm)
Arkell 1947a, plate 78, fig. 2; text-fig. 135; p. 376.
Ampthill Clay, *decipiens* Zone.
Reservoir site, Long Stanton, Cambridgeshire.
Survey Collection (W. Dewar) 1932.
Dw 2706

Perisphinctes sp.
Arkell 1935b, p. 67.
Perisphinctes (Ampthillia) ampthillensis Arkell.
Arkell 1947a, p. 361.
Ampthill Clay.
Reservoir site, Long Stanton, Cambridgeshire.
Survey Collection (W. Dewar) 1932.
Dw 2750, 2752, 2753, 2757

Perisphinctes sp.
Arkell 1935b, p. 67.
Perisphinctes (Ampthillia) ampthillensis Arkell HOLOTYPE
Arkell 1947a, plate 75, fig. 8; pp. 359-361.
Arkell 1957, fig. 412, 1; p. L322.
Pleistocene drift, derived from Ampthill Clay. Lincolnshire.
E.C.H. Day Collection, purchased ?1871.
GSM 58060

Perisphinctes (Ampthillia) ampthillensis Arkell
Arkell 1947a, p. 361.
Ampthill Clay, ?*pseudocordata* Zone.
Boxworth, Cambridgeshire.
Survey Collection (C.B. Wedd) 1900.
CBW 101

Perisphinctes sp.
Arkell 1935b, plate 3, fig. 5.
Arkell 1947a, plate 78, fig. 13.
Reservoir site, Long Stanton, Cambridgeshire.
Survey Collection (W. Dewar) 1932.
GSM 54900 [formerly Dw 2731]

Dichotomoceras strumatum S. S. Buckman
HOLOTYPE
S. S. Buckman 1927, plates DCCXLVII A-D.
Perisphinctes (Perisphinctes) strumatus (S. S. Buckman)
Arkell 1947a, plate 77, fig. 3, pp. 365-366.
Pleistocene drift, derived from Ampthill Clay. Sharnbrook, Bedford.
S. S. Buckman Collection, ex T. Wright, purchased 1928.
GSM 49326

Ringsteadia anglica Salfeld SYNTYPE
Salfeld 1917, plate 13; pp. 76-77.
Corallian, ?Westbury Ironstone, *pseudocordata* Zone.
Westbury, Wiltshire.
Survey Collection (H. B. Woodward) 1885.
GSM 25502 [formerly 2646 HBW]

Ringsteadia anglica Salfeld SYNTYPE
Salfeld 1917, p. 76.
Corallian, *pseudocordata* Zone.
Osmington, Dorset.
F. Gordon Collection, purchased 1895.
GSM 5776

Ringsteadia anglica Salfeld SYNTYPE
Salfeld 1917, pp. 76, 77.
Corallian, *pseudocordata* Zone.
Ringstead Bay, Dorset.
Museum Collection.
GSM 25479

Ringsteadia pseudocordata (Blake)
Salfeld 1917, p. 80.
Corallian, *pseudocordata* Zone.
Red Cliff, Weymouth, Dorset.
T. Reynolds Collection, presented ?1851.
GSM 25498

Ringsteadia pseudocordata (Blake)
Salfeld 1917, p. 80.
Corallian, *pseudocordata* Zone.
Near Osmington, Dorset.
H. Smith Collection, purchased 1890.
GSM 3864

Ammonites pseudocordatus Blake & Hudleston HOLOTYPE
Blake and Hudleston 1877, plate 13, fig. 1; p. 392.
Ringsteadia pseudocordata (Blake & Hudleston) HOLOTYPE
Salfeld 1913, p. 427.
Salfeld 1914, p. 129.
S. S. Buckman 1925, plates DLX A, B.
Arkell 1936b, pp. 149, 150.
Arkell 1940, p.lxv.
Arkell 1956b, plate 39, fig. 2.
Corallian, Westbury Ironstone, *pseudocordata* Zone.
Westbury, Wiltshire.
W.H. Hudleston Collection, presented by Miss C.A. Raisin 1920.
GSM 46264

Perisphinctes wartae Bukowski
Salfeld 1914, p. 249.
Arkell 1933, pp. 376, 389.
Perisphinctes (Perisphinctes) wartaeformis Arkell HOLOTYPE
Arkell 1947a, plate 77, fig. 5; text-fig. 129 (as **P. subwartaeformis)**; p. 367.
Corallian, Westbury Ironstone, *pseudocordata* Zone.
Ironworks, Westbury, Wiltshire.
W. Cunnington Collection, purchased 1875.
GSM 25484

Perisphinctes (Perisphinctes) waltonensis Arkell HOLOTYPE
Arkell 1947a, plate 77, fig. 2; pp. 364, 365.
Ampthill Clay, *pseudocordata* Zone.
Cutting, Great Northern Railway, Wood Walton, Cambridgeshire [Huntingdonshire].
T. Reynolds Collection, presented ?1851.
GSM 58499

Prionodoceras superstes (Phillips)
S. S. Buckman 1923, plate CDXXII.
Arkell 1933, p. 462.
Ampthill Clay.
Rids Hill Brickfield, Brill, Buckinghamshire.
S. S. Buckman Collection, purchased 1924.
GSM 47202

Amoeboceras (Prionodoceras) marstonense Spath HOLOTYPE
Spath 1935, plate 4; p. 20.
Corallian, *pseudocordata* Zone.
Marston, Wiltshire.
L. F. Spath Collection, purchased 1943.
GSM 72210

Perisphinctes (Microbiplices)
Arkell 1936a, p.xli.
Microbiplices anglicus Arkell HOLOTYPE
Arkell 1947a, plate 76, fig. 7; p. 378.
Perisphinctes (Microbiplices) anglicus Arkell HOLOTYPE
Malinowska 1972b, p. 26.
Corallian, Sandsfoot Grits, *pseudocordata* Zone.
Near Weymouth, Dorset.
Museum Collection.
GSM 30627

?Klematosphinctes sp.
Spath 1931, p. 323.
Corallian, Sandsfoot Grits, *pseudocordata* Zone.
Weymouth, Dorset.
L. F. Spath Collection, purchased 1943.
GSM 72184

Divisosphinctes sp.
Spath 1931, p. 322.
Corallian, Sandsfoot Grit, *pseudocordata* Zone.
East of Red Cliff, Weymouth, Dorset.
L. F. Spath Collection, purchased 1943.
GSM 72183

Cardioceras (Cawtoniceras) blakei Spath HOLOTYPE
Spath 1935, plate 13, fig. 4; p. 16.
Arkell 1941, p.lxxviii.
Pleistocene drift, derived from Ampthill Clay, *?pseudocordata* Zone.
?Bedfordshire.
L.F. Spath Collection, purchased 1943.
GSM 72203

KIMMERIDGIAN STAGE

Pictonia densicostata Salfeld
S. S. Buckman 1924, plate DXXXIII.
Kimmeridge Clay, *baylei* Zone.
Ringstead Bay, Dorset.
Museum Collection.
GSM 25481

Pictonia sp.
Arkell 1935b, plate A fig. 5; p.xiii.
Basal Kimmeridge Clay, *baylei* Zone.
Wootton Bassett, Wiltshire.
Museum Collection
GSM 25487

Cardioceras cricki Salfeld
Salfeld 1915, plate 19 figs. 3a-c; pp.191-193.
Kimmeridge Clay, *cymodoce* Zone.
Market Rasen, Lincolnshire.
Museum Collection.
GSM 25563
[specimen had decomposed in 1930]

Cardioceras cricki Salfeld
Salfeld 1915, plate 19, fig. 6; pp. 191-193.
Kimmeridge Clay, *cymodoce* Zone.
Market Rasen, Lincolnshire.
Museum Collection.
GSM 25564

Cardioceras cricki Salfeld
Salfeld 1915, plate 19, fig. 4; pp. 191-193.
Market Rasen,Lincolnshire.
Museum Collection.
GSM 25565

Cardioceras cricki Salfeld
Salfeld 1915, plate 19, fig. 5; pp. 191-193.
Kimmeridge Clay, *cymodoce* Zone.
Market Rasen, Lincolnshire.
Museum Collection.
GSM 25566
[specimen had decomposed in 1930]

Cardioceras kitchini Salfeld
Salfeld 1915, plate 19, fig. 8; pp. 189-191.
Kimmeridge Clay, *cymodoce* Zone.
Market Rasen, Lincolnshire.
Museum Collection.
GSM 25553

Cardioceras kitchini Salfeld
Salfeld 1915, plate 19, fig. 9; pp. 189-191.
Kimmeridge Clay, *cymodoce* Zone.
Market Rasen, Lincolnshire.
Museum Collection.
GSM 25554
[specimen had decomposed in 1930]

Cardioceras kitchini Salfeld
Salfeld 1915, plate 19, fig. 10; pp. 189-191.
Kimmeridge Clay, *cymodoce* Zone.
Market Rasen, Lincolnshire.
Museum Collection.
GSM 25555
[specimen had decomposed in 1930]

Cardioceras kitchini Salfeld
Salfeld 1915, plate 19, fig. 11; pp. 189-191.
Kimmeridge Clay, *cymodoce* Zone.
Market Rasen, Lincolnshire.
Museum Collection.
GSM 25556

Cardioceras kitchini Salfeld
Salfeld 1915, plate 19, fig. 12; pp. 189-191.
Kimmeridge Clay, *cymodoce* Zone.
Market Rasen, Lincolnshire.
Museum Collection.
GSM 25557

Cardioceras kitchini Salfeld
Salfeld 1915, plate 19, fig. 13; pp. 189-191.
Kimmeridge Clay, *cymodoce* Zone.
Market Rasen, Lincolnshire.
Museum Collection.
GSM 25558

Cardioceras kitchini Salfeld
Salfeld 1915, plate 19, fig. 16; pp. 189-191.
Kimmeridge Clay, *cymodoce* Zone.
Market Rasen, Lincolnshire.
Museum Collection.
GSM 25561

Cardioceras kitchini Salfeld
Salfeld 1915, plate 19, fig. 17; pp. 189-191.
Kimmeridge Clay, *cymodoce* Zone.
Market Rasen, Lincolnshire.
Museum Collection.
GSM 25562

Plasmatites crenulatus S. S. Buckman HOLOTYPE
S. S. Buckman 1925, plate DCXVIII.
Amoeboceras crenulatum (S. S. Buckman) HOLOTYPE
Arkell 1935b, p.lxxxii.
Basal Kimmeridge Clay.
[Locality given by Buckman as 'Bowood, Wilts.' but Arkell believed that he had in fact acquired the specimen from John Spencer of Bowood, and that it came from the brickworks at Wootton Bassett, Wiltshire.]
S. S. Buckman Collection, purchased 1926.
GSM 30523

Rasenia sp.
Spath 1935, plate 13, fig. 2 [suture line].
Kimmeridge Clay, *cymodoce* Zone.
Market Rasen, Lincolnshire.
L. F. Spath Collection, purchased 1943.
GSM 72202

Rasenia similis Spath
Birkelund, Thusu and Vigran 1978, p. 51.
Glacial Drift, derived from Kimmeridge Clay, *cymodoce* Zone.
Brigg, Humberside [Lincolnshire].
Museum Collection.
GSM 30740

Triozoites seminudatus S. S. Buckman HOLOTYPE
S. S. Buckman 1924, plate CDXCIV.
Arkell 1957, fig. 416, 3; p. L324.
Kimmeridge Clay, *cymodoce* Zone.
Ringstead Bay, Dorset.
S. S. Buckman Collection, purchased 1926.
GSM 47535

Aulacostephanus (Aulacostephanoides) mutabilis (J. Sowerby)
Ziegler 1962, plate 4, figs. 6, 7, 10; text-fig. 12, p. 37; text-fig. 18a, p. 39.
Kimmeridge Clay, *mutabilis* Zone.
Tealby, Lincolnshire [but the Donations Register entry gives the locality as Horncastle, Lincolnshire].
J. W. Judd Collection, presented 1867.
GSM 30738

Aulacostephanus (Xenostephanus) sp.
Kent and Casey 1963, p. 58.
Elsham Sandstone, *mutabilis* Zone.
Quarry at S end of village, Elsham, Lincolnshire.
Survey Collection (R. Casey) 1962.
CE 3106, 3123

Aulacostephanus (Xenostephanus) sp.
Kent and Casey 1963, p. 58.
Elsham Sandstone, *mutabilis* Zone.
Quarry at S end of village, Elsham, Lincolnshire.
P. E. Kent Collection, presented 1962.
Zm 5967, 5968

Aulacostephanus (Xenostephanus) sp.
Kent and Casey 1963, p. 59.
Elsham Sandstone, *mutabilis* Zone.
Gallows Farm, Wrawby, Lincolnshire.
P. E. Kent Collection, presented 1962.
Zm 5974-5976, 5979

"Holcostephanus" witteanus (Oppel)
Kitchin *in* Lamplugh and Kitchin 1911, pp. 188, 119.
Rasenia witteana (Oppel)
Lamplugh, Kitchin and Pringle 1923, p. 220.
Kimmeridge Clay, *mutabilis* Zone.
Simpson (No. 2) shaft, Dover Colliery, Kent.
Survey Collection (G. W. Lamplugh) 1899.
L 1792

"Holcostephanus" cf. **witteanus** (Oppel)
Kitchin *in* Lamplugh and Kitchin 1911, p. 118.
Rasenia cf. **witteana** (Oppel)
Lamplugh, Kitchin and Pringle 1923, p. 220.
Aulacostephanus (Xenostephanus) sp.
Kent and Casey 1963, p. 61.
Kimmeridge Clay, *mutabilis* Zone.
Simpson (No.2) shaft, Dover Colliery, Kent.
Survey Collection (G.W. Lamplugh) 1899.
GSM 108002, 108005 [formerly L 1796, L 1820]

"Holocostephanus" cf. **trimerus** (Oppel)
Kitchin *in* Lamplugh and Kitchin 1911, p. 118.
Rasenia cf. **trimerus** (Oppel)
Lamplugh, Kitchin and Pringle 1923, p. 220.
Aulacostephanus (Xenostephanus) sp.
Kent and Casey 1963, p. 61.
Kimmeridge Clay, *mutabilis* Zone.
Simpson (No.2) shaft, Dover Colliery, Kent.
Survey Collection (G.W. Lamplugh) 1899.
GSM 108001, 108003 [formerly L 1795, L 1797]

"Holcostephanus" molenai Canavari
Kitchin *in* Lamplugh and Kitchin 1911, p. 118.
Aulacostephanoides cf. **attenuatus** Ziegler
Kent and Casey 1963, p. 61.
Kimmeridge Clay, *mutabilis* Zone.
Simpson (No.2) shaft, Dover Colliery, Kent.
Survey Collection (G.W. Lamplugh) 1899.
GSM 108004

"Holcostephanus" cf. **stephanoides** (Oppel)
Kitchin *in* Lamplugh and Kitchin 1911, p. 118.
Rasenia cf. **stephanoides** (Oppel)
Lamplugh, Kitchin and Pringle 1923, p. 220.
Kimmeridge Clay, *mutabilis* Zone.
Simpson (No.2) shaft, Dover Colliery, Kent.
Survey Collection (G.W. Lamplugh) 1899.
L 1842

Hoplites sp.
Danford 1906, plate 14, fig. 1; p. 103.
Aulacostephanus pseudomutabilis (Loriol)
Arkell 1933, plate 33, fig. 3.
Aulacostephanus (Aulacostephanus) fallax Ziegler HOLOTYPE
Ziegler 1962, plate 16, fig. 4; plate 17, fig. 7; p. 120.
Kimmeridge Clay, *autissiodorensis* Zone.
Speeton, Yorkshire.
C.G. Danford Collection, purchased 1906
GSM 18150

Aulacostephanus (Aulacostephanus) fallax Ziegler PARATYPE
Ziegler 1962, plate 17, fig. 8; text-fig. 64; p. 120.
Kimmeridge Clay, *autissiodorensis* Zone.
Speeton, Yorkshire.
C.G. Danford Collection, purchased 1906.
GSM 21547

Aulacostephanus (Aulacostephanus) autissiodorensis (Cotteau)
Ziegler 1962, text-fig. 49B; p. 100.
Kimmeridge Clay, *autissiodorensis* Zone.
Speeton, Yorkshire.
C.G. Danford Collection, purchased 1906.
GSM 18162

Perisphinctes lacertosus Dumortier & Fontannes
Danford 1906, plate 14, fig. 4; p. 103.
Kimmeridge Clay, *autissiodorensis* Zone.
Speeton, Yorkshire.
C.G. Danford Collection, purchased 1906.
GSM 18151

Gravesia sp.
Arkell 1933, p. 457.
Kimmeridge Clay, *elegans* Zone.
Swindon, Wiltshire.
W.H. Hudleston Collection presented by Miss C.A. Raisin 1920.
Y 815

Sphinctoceras distans Neaverson HOLOTYPE
Neaverson, 1925, plate 4, fig. 3; text-fig. B 12-15; pp. 23, 24.
Allovirgatites distans (Neaverson) HOLOTYPE
S. S. Buckman 1927, plates DCXXXVIII C,D.
Sphinctoceras distans Neaverson HOLOTYPE
Arkell 1933, p. 461.
Virgatosphinctoides distans (Neaverson) HOLOTYPE
Spath 1936b, p. 14.
Kimmeridge Clay, Nodule Bed, *wheatleyensis* Zone.
Brickyard at NW of Shotover Hill, above Headington Quarry, Oxford.
S. S. Buckman Collection, purchased 1914.
GSM 27817

Allovirgatites distans (Neaverson)
S. S. Buckman 1926, plates DCXXXVIII A, B; p. 9.
Virgatosphinctoides
Spath 1936, p. 14.
Kimmeridge Clay, Upper Nodule Bed, *wheatleyensis* Zone.
Brickyard, Wheatley, Oxfordshire.
J. Pringle Collection, presented 1925.
GSM 37483

?Aulacosphinctes contiguus S. S. Buckman
Pringle 1926, p. 68.
Allovirgatites tutcheri Neaverson
S. S. Buckman 1926, plate DCXCII; p. 9.
Kimmeridge Clay, *wheatleyensis* Zone.
Chawley Brickyard, Cumnor Hurst, Berkshire
Survey Collection (S. W. Hester) 1924.
GSM 37486 [formerly SH 4724]

Allovirgatites woodwardi Neaverson HOLOTYPE
Neaverson 1925, plate 3, fig. 1; p. 31.
Arkell 1933, p. 461.
Kimmeridge Clay, *wheatleyensis* Zone.
Wheatley, Oxfordshire.
Survey Collection (H. B. Woodward) 1903.
GSM 32069 [formerly HBW 1415]

Pectinatites (Virgatosphinctoides) woodwardi (Neaverson)
Cope 1974, plate 3, fig. 3.
Kimmeridge Clay, *wheatleyensis* Zone.
Hunstanton borehole, Hunstanton, Norfolk.
Survey Collection 1970.
BDD 3767

Allovirgatites woodwardi Neaverson
S. S. Buckman 1926, plate DCXXXVII.
Kimmeridge Clay, Nodule Bed, *wheatleyensis* Zone.
Wheatley, Oxfordshire.
S. S. Buckman Collection, purchased 1927.
GSM 47836

Pectinatites (Virgatosphinctoides) wheatleyensis (Neaverson)
Cope 1974, plate 2, fig. 3.
Kimmeridge Clay, *wheatleyensis* Zone.
Gayton borehole, Gayton, Norfolk.
Survey Collection, 1970.
BDB 9143

Pectinatites (Virgatosphinctoides) cf. **pseudoscruposus** (Spath)
Cope 1974, plate 3, fig. 1.
Kimmeridge Clay, *wheatleyensis* Zone.
Gayton borehole, Gayton, Norfolk.
Survey Collection 1970.
BDB 9134

Pectinatites (Virgatosphinctoides) pseudoscruposus (Spath)
Cope 1974, plate 3, fig. 2.
Kimmeridge Clay, *wheatleyensis* Zone.
Gayton borehole, Gayton, Norfolk.
Survey Collection 1970.
BDB 9151

Pectinatites (Virgatosphinctoides) cf. **encombensis** Cope
Cope 1974, plate 2, fig. 1.
Kimmeridge Clay, *hudlestoni* Zone.
Skegness borehole, Skegness, Lincolnshire.
Survey Collection 1970.
BDF 5588

Pectinatites (Virgatosphinctoides) reisiformis Cope.
Cope 1974, plate 2, fig. 2.
Kimmeridge Clay, *hudlestoni* Zone.
Hunstanton borehole, Hunstanton, Norfolk.
Survey Collection 1970.
BDD 3671

Pectinatites (Pectinatites) eastlecottensis (Salfeld)
Cope 1974, plate 1, fig. 1.
Kimmeridge Clay, *pectinatus* Zone.
Skegness borehole, Skegness, Lincolnshire.
Survey Collection 1970.
BDF 5533

Pectinatites (Pectinatites) cornutifer (S. S. Buckman)
Cope 1974, plate 1, fig. 2.
Kimmeridge Clay, *pectinatus* Zone.
Skegness borehole, Skegness, Lincolnshire.
Survey Collection 1970.
BDF 5531

Pectinatites aulacophorus S. S. Buckman
Neaverson 1925, text-fig. A, 15; p. 16.
Kimmeridge Clay, *pectinatus* Zone.
Kimmeridge Shale Works, Kimmeridge, Dorset.
W. H. Hudleston Collection, presented by Miss C.A. Raisin 1920.
GSM 32071 [formerly Y 1667]

Pectinatites aulacophorus S. S. Buckman
Neaverson 1925, plate 1, fig. 5; p. 15.
Kimmeridge Clay, *pectinatus* Zone.
Kimmeridge Shale Works, Kimmeridge, Dorset.
W. H. Hudleston Collection, presented by Miss C.A. Raisin 1920.
GSM 32072 [formerly Y 1669]

Pectinatites aulacophorus S. S. Buckman HOLOTYPE
S. S. Buckman 1923, plate CCCLXXXI.
Neaverson 1925, pp. 15, 16.
Johnstone 1927, text-fig. 75.
Upper Cemetery Beds ("Lower Portland Sands", Hudleston's bed 'Da'), *pectinatus* Zone.
Swindon, Wiltshire.
W. H. Hudleston Collection, presented by Miss C.A. Raisin 1920.
GSM 45938

Pectinatites pectinatus (Phillips)
S. S. Buckman 1922a, plate CCCLIV A.
Arkell 1933, p. 461.
Kimmeridge Clay, *pectinatus* Zone.
Headington, Oxford.
S. S. Buckman Collection, purchased 1924.
GSM 47154

Pectinatites pectinatus (Phillips)
S. S. Buckman 1922a, plate CCCLIV B.
Cemetery Beds, *pectinatus* Zone.
Swindon, Wiltshire.
Presented by C. P. Chatwin and J. Pringle, 1922.
GSM 31670

Pectinatites pectinatus (Phillips)
S. S. Buckman, 1926, plate CCCLIV C.
Arkell 1933, p. 457.
Shotover Grit Sands, *pectinatus* Zone.
Shotover Brickyard, Oxfordshire.
S. S. Buckman Collection, purchased 1927.
GSM 47760

Pectinatites (Keratinites) sp. juv.
Spath 1936b, plate 6, fig. 4; p. 38.
Shotover Grit Sands, *pectinatus* Zone.
Near Oxford.
L.F. Spath Collection, purchased 1943.
GSM 72222

Pectinatites (Keratinites) sp. juv.
Spath 1936b, plate 15, fig. 2; p. 38.
Shotover Grit Sands, *pectinatus* Zone.
Near Oxford.
L.F. Spath collection, purchased 1943.
GSM 72221

Pectinatites pyriticus Neaverson HOLOTYPE
Neaverson 1925, plate 1, fig. 4; text-fig. A14; p. 17.
Kimmeridge Oil Shales, *pectinatus* Zone.
Kimmeridge Shale Works, Dorset.
W.H. Hudleston Collection presented by
Miss C.A. Raisin 1920.
GSM 32073 [formerly Y 1670]

Keratinites proboscide S. S. Buckman HOLOTYPE
S. S. Buckman 1926, plate DCLI.
Wheatley Sands, *pectinatus* Zone.
Brickyard, Wheatley, Oxfordshire.
S.S. Buckman Collection, purchased 1927.
GSM 47845

Keratinites cornutifer S. S. Buckman HOLOTYPE
S. S. Buckman 1925, plate DCII
Kimmeridge Clay, *pectinatus* Zone
Swindon, Wiltshire.
W. Cunnington Collection, purchased 1875.
GSM 30757

Keratinites cornutifer S. S. Buckman
S. S. Buckman 1926, plate DCII A.
Shotover Grit Sands, *pectinatus* Zone.
Brickyard, Shotover, Oxfordshire.
S.S. Buckman Collection, purchased 1927.
GSM 47780

Keratinites naso S. S. Buckman HOLOTYPE
S. S. Buckman 1926, plate DCLII.
'Keratinites' naso S. S. Buckman HOLOTYPE
Arkell 1933, pp. 447, 461.
Shotover Grit Sands, *pectinatus* Zone.
Brickyard, Shotover, Oxfordshire.
S.S. Buckman Collection, purchased 1927.
GSM 47846

Keratinites naso S. S. Buckman
S.S. Buckman 1928, plate DCLII A.
Shotover Grit Sands, *pectinatus* Zone.
Brickyard, Shotover, Oxfordshire.
S.S. Buckman Collection, purchased 1928.
GSM 49357

Keratinites nasutus S. S. Buckman HOLOTYPE
S.S. Buckman 1926, plate DCLXIV.
'Keratinites' nasutus S.S. Buckman HOLOTYPE
Arkell 1933, p. 447.
Wheatley Sands, *pectinatus* Zone.
Brickyard, Wheatley, Oxford.
S.S. Buckman Collection, ex J. Buckman,
purchased 1927.
GSM 47851

Keratinites keratophorus S. S. Buckman HOLOTYPE
S. S. Buckman 1925, plate DCI.
Wheatley Sands, *pectinatus* Zone.
Brickyard, Wheatley, Oxford.
S. S. Buckman Collection, purchased 1927.
GSM 47779

Pectinatites scalariformis S. S. Buckman HOLOTYPE
S. S. Buckman 1927, plate DCCV.
Wheatley Sands, *pectinatus* Zone.
Brickyard, Wheatley, Oxford.
S. S. Buckman Collection, purchased 1928.
GSM 49295

Wheatleyites reductus S. S. Buckman HOLOTYPE
S. S. Buckman 1923, plate CCCLXXXIV.
Shotoverites reductus (S. S.Buckman) HOLOTYPE
S. S. Buckman 1926, pp. 8, 9, 15.
Wheatley Sands, *pectinatus* Zone.
Brickyard, Wheatley, Oxford.
S. S. Buckman Collection, presented 1924.
GSM 47177

Wheatleyites tricostulatus S. S. Buckman HOLOTYPE
S. S. Buckman 1923, plate CCCLXV.
S. S. Buckman 1926, p. 9.
?Pectinatites (Wheatleyites) tricostulatus
(S. S. Buckman) HOLOTYPE
Arkell 1957, fig. 431, 8; p. L330.
Wheatley Sands, *pectinatus* Zone.
Brickyard, Wheatley, Oxford.
S. S. Buckman Collection, purchased 1924.
GSM 47163

Wheatleyites opulentus S. S. Buckman HOLOTYPE
S. S. Buckman 1923, plate CCCLXXXIII A.
S. S. Buckman 1926, p. 9.
Wheatley Sands, *pectinatus* Zone.
Brickyard, Wheatley, Oxford.
S. S. Buckman Collection, purchased 1924.
GSM 47176

Wheatleyites opulentus S. S. Buckman PARATYPE
S. S. Buckman 1923, plate CCCLXXXIII B.
S. S. Buckman 1926, p. 9.
"Portland Sands" of Swindon, *pectinatus* Zone.
Swindon, Wiltshire.
W. H. Hudleston Collection, presented by
Miss C.A. Raisin 1920.
GSM 45936

Wheatleyites rarescens S. S. Buckman HOLOTYPE
S. S. Buckman 1925, plate DLXI A.
S. S. Buckman 1926, p. 9.
Wheatley Sands, *pectinatus* Zone.
Brickyard, Wheatley, Oxford.
S. S. Buckman Collection, purchased 1926.
GSM 47565

Wheatleyites rarescens S. S. Buckman PARATYPE
S. S. Buckman 1925, plate DLXI B.
Wheatley Sands, *pectinatus* Zone.
Brickyard, Wheatley, Oxford.
S. S. Buckman Collection, purchased 1925.
GSM 47566

Subplanites pseudoscruposus Spath HOLOTYPE
Spath 1936b, text-fig. 2; p. 173.
Kimmeridge Clay, shales in main bed of Oil Shales.
Corton Oil Works, Upwey, Dorset.
Survey Collection (J. Pringle) 1918
GSM 51252

Shotoverites pringlei S. S. Buckman HOLOTYPE
S. S. Buckman 1925, plate DLXII.
S. S. Buckman 1926, pp. 9, 15, 24.
Paravirgatites pringlei (S. S. Buckman) HOLOTYPE
Arkell 1933, p. 461.
Paravirgatites paravirgatus (S. S. Buckman)
Spath 1936b, p. 40.
Doggers between Shotover Fine and Grit Sands, *pectinatus* Zone.
Shotover Brickyard, Oxfordshire.
Survey Collection (J. Pringle) 1924.
GSM 37363 [formerly Pe 2179]

Shotoverites pringlei S. S. Buckman
S. S. Buckman 1926, plates DLXII A, B.
Dogger in Shotover Grit Sands, *pectinatus* Zone.
North side of Shotover Brickyard, Oxfordshire.
S. S. Buckman Collection, purchased 1928.
GSM 49277

Paravirgatites paravirgatus S. S. Buckman HOLOTYPE
S. S. Buckman 1922a, plate CCCVIII.
S. S. Buckman 1926, p. 14.
Arkell 1933, p. 461.
Pavlovia (Paravirgatites) paravirgatus (S. S. Buckman) HOLOTYPE
Arkell 1957, fig. 435, 3; p. L332.
Shotover Grit Sands, *pectinatus* Zone.
Sandpit near waterworks, Shotover, Oxfordshire.
S. S. Buckman Collection, purchased 1924.
GSM 47125

Paravirgatites kimmeridgensis Neaverson HOLOTYPE
Neaverson 1925, plate 4, fig. 4; p. 33.
S. S. Buckman 1926, p. 15.
Kimmeridge Clay, Oil Shale, *pectinatus* Zone.
Kimmeridge Bay, Dorset.
S. S. Buckman Collection, purchased 1914.
GSM 27959

Pavlovia (Lydistratites) nobilis Spath HOLOTYPE
Spath 1936b, plate 5, fig. 6.
Hartwell Clay, *pallasioides* Zone.
Aylesbury, Buckinghamshire.
L. F. Spath Collection, purchased 1943.
GSM 72213

Pavlovia (Lydistratites) variabilis (Neaverson)
Spath 1936b, p. 38.
Hartwell Clay, *pallasioides* Zone.
Hartwell, Buckinghamshire.
L. F. Spath Collection, purchased 1943.
GSM 72219

Paravirgatites infrequens S. S. Buckman HOLOTYPE
S. S. Buckman 1925, plate DCIII.
Spath 1936b, p. 30.
Thame Sands, near top, *pectinatus* Zone, *paravirgatus* Subzone.
Sand pit near former Smallpox Hospital, Moreton Farm, Thame, Oxfordshire.
S. S. Buckman Collection, purchased 1927.
GSM 47781

Paravirgatites desideratus S. S. Buckman HOLOTYPE
S. S. Buckman 1923, plate CCCLXXXII.
Pavlovia (Pallasiceras) of rotunda (J. Sowerby) group
Spath 1936b, pp. 30, 42.
Thame Sands, *pectinatus* Zone, *paravirgatus* Subzone.
Long Crendon, Buckinghamshire.
W. H. Hudleston Collection, presented by Miss C. A. Raisin 1920.
GSM 45934

Ammonites biplex J. Sowerby
?Woodward 1895, text-fig. 72; p. 156.
Holcosphinctes pallasioides Neaverson HOLOTYPE
Neaverson 1925, plate 3, fig. 5; text-fig. B10; pp. 35, 36.
S. S. Buckman 1928, p. 14.
'Holcosphinctes' pallasioides Neaverson HOLOTYPE
Arkell 1933, p. 464.
Pavlovia pallasioides (Neaverson) HOLOTYPE
Arkell 1956b, plate 41, fig. 4.
Hartwell Clay, *pallasioides* Zone.
Hartwell, Buckinghamshire.
Presented by a Mrs Smyth 1850.
GSM 30721

Holcosphinctes pallasioides Neaverson
S. S. Buckman 1925, plate DLXIX.
S. S. Buckman 1926, p. 14.
Spath 1936b, p. 27.
Hartwell Clay, *pallasioides* Zone.
Brickyard by Lion Spring, Long Crendon, Buckinghamshire.
S. S. Buckman Collection, purchased 1926.
GSM 47571

Pallasiceras gracile Neaverson HOLOTYPE
Neaverson 1925, plate 1, fig. 8; p. 20.
Arkell 1933, p. 447.
Kimmeridge Clay, *rotunda* Zone.
Chapman's Pool, Kingston and Worth Matravers, Dorset.
Survey Collection (J. Pringle) 1922.
GSM 32419 [formerly Pe 2051]

Pallasiceras gracile Neaverson PARATYPE
Neaverson 1925, plate 1, fig. 9.
Arkell 1933, p. 447.
Kimmeridge Clay, *rotunda* Zone.
Chapman's Pool, Kingston and Worth Matravers, Dorset.
Survey Collection (J. Pringle) 1922.
GSM 32420 [formerly Pe 2049]

Lydistratites lyditicus S. S. Buckman
S. S. Buckman 1926, plates CCCLIII C,D.
Arkell 1933, p. 447.
Pallasiceras sp.
Spath 1936b, pp. 27, 45.
Kimmeridge Clay, Nodule Bed, *rotunda* Zone.
Chapman's Pool, Kingston and Worth Matravers, Dorset.
S. S. Buckman Collection, ex Miss E. R. Thompson, purchased 1927.
GSM 47759

Lydistratites trigonalis S. S. Buckman HOLOTYPE
S. S. Buckman 1926, plates DCLXXIV A, B.
Spath 1936b, p. 27.
Kimmeridge Clay, Nodule Bed, *rotunda* Zone.
Chapman's Pool, Kingston and Worth Matravers, Dorset.
S. S. Buckman Collection, purchased 1928.
GSM 49273

Lydistratites gibbosus S. S. Buckman HOLOTYPE
S. S. Buckman 1926, plates DCXXXIX A-C.
Arkell 1933, p. 447.
Spath 1936b, p. 27.
Kimmeridge Clay, Nodule Bed, *rotunda* Zone.
Chapman's Pool, Kingston and Worth Matravers, Dorset.
S. S. Buckman Collection, purchased 1927.
GSM 47837

Lydistratites gibbosus S. S. Buckman PARATYPE
S. S. Buckman 1927, plate DCXXXIX D.
Kimmeridge Clay, Nodule Bed, *rotunda* Zone.
Chapman's Pool, Kingston and Worth Matravers, Dorset.
S. S. Buckman Collection, purchased 1928.
GSM 49290

Pallasiceras concinnum Neaverson HOLOTYPE
Neaverson 1925, plate 1, fig. 7; text-fig. A11; p. 19.
Arkell 1933, p. 447.
Kimmeridge Clay, *rotunda* Zone.
Chapman's Pool, Kingston and Worth Matravers, Dorset.
Survey Collection (J. Pringle) 1922.
GSM 32418 [formerly Pe 2047]

Pavlovia (Pallasiceras) aff. **concinna** (Neaverson)
Spath 1936b, plate 5, fig. 5.
Kimmeridge Clay, *rotunda* Zone.
Chapman's Pool, Kingston and Worth Matravers, Dorset.
L. F. Spath Collection, purchased 1943.
GSM 72212

Pavlovia (Pallasiceras) concinna (Neaverson)
Spath 1936b, plate 10, fig. 2; p. 42. [the explanation to plate 10 gives the name as *Pavlovia (Pallasiceras) rotunda* (J. Sowerby)].
Kimmeridge Clay, *rotunda* Zone.
Chapman's Pool, Kingston and Worth Matravers, Dorset.
L. F. Spath Collection, purchased 1943.
GSM 72216

Pallasiceras rotundum (J. Sowerby) and
?Pallasiceras gracile Neaverson and
Lydistratites gibbosus S. S. Buckman
S. S. Buckman 1926, plates DXC A-C.
Kimmeridge Clay, Nodule Bed, *rotunda* Zone.
Worth Matravers, Dorset.
S. S. Buckman Collection, purchased 1927.
Large nodule numbered GSM 47772 and 47773.

Virgatites stschukinensis (Mikhal'skiy) LECTOTYPE
Arkell 1956b, plate 45, fig. 2.
Middle Volgian Beds.
Moscow region, USSR.
A. P. Pavlov Collection, presented 1891.
FOR 381

PORTLANDIAN STAGE

Epivirgatites sp.
Casey 1967, p. 131.
Portland Sands, *albani* Zone.
Gad Cliff, Tyneham, Dorset.
Survey Collection (H. B. Woodward) 1884.
1718 HBW

Epivirgatites sp.
Casey 1967, p. 131.
albani Zone.
Blacknor (or Black Nore), Portland, Dorset.
Geological Society Collection, ex W. Buckland, presented 1911.
Geol Soc Coll 2910

Epivirgatites sp.
Casey 1967, p. 131.
Stinkstones, *albani* Zone.
Hounstout, Kingston, Dorset.
L. F. Spath Collection, purchased 1943.
GSM 72954

Pavlovia (Lydistratites) vulgaris Spath HOLOTYPE
Spath 1936b, plate 17, fig. 5; p. 31.
Epivirgatites vulgaris (Spath) HOLOTYPE
Casey 1967, pp. 131, 132.
Portland Sands, *albani* Zone.
Hounstout, Kingston, Dorset.
L. F. Spath Collection, purchased 1943.
GSM 72215

Pavlovia (Lydistratites) vulgaris Spath PARATYPE
Spath 1936b, plate 9, fig. 2.
Epivirgatites vulgaris (Spath) PARATYPE
Casey 1967, pp. 131, 132.
Portland Sands, *albani* Zone.
Hounstout, Kingston, Dorset.
L. F. Spath Collection, purchased 1943.
GSM 72214

Epivirgatites cf. **vulgaris** (Spath)
Casey 1967, p. 131.
albani Zone.
Penshurst borehole, Kent.
Survey Collection (J. Rhodes) 1899.
GSM 102190, 102195

Epivirgatites vulgaris (Spath)
Casey 1967, p. 131.
albani Zone.
Cliff below St. Alban's Head Coastguard Station, Worth Matravers, Dorset.
Survey Collection, (J. Pringle) 1922.
Pe 2071

Progalbanites albani (Arkell)
Spath 1936b, plate 24, fig. 2; p. 30.
Portland Sands, *albani* Zone.
Hounstout, Kingston, Dorset.
L. F. Spath Collection, purchased 1943.
GSM 72234

Progalbanites albani (Arkell)
Spath 1936b, plate 23, fig. 2.
Portland Sands, *albani* Zone.
Hounstout, Kingston, Dorset.
L. F. Spath Collection, purchased 1943.
GSM 72233

Progalbanites albani (Arkell)
Spath 1936b, plate 20, fig. 2; p. 30.
Portland Sands, *albani* Zone.
Hounstout, Kingston, Dorset.
L. F. Spath Collection, purchased 1943.
GSM 72234

Virgatites scythicus (Mikhal'skiy)
S. S. Buckman 1926, plate DCLXXV.
Arkell 1933, pp. 445, 481, 491.
Arkell 1935a, p. 339.
Progalbanites scythicus (S. S. Buckman *non* Mikhal'skiy)
Spath 1936b, pp. 19, 30.
Portland Sands, *albani* Zone.
Hounstout, Kingston, Dorset.
S. S. Buckman Collection, purchased 1928.
GSM 49274

Virgatites pallasianus (d'Orbigny)
S. S. Buckman 1926, plate DCXCIII.
Portland Sands, *albani* Zone.
Hounstout, Kingston, Dorset.
S. S. Buckman Collection, purchased 1928.
GSM 49288

Pavlovia (Lydistratites) worthensis Spath HOLOTYPE
Spath 1936b, plate 18, fig. 6,; p. 30.
Arkell 1947b, p. 93.
Casey 1967, p. 132.
Portland Sands, *albani* Zone.
Hounstout, Kingston, Dorset.
L. F. Spath Collection, purchased 1943.
GSM 72220

Crendonites pregorei Spath HOLOTYPE
Spath 1936b, plate 22, fig. 2; p. 30.
Portland Sands, *albani* Zone.
Hounstout, Kingston, Dorset.
L. F. Spath Collection, purchased 1943.
GSM 72229

Glaucolithites glaucolithus S. S. Buckman HOLOTYPE
S. S. Buckman 1922a, plates CCCVI A, B.
Arkell 1933, plate 40, fig. 2; pp. 481, 514.
Arkell 1935a, p. 338.
Arkell 1957, fig. 437; p. L334.
Glauconitic Stone, *glaucolithus* Zone.
Long Crendon (NW pit), Buckinghamshire.
S. S. Buckman Collection, purchased 1924.
GSM 47123

Lydistratites lyditicus S. S. Buckman HOLOTYPE
S. S. Buckman 1922a, plate CCCLIII A.
Neaverson 1925, p. 18.
S. S. Buckman 1926, pp. 14, 29.
Arkell 1933, p. 514.
Spath 1936b, pp. 27, 45.
Upper Lydite Bed, *glaucolithus* Zone.
Well, Barrel Hill, Long Crendon, Buckinghamshire.
S. S. Buckman Collection, purchased 1925.
GSM 47153

Behemoth lapideus S. S. Buckman HOLOTYPE
S. S. Buckman 1922a, plates CCCXLII A, B.
Arkell 1933, p. 514.
Spath 1936b, p. 32.
Blue Bed Building Stone, *glaucolithus* Zone.
Barley Hill, Thame, Oxfordshire.
S. S. Buckman Collection, purchased 1924.
GSM 47146

Behemoth lapideus S. S. Buckman PARATYPE
S. S. Buckman 1924, plate CCCXLII C.
Arkell 1933, p. 514.
Blue Bed, *glaucolithus* Zone.
Temporary exposure near Police Station, Chinnor Road, Thame, Oxfordshire.
S. S. Buckman Collection, purchased 1926.
GSM 47529

Behemoth megasthenes S. S. Buckman HOLOTYPE
S. S. Buckman 1922a, plates CCCVA, A*, B.
Behemoth megastenes [sic.] S. S. Buckman HOLOTYPE
Roman 1938, p. 295.
Glauconitic Stone, *glaucolithus* Zone.
Works to north of Station, Haddenham, Buckinghamshire.
S. S. Buckman, ex S. Jackson, purchased 1924.
GSM 47122

Leucopetrites caementarius S. S. Buckman HOLOTYPE
S. S. Buckman 1926, plate DCLXXVII.
Arkell 1933, p. 491.
Arkell 1935a, p. 338.
Spath 1936, p. 32.
Glaucolithites caementarius (S. S. Buckman) HOLOTYPE
Wimbledon and Cope 1978, p. 184.
White Cementstone, *glaucolithus* Zone.
S. S. Buckman Collection, ex C. H. Waddington, purchased 1928.
GSM 49276

Behemoth ("Leucopetrites") caementarius (S. S. Buckman)
Spath 1936, p. 32.
White Cementstone, *glaucolithus* Zone.
Hounstout, Kingston, Dorset.
L. F. Spath Collection, purchased 1943.
GSM 72231

Leucopetrites leucus S. S. Buckman HOLOTYPE
S. S. Buckman 1922a, plates CCCVII A, B.
S. S. Buckman 1926, p. 36.
Arkell 1933, p. 514.
Spath 1936b, p. 32.
Glauconitic Beds, Green Marl, *glaucolithus* Zone.
Long Crendon (NW pit), Buckinghamshire.
S. S. Buckman Collection, ex A. J. Webb, purchased 1924.
GSM 47124

Leucopetrites leucus S. S. Buckman PARATYPE
S. S. Buckman 1925, plate CCCVII C.
Arkell 1933, p. 514.
Spath 1936b, p. 32.
Glauconitic Beds, Green Marl, *glaucolithus* Zone.
Long Crendon (NW pit), Buckinghamshire.
S. S. Buckman Collection, purchased 1926.
GSM 47528

Hydrostratites bifurcus S. S. Buckman HOLOTYPE
S. S. Buckman 1926, plate DCLXXVI; p. 38.
Arkell 1933, p. 514.
Spath 1936b, p. 32.
Glauconitic Beds, Waterstone, *glaucolithus* Zone.
Long Crendon (NW pit), Buckinghamshire.
S. S. Buckman Collection, purchased 1928.
GSM 49275

Gyromegalites polygyralis S. S. Buckman HOLOTYPE
S. S. Buckman 1925, plates DCXX A, B.
Arkell 1933, p. 507.
Wimbledon 1976, p. 9.
Glaucolithites polygyralis (S. S. Buckman) HOLOTYPE
Wimbledon and Cope 1978, p. 184.
Sandy bed below the Cockly Bed, *glaucolithus* Zone.
Okus Quarry, Swindon, Wiltshire.
S. S. Buckman Collection, ex C. H. Gore, purchased 1927.
GSM 47824

Simotoichites simus S. S. Buckman HOLOTYPE
S. S. Buckman 1923, plate CDIIA.
Spath 1936b, p. 32.
Arkell 1957, p. L334.
?Glauconitic Stone, *glaucolithus* Zone.
?Brill (but found on a pile of stones at Oakley), Buckinghamshire.
S. S. Buckman Collection, ex J. C. Kirby, purchased 1924.
GSM 47191

Aquistratites aquator S. S. Buckman HOLOTYPE [with brachiopod **Orbiculoidea glabella** S. S. Buckman HOLOTYPE]
S. S. Buckman 1924, plates DXXXIV A, B.
Glaucolithites aquator (S. S. Buckman) HOLOTYPE
Wimbledon and Cope 1978, p. 184.
Glauconitic Beds, Waterstone, *glaucolithus* Zone.
Long Crendon (NW pit), Buckinghamshire.
S. S. Buckman Collection, purchased 1926.
GSM 47553

Crendonites subgorei Spath HOLOTYPE
Spath 1936b, plate 9, fig. 5; p. 62.
glaucolithus or *okusensis* Zone.
Swindon, Wiltshire.
L. F. Spath Collection, purchased 1943.
GSM 72227

Ammonites triplicatus Pavlov
Pavlov 1889, plate 2, fig. 3.
Portland Stone.
Portland, Dorset.
C. Westendarp Collection, presented 1884.
GSM 225

Kerberites okusensis Salfeld
S. S. Buckman 1925, plates DLXX A, B.
Cockly Bed, *okusensis* Zone.
Okus Quarry, Swindon, Wiltshire.
S. S. Buckman Collection, purchased 1926.
GSM 47572
[This specimen has not been traced]

Kerberites virguloides Spath HOLOTYPE
Spath 1936b, plate 27, fig. 4; p. 34.
Cockly Bed, *okusensis* Zone.
Swindon, Wiltshire.
L. F. Spath Collection, purchased 1943.
GSM 72224

Kerberites kerberus S. S. Buckman
S. S. Buckman 1926, plates DXX A, B.
Arkell 1933, pp. 507, 513.
Cockly Bed, *okusensis* Zone.
Okus Quarry, Swindon, Wiltshire.
J. Pringle Collection, presented 1923.
GSM 32394

Kerberites sp. juv. (**"portlandiensis"** Cox)
Spath 1936b, plate 7, fig. 6; p. 34.
?Sandy limestone below the Cockly Bed, *?okusensis* Zone.
Swindon, Wiltshire.
L. F. Spath Collection, purchased 1943.
GSM 72225

Polymegalites polypreon S. S. Buckman HOLOTYPE
S. S. Buckman 1925, plates DXCI A, B.
Soft bed below the Cockly Bed, *okusensis* Zone.
Okus Quarry, Swindon, Wiltshire.
S. S. Buckman Collection, purchased 1927.
GSM 47774

Gyromegalites polygyralis S. S. Buckman PARATYPE
S. S. Buckman 1927, plates DCXX C, D.
Wimbledon 1976, p. 6.
Green Bed, Main Building Stone, *okusensis* Zone.
Chilmark, Tisbury, Wiltshire.
S. S. Buckman Collection, purchased 1928.
GSM 49311

Perisphinctes lomonosowi Vishnyakov
Nikitin 1889, p. 47.
Lomonosovella lomonosovi (Vishnyakov)
Casey 1962, p. 99.
Cockly Bed, *okusensis* Zone.
Okus Quarry, Swindon, Wiltshire.
H. Lance Gray Collection, purchased 1929.
GSM 49715

Crendonites leptolobatus S. S. Buckman HOLOTYPE
S. S. Buckman 1923, plate CDI.
'Crendonites' leptolobatus S. S. Buckman HOLOTYPE
Arkell 1933, p. 513.
Crendonites leptobatus [sic] S. S. Buckman HOLOTYPE
Roman 1938, p. 295.
[Crendon Sands] Rubbly Limestones, *okusensis* Zone.
Long Crendon (NW pit), Buckinghamshire.
S. S. Buckman Collection, purchased 1924.
GSM 47189

Crendonites cf. **lesliei** Spath
Spath 1936b, p. 63.
?*okusensis* Zone.
Okus Quarry, Swindon, Wiltshire.
L. F. Spath Collection, purchased 1943.
GSM 72228

Crendonites aff. **transitorius** Spath
Spath 1936b, plate 7, fig. 7; p. 64.
?*okusensis* Zone.
Swindon, Wiltshire.
L. F. Spath Collection, purchased 1943.
GSM 72226

Kerberites kerberus S. S. Buckman
Spath 1936b, plate 18, fig. 2; p. 34.
kerberus Zone.
?Buckinghamshire.
L. F. Spath Collection, purchased 1943.
GSM 72223

Kerberites cf. **kerberus** S. S. Buckman
Casey 1973, plate 8, fig. 6; p. 230.
Lower Spilsby Sandstone Basement Bed, ex *kerberus* Zone.
No.2 well, Fordington, Lincolnshire.
A. Templeman Collection, presented by Sir George Taylor 1967.
Zq 275

Simotoichites simus S. S. Buckman PARATYPE
S. S. Buckman 1923, plate CDII B
?Crendon Sand, *kerberus* Zone.
Long Crendon (NW pit), Buckinghamshire.
S. S. Buckman Collection, purchased 1924.
GSM 47190

Galbanites fasciger S. S. Buckman HOLOTYPE
S. S. Buckman 1923, plate CDLI.
Creamy Limestones, Lower Witchett, *kerberus* Zone.
Barrel Hill, Long Crendon, Buckinghamshire.
S. S. Buckman Collection, purchased 1924.
GSM 37302

Galbanites mikrolobus S. S. Buckman HOLOTYPE
S. S. Buckman 1923, plate CDXXIX.
Creamy Limestones, Soft Rock, *kerberus* Zone.
Barrel Hill, Long Crendon, Buckinghamshire.
S. S. Buckman Collection, purchased 1925.
GSM 37296

Galbanites cretarius S. S. Buckman HOLOTYPE
S. S. Buckman 1925, plate DCXXI.
Wimbledon 1976, p. 6.
Titanites giganteus (J. Sowerby)
Wimbledon and Cope 1978, p. 188.
Chalky Series, *kerberus* Zone.
Chilmark, Teffont Evias, Tisbury, Wiltshire.
S. S. Buckman Collection, ex T. T. Gething, purchased 1927.
GSM 47825

Galbanites galbanus S. S. Buckman HOLOTYPE
S. S. Buckman 1922a, plate CCCLV A.
S. S. Buckman 1923, plate CCCLV B.
Roman 1938, p. 297.
Creamy Limestones, Blue and Cream Bed, *kerberus* Zone.
Works north of station, Haddenham, Buckinghamshire.
S. S. Buckman Collection, ex S. Jackson, purchased 1924.
GSM 47155

Vaumegalites vau S. S. Buckman HOLOTYPE
S. S. Buckman 1924, plate DXXXVI.
Arkell 1933, p. 514.
Creamy Limestones, Bottom Bed, Hard Brown, *kerberus* Zone.
Barrel Hill, Long Crendon, Buckinghamshire.
S. S. Buckman Collection, purchased 1926.
GSM 47554

Glottoptychinites glottodes S. S. Buckman HOLOTYPE
S. S. Buckman 1923, plate CDIII.
Arkell 1957, fig. 435, 5; p.L 334.
Casey 1973, p. 232.
Creamy Limestones, base of Upper Witchett, *kerberus* Zone.
Barrel Hill, Long Crendon, Buckinghamshire.
S. S. Buckman Collection, purchased 1924.
GSM 47192

Glottoptychinites audax S. S. Buckman HOLOTYPE
S. S. Buckman 1927, plates DCCXVII A, B.
Arkell 1933, p. 511.
Arkell 1935a, p. 335.
Creamy Limestones, Upper Witchett, *kerberus* Zone.
West of Coney Hill, Over Winchendon, Buckinghamshire.
S. S. Buckman Collection, purchased 1928.
GSM 49309

Briareites polymeles S. S. Buckman HOLOTYPE
S. S. Buckman 1921, plates CCLVII A, B, C.
Arkell 1933, p. 512.
Creamy Limestones, Building Stone, *kerberus* Zone.
Scotsgrove, Haddenham, Buckinghamshire.
S. S. Buckman Collection, ex Capt. Ashton, purchased 1922.
GSM 32058

Hippostratites hippocephaliticus S. S. Buckman HOLOTYPE
S. S. Buckman 1924, plates CDXCV A, B.
Creamy Limestones, "Osses Ed" Bed, *kerberus* Zone.
Scotsgrove, Haddenham, Buckinghamshire.
S. S. Buckman Collection, purchased 1926.
GSM 47536

Hippostratites rhedarius S. S. Buckman HOLOTYPE
S. S. Buckman 1924, plate DXIV.
Creamy Limestones, "Osses Ed" Bed, *kerberus* Zone.
Barrel Hill, Long Crendon, Buckinghamshire.
S. S. Buckman Collection, purchased 1926.
GSM 47546

Gigantites giganteus (J. Sowerby)
S. S. Buckman 1921, plates CCLVI A, B.
Arkell 1933, p. 512.
House 1958, pp. 18-19.
Titanites giganteus (J. Sowerby)
Wimbledon and Cope 1978, pp. 188, 189.
Creamy Limestones, Hard Lime or Blue Bed, *kerberus* Zone.
Barrel Hill, Long Crendon, Buckinghamshire.
S. S. Buckman Collection, ex H. Dodwell, purchased 1922.
GSM 32057

Gigantites pachymeres S. S. Buckman HOLOTYPE
S. S. Buckman 1925, plate DXC11 A, B.
Creamy Limestones, Blue Bed, *kerberus* Zone.
Quarry in railway cutting north of station, Haddenham, Buckinghamshire.
S. S. Buckman Collection, purchased 1925.
GSM 47775

Gigantites zeta S. S. Buckman HOLOTYPE
S. S. Buckman 1923, plates CDLII A, B.
Creamy Limestones, Blue Bed, *kerberus* Zone.
Barrel Hill, Long Crendon, Buckinghamshire.
S. S. Buckman Collection, purchased 1925.
GSM 37303

Titanites titan S. S. Buckman HOLOTYPE
S. S. Buckman 1921, plates CCXXXI A, B.
Arkell 1957, fig. 435, 2; p. L334.
House 1958, p. 19.
Creamy Limestones, *kerberus* Zone.
Near Baggle Hill, Notley Abbey, Haddenham, Buckinghamshire.
S. S. Buckman Collection, ex H. Reynolds, purchased 1922.
GSM 32044

Trophonites trophon S. S. Buckman HOLOTYPE
S. S. Buckman 1922a, plates CCCXXV A, B.
Arkell 1933, p. 512.
Spath 1936b, p. 33.
Creamy Limestones, Soft Rock, *kerberus* Zone.
Barrel Hill, Long Crendon, Buckinghamshire.
S. S. Buckman Collection, purchased 1924.
GSM 47139

Trophonites imperator S. S. Buckman HOLOTYPE
S. S. Buckman 1922a, plates CCCXLIII A, B.
Creamy Limestones, Soft Rock, *kerberus* Zone.
Barrel Hill, Long Crendon, Buckinghamshire.
S. S. Buckman Collection, purchased 1924.
GSM 47147

Trophonites pseudogigas (Blake) NEOTYPE
S. S. Buckman 1923, plates CCCLXXXV A, B.
Arkell 1933, pp. 481, 512.
Arkell 1935a, p. 336.
Spath 1936b, p. 33.
Creamy Limestones, Soft Rock, *kerberus* Zone.
Barrel Hill, Long Crendon, Buckinghamshire.
S. S. Buckman Collection, purchased 1924.
GSM 47178

Pleuromegalites forticosta S. S. Buckman HOLOTYPE
S. S. Buckman 1924, plate DXIII.
Arkell 1933, p. 512.
Creamy Limestones, Lower Witchett, *kerberus* Zone.
Barrel Hill, Long Crendon, Buckinghamshire.
S. S. Buckman Collection, purchased 1926.
GSM 47544

Pleuromegalites forticosta S. S. Buckman PARATYPE
S. S. Buckman 1925, plate DXIII A.
Creamy Limestones, Lower Witchett, *kerberus* Zone.
Barrel Hill, Long Crendon, Buckinghamshire.
S. S. Buckman Collection, purchased 1926.
GSM 47545

Crendonites sp.
Spath 1947, p. 26.
Casey 1973, p. 206.
Basal nodule bed, Lower Spilsby Sandstone, ex *kerberus* Zone.
Nettleton Mine, Lincolnshire.
C. W. Wright Collection, presented 1962.
GSM 107956

Kerberites sp.
Spath 1947, p. 26.
Casey 1973, p. 206.
Basal nodule bed, Lower Spilsby Sandstone, ex *kerberus* Zone.
Nettleton Mine, Lincolnshire.
C. W. Wright Collection, presented 1962.
GSM 107957

Kerberites sp.
Casey 1973, p. 208.
?Titanites sp.
Wimbledon and Cope 1978, p. 185.
Portland Stone, Shrimp Bed, *anguiformis* Zone.
Swanworth Quarry, Worth Matravers, Dorset.
A. J. Wilkinson Collection, presented 1965.
GSM 109556

Paracraspedites oppressus Casey HOLOTYPE
Casey 1973, plate 1, fig. 1; p. 230.
Portland Stone, Shrimp Bed, *oppressus* Zone.
St. Alban's Head, Worth Matravers, Dorset.
W. Heap Collection, presented 1946.
GSM 87564

Paracraspedites oppressus Casey
Casey 1973, plate 1, fig. 2; p. 230.
Drift ex Basement Bed, Lower Spilsby Sandstone, *oppressus* Zone.
British Industrial Sand Pit, Bawsey, Norfolk.
Survey Collection (R. Casey and D. E. Butler) 1962.
CE 3592

Paracraspedites sp.
Casey 1973, plate 1, fig. 3.
Base of Roxham Beds, *oppressus* Zone.
No.4 gas feeder main trench, Manor Farm, North Runcton, Norfolk.
Survey Collection (R. Casey, R. W. Gallois and E. P. Smith) 1970.
CE 5744

cf. **Craspedites okensis** (d'Orbigny)
Casey 1962, p. 98.
Near base of the Lower Spilsby Sandstone, *primitivus* Zone.
Goulceby, Lincolnshire.
R. G. Thurrell Collection, presented 1962.
GSM 100513

Subcraspedites (Swinnertonia) primitivus Swinnerton
Casey 1973, text-fig. 4g; p. 238.
Lower Spilsby Sandstone, *primitivus* Zone.
Nettleton Top Barn, Lincolnshire.
H. H. Swinnerton Collection.
GSM 114815

Subcraspedites primitivus Swinnerton
Spath 1947, text-figs. 6 c, d.
Subcraspedites (Swinnertonia) primitivus Swinnerton
Casey 1973, text-fig. 4d; p. 238.
Lower Spilsby Sandstone, *primitivus* Zone.
Nettleton Top Barn, Lincolnshire.
C. W. Wright Collection, presented 1962.
GSM 107961

Subcraspedites (Swinnertonia) primitivus Swinnerton
Casey 1973, text-fig. 4e; p. 238.
Lower Spilsby Sandstone, *primitivus* Zone.
Nettleton Top Barn, Lincolnshire.
C. W. Wright Collection, presented 1962.
GSM 107958

Subcraspedites (Swinnertonia) sp. juv.
Casey 1973, plate 4, fig. 5; text-fig. 4f; p. 238.
Lower Spilsby Sandstone, *primitivus* Zone.
Nettleton Top Barn, Lincolnshire.
H. H. Swinnerton Collection.
GSM 114744

Subcraspedites (Swinnertonia) sp. juv.
Casey 1973, plate 4, fig. 4.
Lower Spilsby Sandstone, *primitivus* Zone.
No.2 well, Fordington, Lincolnshire.
A. Templeman Collection, presented by Sir George Taylor 1967.
Zq 280

Subcraspedites (Swinnertonia) subundulatus Swinnerton
Casey 1973, text-fig. 4h; p. 238.
Lower Spilsby Sandstone, *primitivus* Zone.
Nettleton, Lincolnshire.
H. H. Swinnerton Collection.
GSM 114816

Subcraspedites (Swinnertonia) subundulatus Swinnerton
Casey 1973, plate 4, fig. 1.
Lower Spilsby Sandstone, *primitivus* Zone.
No.2 well, Fordington, Lincolnshire.
H. H. Swinnerton Collection.
GSM 114742

Subcraspedites (Swinnertonia) cristatus Swinnerton
Casey 1973, plate 4, fig. 2.
Lower Spilsby Sandstone, *primitivus* Zone.
No.2 well, Fordington, Lincolnshire.
H. H. Swinnerton Collection.
GSM 114743

Subcraspedites (Subcraspedites) sowerbyi Spath
Casey 1973, text-fig. 41; p. 236.
Lower Spilsby Sandstone, *preplicomphalus* Zone.
Old Bolingbroke church, near Spilsby, Lincolnshire.
Survey Collection (J. Rhodes) 1884.
GSM 114817

Subcraspedites (Subcraspedites) sowerbyi Spath
Casey 1973, plate 5, fig. 1; p. 236.
Lower Spilsby Sandstone (erratic block), *preplicomphalus* Zone.
British Industrial Sand pit, Bawsey, Norfolk.
Survey Collection (R. Casey and D. E. Butler) 1962.
CE 3188

Subcraspedites (Subcraspedites) sowerbyi Spath
Casey 1973, plate 5, fig. 2; text-fig. 4k, p. 236.
Lower Spilsby Sandstone, *preplicomphalus* Zone.
Field NE of Goulceby, near Horncastle, Lincolnshire.
R. G. Thurrell Collection, presented 1962.
GSM 100514

Subcraspedites (Subcraspedites) sowerbyi Spath
Casey 1973, plate 3, fig. 3.
Lower Spilsby Sandstone, *preplicomphalus* Zone.
Old Bolingbroke, near Spilsby, Lincolnshire.
Survey Collection (J. Rhodes) 1884.
GSM 114733

Subcraspedites (Subcraspedites?) claxbiensis Spath
Casey 1973, plate 4, fig. 7; p. 238.
Base of Albian Carstone, derived from Lower Spilsby Sandstone, *preplicomphalus* Zone.
Nettleton valley, Lincolnshire.
P. F. Rawson Collection, presented 1972.
GSM 114735

Subcraspedites (Subcraspedites) sp. nov. cf. **claxbiensis** Spath
Casey 1973, plate 3, fig. 1; p. 238.
Lower Spilsby Sandstone, *preplicomphalus* Zone.
Field NE of Goulceby, near Horncastle, Lincolnshire.
R. G. Thurrell Collection, presented 1962.
GSM 100516

Subcraspedites (Subcraspedites) preplicomphalus Swinnerton
Casey 1973, plate 3, fig. 4, text-fig. 4m; p. 238.
Lower Spilsby Sandstone (erratic block), *preplicomphalus* Zone.
British Industrial Sand pit, Bawsey, Norfolk.
Survey Collection (R. Casey and D. E. Butler) 1962.
CE 3157

Subcraspedites (Subcraspedites) sp. juv.
Casey 1973, plate 4, fig. 6; p. 236.
Lower Spilsby Sandstone, *preplicomphalus* Zone.
Old Bolingbroke, near Spilsby, Lincolnshire.
Survey Collection (J. Rhodes) 1884.
GSM 114734

Craspedites group of **subditus** (Trautschold)
Casey 1962, p. 98.
Craspedites thurrelli Casey HOLOTYPE
Casey 1973, plate 5, fig. 4; p. 234.
c.3m above base of Spilsby Sandstone, *preplicomphalus* Zone.
Field NE of Goulceby, near Horncastle, Lincolnshire.
R. G. Thurrell Collection, presented 1962.
GSM 100512

Craspedites parakaschpurensis Gerasimov
Casey 1973, plate 2, fig. 3.
Upper Volgian Beds, *nodiger* Zone = *preplicomphalus* Zone.
Kashpir, near Moscow, USSR.
A. P. Pavlov Collection, presented 1891.
FOR 390

Craspedites plicomphalus (J. Sowerby)
Casey 1973, plate 2, fig. 2; text-fig. 4b; pp. 232, 236.
Lower Spilsby Sandstone, *preplicomphalus* Zone.
Spilsby Hill, Old Bolingbroke, Spilsby, Lincolnshire.
H. H. Swinnerton Collection.
GSM 114729

Subcraspedites (Volgidiscus) aff. **lamplughi** Spath
Casey 1973, plate 4, fig. 8; p. 239.
Basal nodule bed of Mintlyn Beds, derived from Runcton Beds, *lamplughi* Zone.
Fenland Flood Relief Channel, West Dereham, Norfolk.
Survey Collection (R. Casey and D. E. Butler) 1961.
CE 1966

Subcraspedites (Volgidiscus) lamplughi Spath
Casey 1973, plate 4, fig. 9; p. 239.
Basal nodule bed of Mintlyn Beds, derived from Runcton Beds, *lamplughi* Zone.
Fenland Flood Relief Channel, West Dereham, Norfolk.
Survey Collection (R. Casey and D. E. Butler) 1961.
CE 1903

Subcraspedites (Volgidiscus) lamplughi Spath
Casey 1973, text-fig. 5j; p. 239.
Nodule band, Mintlyn Beds, derived from Runcton Beds, *lamplughi* Zone.
Fenland Flood Relief Channel, West Dereham, Norfolk.
Survey Collection (R. Casey, D. E. Butler and C. J. Wood) 1961.
CE 1886

Subcraspedites (Volgidiscus) aff. **lamplughi** Spath
Casey 1973, plate 5, fig. 3; p. 239.
Lower Spilsby Sandstone, *lamplughi* Zone.
Nettleton Top Barn, Lincolnshire.
S.R.A. Kelly Collection, presented 1972.
GSM 114731

Subcraspedites (Volgidiscus) sp. nov.
Casey 1973, text-fig. 5i.
Base of Carstone, derived from Spilsby Sandstone, *lamplughi* Zone.
Nettleton Top Barn, Lincolnshire.
Survey Collection (V. Wilson) 1942.
VW 565

SPECIMENS IN EDINBURGH

HETTANGIAN STAGE

Psiloceras aequabile S. S. Buckman HOLOTYPE
Buckman 1923, plate CCCXC.
Lower Lias, *planorbis* Zone.
Aird na Iolaire, Ardmeanach, Mull.
GSE 3439 [formerly M 3328 f]

Ammonites (Aegoceras) angulatus Schlotheim
Peach, Gunn and Newton 1901, plate 9, fig. 1.
Lower Lias, *angulata* Zone.
Ballymichael Glen, Arran.
GSE 5455 [formerly M 2971 e]

SINEMURIAN STAGE

Echioceras boreale S. S. Buckman HOLOTYPE
S. S. Buckman 1914, p. 96d.
Trueman and Williams 1925, p. 710.
Getty 1973, pl. 2, fig. 1.
Lower Lias, *raricostatum* Zone.
Allt Fearns, Raasay.
GSE 2398

Echioceras exortum (Simpson)
Trueman and Williams 1925, plate 1, fig. 11; p. 711.
Lower Lias, Pabba Shales.
Allt Fearns, Raasay.
GSE 10094

Echioceras parvum Trueman and Williams HOLOTYPE
Trueman and Williams 1925, plate 1, fig. 10; pp. 710-711.
Lower Lias, Pabba Shales.
Allt Fearns, Raasay.
GSE 10095

Echioceras robustum (Quenstedt)
Trueman and Williams 1925, plate 3, fig. 5; p. 710.
Lower Lias, Pabba Shales.
Allt Fearns, Raasay.
GSE 10092, 10093

Echioceras polygyratum S. S. Buckman HOLOTYPE
S. S. Buckman 1914, p. 96c.
Euechioceras polygyratum (S. S. Buckman) HOLOTYPE
Trueman and Williams 1925, p. 728.
Lower Lias, *raricostatum* Zone.
Near the source of Hallaig Burn, Raasay.
GSE 2411 [formerly T 330 e]

Echioceras scoticum S. S. Buckman HOLOTYPE
S. S. Buckman 1914, p. 96c.
Euechioceras scoticum (S. S. Buckman) HOLOTYPE
Trueman and Williams 1925, p. 728.
Lower Lias, *raricostatum* Zone.
Allt Fearns, Raasay.
GSE 2418 [formerly T 4491 d]

Echioceras subobsoletum S. S. Buckman HOLOTYPE
S. S. Buckman, 1914, p. 96c
Euechioceras subobsoletum (S. S. Buckman) HOLOTYPE
Trueman and Williams, 1925, p. 727.
Leptechioceras subobsoletum (S. S. Buckman) HOLOTYPE
Getty 1973, plate 2, fig. 9.
Lower Lias, *raricostatum* Zone.
Allt Fearns, Raasay
GSE 2421 [formerly T3662d]

Euechioceras dubium Trueman and Williams HOLOTYPE
Trueman and Williams 1925, plate 2, fig. 3; p. 728.
Lower Lias, Pabba Shales.
Near the source of Hallaig Burn, Raasay.
GSE 10096

Leptechioceras pumilum Trueman and Williams HOLOTYPE
Trueman and Williams 1925, plate 2, fig. 7, p. 731.
Lower Lias, *raricostatum* Zone.
Carsaig, Mull.
GSE 2471

Echioceras cf. **ophioides** (d'Orbigny)
S. S. Buckman 1914, p. 96c.
Lower Lias, *raricostatum* Zone.
Near the source of Hallaig Burn, Raasay.
GSE 2413 [formerly T 326 e]

TOARCIAN STAGE

Dactylioceras sp.
Lee and Pringle 1932, p. 187.
Upper Lias.
Shiant Islands.
GSE 2661-2664

BAJOCIAN STAGE

Witchellia aff. **rubra** (S. S. Buckman)
Morton 1975, plate 9, figs. 21, 22, p. 56.
laeviuscula Zone.
Fallen blocks, shore between Bearreraig Bay and Holm Island, Skye.
GSE 2968

Sonninia (Sonninia) cf. **propinquans** (Bayle)
Morton 1975, plate 14, figs. 3, 4; p. 68.
Massive Sandstone, *sauzei* Zone, *sauzei* Subzone.
Fallen blocks, shore north side of Bearreraig Bay, Skye.
GSE 2972

Sonninia (Sonninia) cf. **propinquans** (Bayle)
Morton 1975, plate 14, figs. 1, 2; p. 68.
Massive Sandstone, *sauzei* Zone, *sauzei* Subzone.
Fallen blocks, shore north side of Bearreraig Bay, Skye.
GSE 2973

Sonninia (Sonninia) cf. **propinquans** (Bayle)
Morton 1975, plate 12, figs. 5, 8; text-fig.5I; pp. 68, 70.
Massive Sandstone, *sauzei* Zone, *sauzei* Subzone.
Fallen blocks, shore between Bearreraig Bay and Holm Island, Skye.
GSE 3060

Sonninia (Sonninia) cf. **propinquans** (Bayle)
Morton 1975, p. 68.
Massive Sandstone, *sauzei* Zone, *sauzei* Subzone.
Fallen blocks, shore north side of Bearreraig Bay, Skye.
GSE 2974, 2976-2978, 3020

Sonninia (Papilliceras) arenata (Quenstedt)
Morton 1975, plate 12, figs. 1, 2; p. 73.
Massive Sandstone, *sauzei* Zone, *sauzei* Subzone.
Fallen blocks, shore between Bearreraig Bay and Holm Island, Skye.
GSE 2912

Sonninia (Papilliceras) arenata (Quenstedt)
Morton 1975, pp. 73, 76.
Massive Sandstone, *sauzei* Zone, *sauzei* Subzone.
Fallen blocks, shore between Bearreraig Bay and Holm Island, Skye.
GSE 2911, 7102

Sonninia (Papillicera) mesacantha (Waagen)
Morton 1975, p. 76.
Massive Sandstone, *sauzei* Zone, *sauzei* Subzone.
Fallen blocks, shore between Bearreraig Bay and Holm Island, Skye.
GSE 2913

Sonninia (Papilliceras) mesacantha (Waagen)
Morton 1975, p. 76.
Massive Sandstone, *sauzei* Zone, *sauzei* Subzone.
Fallen blocks, Rudha Sughar, Bearreraig, Skye.
GSE 2971

Chondroceras evolvescens (Waagen)
Morton 1971, plate 51, figs. 6, 7; p. 286.
Basal Upper Sandstone, *humphriesianum* Zone.
Shore below Rigg, 200 yards N. of Rigg Burn, Skye.
GSE 13058 [formerly V 1539 c]

Dorsetensia sp.
Morton 1975, p. 82.
Upper Sandstones.
Port nam Marbh, Mull.
GSE 2835, 2836, 2877

Dorsetensia liostraca S. S. Buckman
Morton 1972, p. 506.
sowerbyi or *humphriesianum* Zone.
Beach north of Rigg Burn, Skye.
GSE 7234

Stephanoceras (Stephanoceras) pyritosum (Quenstedt)
Morton 1971, text-fig. 4B; pp. 281-282.
Upper Sandstone, *humphriesianum* Zone.
Shore south of Rigg waterfall, Skye.
GSE 13057 [formerly V 1559 c]

Garantiana (Garantiana) filicosta Bentz
Morton 1971, plate 51, fig. 10; pp. 269, 289-290.
Garantiana Clay, *subfurcatum* Zone.
Storab's Grave, Raasay.
GSE 2888

Garantiana (Garantiana) ? baculata (Quenstedt)
Morton 1971, plate 51, fig. 8; pp. 269, 289-290.
Garantiana Clay, *subfurcatum* Zone.
Storab's Grave, Raasay.
GSE 2889

Garantiana (Garantiana) ?baculata (Quenstedt)
Morton 1971, plate 51, fig. 12; pp. 269, 289-290.
Garantiana Clay, *subfurcatum* Zone.
Storab's Grave, Raasay.
GSE 2921

Garantiana (Garantiana) ?baculata (Quenstedt)
Morton 1971, plate 51, fig. 11; pp. 269, 289-290.
Garantiana Clay, *subfurcatum* Zone.
Storabs Grave, Raasay.
GSE 2922

Garantiana (Garantiana) filicosta Bentz
Morton 1971, plate 51, fig. 15; pp. 269, 289-290.
Garantiana Clay, *subfurcatum* Zone.
Storab's Grave, Raasay.
GSE 2927

Garantiana (Garantiana) filicosta Bentz
Morton 1971, plate 51, fig. 13; pp. 269, 289-290.
Garantiana Clay, *subfurcatum* Zone.
Storab's Grave, Raasay.
GSE 2928

Garantiana (Garantiana) sp.
Morton 1971, plate 51, fig. 16; pp. 269, 290.
Garantiana Clay, *subfurcatum* Zone.
Storab's Grave, Raasay.
GSE 2929

Garantian (Garantiana) sp.
Morton 1971, plate 51, fig. 17; pp. 269, 290.
Garantiana Clay, *subfurcatum* Zone.
Storab's Grave, Raasay.
GSE 2930

Garantiana sp.
Morton 1971, p. 269.
Garantiana Clay, *subfurcatum* Zone.
Storab's Grave, Raasay.
GSE 2926

?Strenoceras sp.
Morton 1971, pp. 269, 290.
Garantiana Clay, *subfurcatum* Zone.
Storabs Grave, Raasay.
GSE 2925

CALLOVIAN STAGE

Proplanulites cf. **auriculatus** S. S. Buckman
S. S. Buckman 1921, p. 37.
Brora Roof Bed, *calloviense* Zone, *koenigi* Subzone.
Shore at Lower Brora, Sutherland.
GSE 3707 [formerly M 1656 g]

Gowericeras childanum S. S. Buckman HOLOTYPE
S. S. Buckman 1923, plate CDIV.
Brora Roof Bed, *calloviense* Zone, *koenigi* Subzone.
Coal pit, Brora, Sutherland.
GSE 3700 [formerly M 1659 g]

Zugokosmoceras zugium S. S. Buckman HOLOTYPE
S. S. Buckman 1923, plate CCCLXXXIX.
Kosmoceras (Zugokosmoceras) grossouvrei
(R. Douvillé)
Arkell 1957, fig. 364, 2; pp. L300-301.
Fascally Shales, *coronatum* Zone, *grossouvrei* Subzone.
North bank of River Brora, Brora, Sutherland.
GSE 3655 [formerly M 308 g]

Zugokosmoceras interpositum S. S. Buckman
HOLOTYPE
S. S. Buckman 1923, plate CDXIX.
Fascally Shales, *coronatum* Zone.
River Brora, Brora, Sutherland.
GSE 5454 [formerly M 385 g]

Sutherlandiceras albisaxaeum S. S. Buckman
HOLOTYPE
S. S. Buckman 1922a, plate CCCXX A.
Lee and Pringle 1932, p. 206.
Eboraciceras albisaxaeum (S. S. Buckman) HOLOTYPE
Meledina 1977, pp. 106-107.
Clyneleish Sandstone, *lamberti* Zone.
Clyneleish Quarry, Brora, Sutherland.
GSE 3704 [formerly M 1498 g]

Sutherlandiceras albisaxaeum S. S. Buckman
PARATYPE
S. S. Buckman 1922a, plate CCCXX B.
Clyneleish Sandstone, *lamberti* Zone.
Clyneleish Quarry, Brora, Sutherland.
GSE 3710 [formerly M 769 g]

Aspidoceras silphouense (Young and Bird)
S. S. Buckman 1923, plate CCCLXIV A.
Aspidoceras clynelishense Arkell HOLOTYPE
Arkell 1939a, pp. 180-181.
Arkell 1940, p. 202.
Arkell 1944, p. 287.
Clyneleish Sandstone, *lamberti* Zone.
Clyneleish Quarry, Brora, Sutherland.
M 766 g

OXFORDIAN STAGE

Aspidoceras (Euaspidoceras) paucituberculatum
Arkell
Arkell 1941, p. 215.
cordatum Zone.
Balintore, Ross.
GSE 3369, 3421

Cardioceras (Cardioceras) costicardia S. S. Buckman
Arkell 1946, p. 321.
cordatum Zone, *costicardia* Subzone.
Beach, Staffin Bay, Skye.
GSE 10352-10354

Cardioceras (Scarburgiceras) excavatoides Maire
Arkell 1946, p. 303.
cordatum Zone, *costicardia* Subzone.
Beach east of Loch Shianta, Staffin Bay, Skye.
GSE 7253, 7254

Perisphinctes (Kranaosphinctes) cf. **kranaus**
(S. S. Buckman)
Arkell 1939, p. 175.
cordatum Zone.
Shore at Port-an-Righ, Balintore, Ross.
GSE 3362

Cardioceras (Scarburgiceras) excavatoides? Maire
Arkell 1947, plate 71, fig. 2.
cordatum Zone.
Staffin Bay, Skye.
GSE 10337

Aspidoceras (Euaspidoceras) perarmatum (J. Sowerby)
Arkell 1941, p. 197.
plicatilis Zone.
Balintore, Ross.
GSE 3169, 3170

Cardioceras (Subvertebriceras) densiplicatum Boden
Arkell 1943, p. 241.
plicatilis Zone, *vertebrale* Subzone.
Ardassie Point, east of Brora, Sutherland.
GSE 10340 [formerly M 1287 g]

Cardioceras (Subvertebriceras) densiplicatum Boden
Arkell 1943, p. 241.
plicatilis Zone, *vertebrale* Subzone.
Clyneleish House, Brora, Sutherland.
GSE 10341 [formerly M 1681 g]

Cardioceras (Subvertebriceras) densiplicatum Boden
Arkell 1943, p. 241.
plicatilis Zone, *vertebrale* Subzone.
Shore at Port-an-Righ, Balintore, Ross.
GSE 10342 [formerly M 3079 g]

Cardioceras (Subvertebriceras) zenaidae Ilovaiskiy
Arkell 1943, p. 243.
plicatilis Zone, *vertebrale* Subzone.
Shore at Port-an-Righ, Balintore, Ross.
GSE 10343 [formerly M 3243 g]

?Cardioceras (Cardioceras) persecans (S. S. Buckman)
Arkell 1946, p. 318.
plicatilis Zone, *vertebrale* Subzone.
Roadside quarry, Uppat House, Brora, Sutherland.
GSE 10346, 10347 [formerly M 861 g, M 866 g]

Cardioceras (Plasmatoceras) popilaniense Boden
Arkell 1942, p. 231.
Ardassie Limestone, *plicatilis* Zone.
Ardassie Point, east of Brora, Sutherland.
GSE 10358, 10359 [formerly M 1013g, M 1218 g]

Cardioceras (Plasmatoceras) popilaniense Boden
Arkell 1942, p. 231.
Staffin Shale, *plicatilis* Zone.
South side of Uig Bay, Trotternish, Skye.
GSE 10360, 10361 [formerly V 567 c, V 580 c]

Perisphinctes (Dichotomosphinctes) buckmani Arkell
Arkell 1938, p. 83.
plicatilis Zone.
Port-an-Righ, Balintore, Ross.
GSE 3167, 3174

Perisphinctes (Arisphinctes) plicatilis (J. Sowerby)
Arkell 1940, p. 149.
plicatilis Zone.
Port-an-Righ, Balintore, Ross.
GSE 3165, 3168

?Cardioceras (Cardioceras) ashtonense Arkell
Arkell 1946, p. 319.
plicatilis Zone.
Bow Buoy Skerry, NNE of Rosemarkie, Skye.
GSE 10348-10351

Cardioceras cf. **excavatum** (J. Sowerby)
S. S. Buckman 1924, p. 48.
Scoticardioceras scoticum S. S. Buckman HOLOTYPE
S. S. Buckman 1925, plate DXCIX.
Cardioceras (Scoticardioceras) excavatum (J. Sowerby) **scoticum** (S. S. Buckman) HOLOTYPE of ssp.
Arkell 1942, text-fig. 77; p. 221-222.
Ardassie Beds, *plicatilis* Zone, *vertebrale* Subzone.
Ardassie Point, east of Brora, Sutherland.
GSE 6794 [formerly M 1069 b]

Cardioceras (Subvertebriceras) densiplicatum Boden
Arkell 1943, plate 53, fig. 7.
plicatilis Zone, *vertebrale* Subzone.
Clyneleish House, Brora, Sutherland.
GSE 10338 formerly M 1682 g]

Cardioceras (Subvertebriceras) densiplicatum Boden
Arkell 1943, plate 53, fig. 8.
plicatilis Zone, *vertebrale* Subzone.
Clyneleish House, Brora, Sutherland.
GSE 10339 [formerly M 1686 g]

Cardioceras (Scoticardioceras) excavatum (J. Sowerby)
Arkell 1942, plate 49, fig. 5.
plicatilis Zone, *vertebrale* Subzone.
Clyneleish House, Brora, Sutherland.
GSE 10357 [formerly M 1685 g]

Cardioceras (Maltoniceras) sp. juv
Arkell 1942, p. 238.
plicatilis Zone, *antecedens* Subzone.
Beach east of Loch Shianta, Staffin Bay, Skye.
GSE 10362-10364 [formerly V 756, 760, 761 c]

Cardioceras (Maltoniceras) sp. juv.
Arkell 1942, p. 238.
plicatilis Zone, *antecedens* Subzone.
Beach east of Digg, Skye.
GSE 10365

Amoeboceras (Prionodoceras) mansoni Pringle HOLOTYPE
Pringle 1936, plate 13, upper fig. ; pp. 308-309.
decipiens Zone (in drift).
Brickyard N of Plaidy station, Aberdeenshire.
GSE 12985 [formerly M 638 d]

Amoeboceras (Prionodoceras) mansoni Pringle PARATYPE
Pringle 1936, plate 13, fig. a.
decipiens Zone.
Shore at Port-an-Righ, Balintore, Ross.
GSE 5436 [formerly M 3311 g]

Amoeboceras (Prionodoceras) mansoni Pringle PARATYPE
Pringle 1936, plate 13, fig. b.
decipiens Zone.
Shore at Port-an-Righ, Balintore, Ross.
GSE 5435 [formerly M 3309 g]

Amoeboceras (Prionoceras) mansoni Pringle PARATYPE
Pringle 1936, plate 13, lower fig.
decipiens Zone (in drift).
Brickyard N of Plaidy station, Aberdeenshire.
GSE 13103 [formerly M 628 d]

Amoeboceras (Prionodoceras) aff. **superstes** (Phillips)
Pringle 1936, plate 14, upper fig.; p. 310.
decipiens Zone (in drift)
Brickyard N of Plaidy station, Aberdeenshire.
GSE 5433

Euaspidoceras aff. **rotari** (Oppel)
Pringle 1936, plate 14, lower fig.; p. 308.
decipiens Zone (in drift).
Brickyard N of Plaidy station, Aberdeenshire.
GSE 5434

KIMMERIDGIAN STAGE

Prionodoceras ogivale S. S. Buckman HOLOTYPE
S. S. Buckman 1923, plate CDXXI.
Kimmeridge Clay.
Shore at Port-an-Righ, Balintore, Ross.
GSE 3098 [formerly M 3296 g]

Amoeboceras sp.
S. S. Buckman 1923, pp. 34, 40.
Amoebites akanthophorus S. S. Buckman HOLOTYPE
S. S. Buckman 1925, plate DL.
Amoeboceras (Amoebites) kitchini (Salfeld)
Arkell 1957, fig. 379, 4; pp. L306, 307.
Kimmeridge Clay.
Shore at Eathie, Cromarty.
GSE 3438 [formerly M 3391 g]

REFERENCES

ARKELL, W. J. 1933. *The Jurassic System in Great Britain.* 681 pp., 41 pls. (Oxford: Clarendon Press.)

— 1935a. The Portland Beds of the Dorset mainland. *Proc. Geol. Assoc.*, Vol. 46, pp. 301–347, pls. 20–26.

— 1935b–1948. A monograph on the ammonites of the English Corallian Beds. 1935b, Part 1, pp. i-xxxii, 1–30, pls. A,B, 1–6; 1936a, Part 2, pp. xxxiii-xlvi, 31–42, pls. C,D, 7–10; 1937a, Part 3, pp. xlvii-liv, 43–67, pls. E,F, 11–13; 1938, Part 4, pp. 69–104, pls. 14–18; 1939a, Part 5, pp. lv-lxiv, 105–190, pls. 19–40; 1940, Part 6, pp. lxv-lxxii, 191–216, pls. 41–47; 1941, Part 7, pp. lxxiii-lxxx, 217–238, pls. 48–51; 1942, Part 8, pp. 239–254, pls. 52–55; 1943, Part 9, pp. lxxxi-lxxxiv, 255–268, pls. 56–60; 1944, Part 10, pp. 269–296, pls. 61–66; 1946, Part 11, pp. 297–332, pls. 67–70; 1947a, Parts 12, 13, pp. 333–378, pls. 71–78; 1948; Part 14, pp. 379–420. *Palaeontogr. Soc. Monogr.*

— 1936b. Ammonite zones of the Upper Oxfordian of Oxford, and the horizons of the Sowerbys' and Buckman's types. *Q. J. Geol. Soc. London*, Vol. 92, pp. 146–187.

— 1937b. Report on ammonites collected at Long Stanton, Cambridgeshire, and the age of the Ampthill Clay. *Summ. Prog. Geol. Surv. G.B.* for 1935, pp. 64–88.

— 1937c. The zonal position of the Elsworth Rock and its alleged equivalent at Upware, Cambridgeshire. *Geol. Mag.*, Vol. 74, pp. 445–458.

— 1939b. The ammonite succession at the Woodham Brick Co.'s pit, Akeman Street Station, Bucks., and its bearing on the classification of the Oxford Clay. *Q. J. Geol. Soc. London*, Vol. 95, pp. 135–222.

— 1947b. The geology of the country around Weymouth, Swanage, Corfe & Lulworth. *Mem. Geol. Surv. G.B.*, Vol. 12, 386 pp., 19 pls., 84 figs.

— 1951a–1958. A monograph of English Bathonian ammonites. 1951a, Parts 1, 2, pp. 1–72, pls. 1–8; 1952, Part 3, pp. 73–102, pls. 9–11; 1954a, Part 4, pp. 103–128, pls. 12–15; 1955, Part 5, pp. 129–140, pls. 16–17; 1956a, Part 6, pp. 141–162, pls. 18–19; 1958, Parts 7, 8, pp. 163–264, pls. 20–33. *Palaeontogr. Soc. Monogr.*

— 1951b. A Middle Bathonian ammonite from Schwandorf, northern Bavaria. *Abh. Schweiz. paläontol. ges.*, Vol. 69, pp. 1–18, pls. 1–3

— 1954b. Three complete sections of the Cornbrash. *Proc. Geol. Assoc.*, Vol. 65, pp. 115–122.

— 1956b. *The Jurassic geology of the world.* 806 pp., 46 pls. (Edinburgh and London: Oliver and Boyd.)

— 1957. in MOORE, R. C. (Editor). *Treatise on Invertebrate Paleontology.* Pt. L, Mollusca 4. Cephalopoda Ammonoidea. 490pp. 588 figs. (Lawrence, Kansas: Geological Society of America and the University of Kansas Press.)

— and DONOVAN, D. T. 1951. Fuller's Earth of the Cotswolds, and its relation to the Great Oolite. *Q. J. Geol. Soc. London*, Vol. 107, pp. 227–253, pls 13–16.

— and PLAYFORD, P. E. 1954. The Bajocian ammonites of Western Australia. *Philos. Trans. R. Soc. London.* Ser. 8, No. 651, Vol. 237, pp. 547–605. pls 27–40, 13 figs.

— RICHARDSON, L. and PRINGLE, J. 1933. Lower Oolites exposed in the Ardley and Fritwell railway cuttings, between Bicester and Banbury, Oxford. *Proc. Geol. Assoc.*, Vol. 44, pp. 340–354, pls. 34, 35.

BASSE, E. 1952. Ammonoidea s.str.. Pp. 581–688, 14 pls., figs. 42–60 *in* PIVETEAU, J. (Editor). *Traité de Paléontologie* [Treatise on Palaeontology], Vol. 2, 790 pp. (Paris: Masson.) [In French.]

— and PERRODON, M. 1951. Macrocéphalitides du sud-ouest de Madagascar, Macrocephalitidae, Eucycloceratidae, Mayaitidae. Récoltes de la mission E. Basse 1930–1931 [Macrocephalitids of the south-west of Madagascar. Macrocephalitidae, Eucycloceratidae, Mayaitidae. Collections of the E. Basse expedition 1930–1931]. *Mém. Soc. Géol. France*, New Ser., Vol. 30, Pts. 3 and 4, Mém. 65, pp. 1–100, pls. 7. [In French.]

BAYER, U. 1969. *Euaptetoceras* und *Eudmetoceras* (Ammonoidea, Hammateceratidae [sic]) aus der *concava*-Zone (Ober-Aalenium) Süddeutschlands [*Euaptetoceras* and *Eudmetoceras* (Ammonoidea, Hammatoceratidae) from the *concava* Zone (Upper Aalenian) of southern Germany]. *Neues Jahrb. Geol. Paläontol. Abh.*, Vol. 133, Pt. 3, pp. 211–222, 4 figs. [In German.]

BEHMEL, H. and GEYER, O. F. 1966. Beiträge zur Stratigraphie und Paläontologie des Juras von Ostspanien. III: Stratigraphie und Fossilführung im Unterjura von Albarracín (Provinz Teruel) [Contributions to the stratigraphy and palaeontology of the Jurassic of eastern Spain. III: Guide to the stratigraphy and fossils in the Lower Jurassic of Albarracín (Teruel province)]. *Neues Jahrb. Geol. Paläontol. Abh.*, Vol. 124, Pt. 1, pp. 1–52, pls. 1–52, 4 figs. [In German.]

BIRKELUND, T., THUSU, B. and VIGRAN, J. 1978. Jurassic–Cretaceous biostratigraphy of Norway, with comments on the British *Rasenia cymodoce* Zone. *Palaeontology*, Vol. 21, pp. 31–63, pls. 1–6, 6 figs.

BLAKE, J. F. 1905. A monograph of the fauna of the Cornbrash. *Monogr. Palaeontogr. Soc.*, 100 pp., 9 pls.

— and HUDLESTON, W. H. 1877. The Corallian rocks of England. *Q. J. Geol. Soc. London*, Vol. 33, pp. 260–405.

BUCKMAN, J. 1844. Appendix of fossil remains from the neighbourhood of Cheltenham. Pp. 68–110 *in* MURCHISON, R. I. *Outline of the geology of the neighbourhood of Cheltenham.* 110 pp., 13 pls., map. (London: Murray.)

— 1858. On the Oolite rocks of Gloucester, Dorset and Somerset. *Q. J. Geol. Soc. London*, Vol. 14, pp. 98–130, pl. 7.

— 1874. On the Cephalopoda Bed and the Oolite Sands of Dorset and part of Somerset. *Proc. Somerset Archaeol. Nat. Hist. Soc.*, Vol. 20, pp. 140–164, 6 figs.

— 1877. The Cephalopoda Beds of Gloucester, Dorset and Somerset. *Q. J. Geol. London*, Vol. 33, pp. 1–9.

— 1881. On the termination of some ammonites from the Inferior Oolite of Dorset and Somerset. *Q. J. Geol. Soc. London*, Vol. 37, pp. 57–66, 7 figs.

BUCKMAN, S. S. 1881. A descriptive catalogue of some species of ammonites from the Inferior Oolite of Dorset. *Q. J. Geol. Soc. London*, Vol. 37, pp. 588–608. 3 figs.

— 1887–1907. A monograph of the ammonites of the Inferior Oolite Series. 1887, pp. 1–24, pls. 1–6; 1888, pp. 25–56, pls. 7–14; 1889a, pp. 57–144, pls. 15–23A; 1890, pp. 145–244, pls. 24–36; 1891, pp. 245–256, pls. 37–44; 1892a, pp. 257–344, pls. 45–76; 1893a, pp. 345–376, pls. 77–92; 1894, pp. 377–456, pls. 93–103; 1898 Supplement, pp. i-xxxii, pls. 1–4; 1899. Supplement, pp. xxxiii-lxix, pls. 5–14; 1904a Supplement, pp. lxv-clxviii, pls. 15–19; 1905a Supplement, pp. clxix-ccviii, pls. 20–24; 1907 Supplement, pp. ccix-cclxii. *Palaeontogr. Soc. Monogr.*

— 1889b. On the Cotteswold, Midford and Yeovil Sands, and the division between Lias and Oolite. *Q. J. Geol. Soc. London*, Vol. 45, pp. 440–473.

— 1889c. The descent of Sonninia and Hammatoceras. *Q. J. Geol. Soc. London*, Vol. 45, pp. 651–663, pl. 22.

— 1889d. On Jurassic ammonites. *Geol. Mag.*, Decade 3, Vol. 6, pp. 200–203.

— 1892b. The morphology of 'Stephanoceras' zigzag. *Q. J. Geol. Soc. London*, Vol. 48, pp. 447–452, pls. 13, 14.

— 1893b. The Bajocian of the Sherborne district: its relation to subjacent and superjacent strata. *Q. J. Geol. Soc. London*, Vol. 49, pp. 479–521. 4 tables.

— 1896. Notes on Jurassic ammonites. *Geol. Mag.*, Decade 4, Vol. 3, pp. 420–421.

— 1903. The Toarcian of Bredon Hill and a comparison with deposits elsewhere. *Q. J. Geol. Soc. London*, Vol. 59, pp. 445–458.

— 1905b. On certain genera and species Lytoceratidae. *Q. J. Geol. Soc. London*, Vol. 61, pp. 142–154, pls. 15–16, 9 figs.

— 1906. Some Lias ammonites: *Schlotheimia* and species of other genera. *Proc. Cotteswold Nat. Field Club*, Vol. 15, pp. 231–254, pls. 10–11.

— 1909–1919. *Yorkshire Type Ammonites*. Vol. 1. 1909, Part 1, pp. i-xii, *i-ii*, pls. I-XI; 1910a, Part 2, pp. xiii-xvi, pls. XII-XXIII; 1911, Parts 3–5, pp. *iii-vi*, pls. XXIV-XLIV; 1912, Parts 6–8, pp. *vii-viii*, appendix pp. A–G, pls. XLV–LXVII. Vol. 2. 1912, Parts 9–11, pp. v-x, *i-viii*, pls. LXVIII–XC; 1914, Parts 12–14, pp. *ix-x*, pls. XCI–CVIII; 1918b, Parts 15–17, pp. *xi-xiv*, pls. CIX–CXIX, CXXIV–CXXIX; 1919, Part 18, pp. *xv-xvi*, appendix pp. A–H, pls. CXX-CXXIII, CXXX. (London: Wheldon and Wesley.) [Continued as *Type Ammonites*, 1919–1930.]

— 1910b. Jurassic (Lias-Oolite) strata of South Dorset; and their correlation. *Q. J. Geol. Soc. London*, Vol. 66, pp. 52–89.

— 1918a. Jurassic chronology: I–Lias. *Q. J. Geol. Soc. London*, Vol. 73, pp. 257–327, pls. 26–31.

— 1919–1930. *Type Ammonites*. Vol. 3. 1919, Parts 19–20, pp. 5–8, pls. CXXXI–CXLVII; 1920, Parts 21–24, pp. 9–30, pls. CXXXIIB, CXXXIX BCDE, CLVI–CXCIV; 1921, Parts 25–30, pp. 1–4, 31–64, pls. CXXXIII B, CXXXIV CD, CXCV–CCLXVI. Vol. 4. 1922a, Parts 31–37, pp. 5–28, pls. CCLXVIII–CCCLXII A; 1923, Parts 38–41, pp. 1–4, 29–68, pls. XVIII A, CCCXXXVII A, CCCXXXVIII A, CCCLV B, CCCLXII B–CDXXII. Vol. 5, 1923, Parts 42–43, pls. CDXXIII–CDLVII; 1924, Parts 44–49, pp. 5–44, pls. LXIV A, X6, 12 figs. *in* BUCKMAN, S. S., JACKSON, J. F., PRINGLE, J., CIX C, CXXVI A, CXCIX C, CCCXLII C, CDLVIII–DXXXVI; 1925, Parts 50–52, pp. 49–88, pls. CLIV A, CLXXIX A, CCLIX C, CCCVII C, CDXL A, CDLXXVI C, DXI C, DXIII A, DXXXI A, DXXVII–DLXXVI; Vol. 6, 1925 Parts 53–55, pls. DXXVIII A, DLXXVII–DCXXI; 1926, Parts 56–61, pp. 5–42, pls. CXXXVIII C, CCCLIII CD, CCCLIV C, DLXII AB, DLXXX C, DXC ABC, DCII A, DCXXII–DCXCIII; 1927, Parts 62–63, pp. 43–46, pls. LXVIII A, CXXXV A, CLVII A, DII A, DVI A, DCXXXIX D, DCXCIV–DCCXVII. Vol. 7. 1927, Parts 64–67, pp. 5–10, pls. XXXI A, LXXXIX A, CDXLVI AB, DVI B, DXVIII AB, DCXX CD, DCXXXVIII CD, DCCXVIII-DCCLX; 1928, Parts 68–70, pp. 11–14, pls. DCCLXXI–DCCLXXIII; 1930 [published posthumously, DAVIES, A. M. (Editor)] Pts. 71–72, pp. 15–78 (Thame and London: Weldon and Wesley.)

— 1922b. Certain Jurassic strata near Eypesmouth (Dorset): the Junction-Bed of Watton Cliff and associated rocks. Pp. 378–436, 12 figs. *in* BUCKMAN, S. S., JACKSON, J. F., PRINGLE, J., SPATH, L. F., and TEMPLEMAN, A. Jurassic Chronology: II - preliminary studies. *Q. J. Geol. Soc. London*, Vol. 78, pp. 378–457, 12 figs., table.

— and WILSON, E. 1896. Dundry Hill: its upper portion, or the beds marked as Inferior Oolite (g^5) on the maps of the Geological Survey. *Q. J. Geol. Soc. London*, Vol. 52, pp. 669–720.

CALLOMON, J. H. 1955. The ammonite succession in the Lower Oxford Clay and Kellaways Beds at Kidlington, Oxfordshire, and the zones of the Callovian Stage. *Philos. Trans. R. Soc. London*, Ser. B, Vol. 239, pp. 215–264, pls. 2–3.

— 1960. New sections in the Corallian Beds around Oxford, and the subzones of the plicatilis Zone. *Proc. Geol. Assoc.*, Vol. 71, pp. 177–208.

— 1971. The type species of *Macrocephalites* Zittel 1884 and the type specimen of *Ammonites macrocephalus* Schlotheim 1813. *Palaeontology*, Vol. 14, pp. 114–130, pls. 15–18, 3 figs.

CARRECK, J. N. 1960. Whitsun field meeting to Weymouth, Abbotsbury and Dorchester, Dorset. *Proc. Geol. Assoc.*, Vol. 71, pp. 341–347.

CASEY, R. 1962. The ammonites of the Spilsby Sandstone, and the Jurassic–Cretaceous boundary. *Proc. Geol. Soc. London*, No. 1598, pp. 95–100.

— 1967. The position of the Middle Volgian in the English Jurassic. *Proc. Geol. Soc. London*, No. 1640, pp. 128–133.

— 1973. The ammonite succession at the Jurassic–Cretaceous boundary in eastern England. Pp. 193–266, 10 pls, *in* The boreal Lower Cretaceous. CASEY, R. and RAWSON, P. R. (Editors). *Spec. Issue Geol. J.*, No. 5, 448 pp. (Liverpool: Seel House.)

CAVE, R. 1977. Geology of the Malmesbury district. *Mem. Geol. Surv. G.B.*, 343 pp, 7 pls., 27 figs.

CONTINI, D. 1969. L'Aalénien et le Bajocien du Jura franc-comtois. [The Aalenian and the Bajocian of the Franche-Comté Jura.] *Ann. Sci. Univ. Besançon Géol.*, 3rd ser., Vol. 11, 240 pp, 56 figs, [In French.]

COPE, J. C. W. 1967. The palaeontology and stratigraphy of the lower part of the Upper Kimmeridge Clay. *Bull. Br. Mus. (Nat. Hist.) Geol.*, Vol. 15, pp. 1–79, 33 pls., 12 figs.

— 1974. Upper Kimmeridgian ammonite faunas of the Wash area and a subzonal scheme for the lower part of the Upper Kimmeridgian. *Bull. Geol. Surv. GB.*, No. 47, pp. 29–37, pls. 1–3.

COX, L. R. and ARKELL, W. J. 1950. Survey of the Mollusca of the British Great Oolite Series: primarily a nomenclatorial revision of the monographs of Morris and Lycett (1851–1855), Lycett (1863) and Blake (1905–1907). *Monogr. Palaeontogr. Soc.*, Pt. 2, pp. 14–24, 49–105.

DANFORD, C. G. 1906. Notes on the Speeton ammonites. *Proc. Yorkshire Geol. Soc.*, Vol. 16, pp. 101–114, pls. 10–14.

DAVIES, A. M. 1907. The Kimmeridge Clay and Corallian Rocks of the neighbourhood of Brill (Buckinghamshire). *Q. J. Geol. Soc. London*, Vol. 63, pp. 29–49, pl. 1, 2 figs.

— and PRINGLE, J. 1913. Two deep borings at Calvert Station (north Buckinghamshire), and on the Palaeozoic floor north of the Thames. *Q. J. Geol. Soc. London*, Vol. 69, pp. 308–340, pls. 33, 34.

DEAN, W. T., DONOVAN, D. T. and HOWARTH, M. K. 1961. The Liassic ammonite zones and subzones of the North-West European Province. *Bull. Br. Mus. (Nat. Hist.) Geol.*, Vol. 4, pp. 435–505, pls. 63–75.
DE LA BECHE, H. T. 1826. On the Lias of the coast, in the vicinity of Lyme Regis, Dorset. *Trans. Geol. Soc. London*, Ser. 2, Vol. 2, pp. 21–30, pls. 3, 4.
DONOVAN, D. T. 1952. The ammonites of the Blue Lias of the Bristol district. *Ann. Mag. Nat. Hist.*, Ser. 12, Vol. 5, pp. 629–655, 717–752, pls. 12, 13, 17–19.
— 1954. Synoptic supplement to T. Wright's 'Monograph on the Lias ammonites of the British Isles' (1878–86). *Monogr. Palaeontogr. Soc.*, 54 pp.
— 1956. The zonal stratigraphy of the Blue Lias around Keynsham, Somerset. *Proc. Geol. Assoc.*, Vol. 66, pp. 182–212.
— 1958. The Lower Lias section at Cannard's Grave, Shepton Mallet, Somerset. *Proc. Bristol Nat. Soc.*, Vol. 29, pp. 393–398.
— 1960. The Lower Liassic ammonites *Neomicroceras* gen. nov. and *Paracymbites*. *Palaeontology*, Vol. 9, pp. 312–318, pl. 53.
— 1973. Systematics of the Lower Liassic Ammonitina. *Paleontol. Contrib. Univ. Kansas*, Pap. 64, 18 pp., 4 pls.
DOUVILLÉ, F. 1943. Révision des genres *Clydoniceras* et *Macrocephalites* [Revision of the genera *Clydoniceras* and *Macrocephalites*]. *Mém. Soc. Géol. France*, New Ser., Vol. 22, No. 48, pp. 3–47, 7 pls., 20 figs, [In French.]
DUMORTIER, E. 1974. *Études paléontologigues sur les dépôts Jurassiques du Basin du Rhône. Pt. 4: Lias supérieur* [Palaeontological studies on the Jurassic deposits of the Rhône basin. Part 4: Upper Lias]. 335 pp. 62 pls, (Paris: Libraire des Sociétés Géologique et Météorologique de France.) [In French.].
EDMUNDS, F. H. and OAKLEY, K. P. 1936 (1st Ed.), 1947 (2nd Ed.). British regional geology: The central England district. *Mem. Geol. Surv. G.B.*, 88 pp., 8 pls., 16 figs.
ELMI, S. 1962. Considérations sur *Choffatia (Subgrossouvria)* (Ammonitina, Pseudoperisphinctinae). *C.R. Somm. Séanc. Soc. Géol. France*, 7th Ser., Vol. 4, pp. 205–206. [In French.]
GABILLY, J. 1975. Évolution et systématique des Phymatoceratinae et des Grammoceratinae (Hildocerataceae Ammonitina) de la région de Thouars, stratotype du Toarcien [Evolution and taxonomy of the Phymatoceratinae and Grammoceratinae (Hildocerataceae Ammonitina) of the Thouars region, stratotype of the Toarcian]. *Mém. Soc. Géol. France*, New Ser., Vol. 54, No. 124, 196 pp., 36 pls., 133 figs, 30 tables [In French.]
— 1976. Le Toarcien à Thouars et dans le centre-ouest de la France. Biostratigraphie-évolution de la faune (Harpoceratinae, Hildoceratinae) [The Toarcian at Thouars and in the centre-west of France. Biostratigraphy – evolution of the fauna (Harpoceratinae, Hildoceratinae)]. *Publ. Com. Fr. Stratigr.*, Les stratotypes français, Vol. 3, 217 pp, 29 pls., 52 figs., 18 tables. [In French.]
GEBHARD, G. and SCHLATTER, R. 1977. Uber das Vorkommen von *Tmaegoceras* Hyatt (Ammonoidea) im Lias Europas [On the occurrence of *Tmaegoceras* HYATT (Ammonoidea) in the European Lias]. *Stuttgarter Beitr. Naturkd.*, Ser.B, Geol. Paläontol., No. 22, pp. 1–15, pl. 1, 3 figs. [In German.].
GÉCZY, B. 1966. Ammonoides jurassiques de Csernye, Montagne Bakony, Hongrie [Jurassic ammonoids of Csernye, Mount Bakony, Hungary]. Part 1 (Hammatoceratidae). *Geol. Hungarica*, Ser. Palaeontol., Pt. 34, 276 pp, 44 pls. [In French; Russian summary.]
— 1967. Ammonoides jurassiques de Csernye, Montagne Bakony, Hongrie [Jurassic ammonoids of Csernye, Mount Bakony, Hungary]. Part 2 (excl. Hammatoceratidae). *Geol. Hungarica*, Ser. Palaeontol., Pt. 35, 413 pp., 65 pls. [In French; Russian summary.]
GETTY, T. A. 1973. A revision of the generic classification of the family Echioceratidae (Cephalopoda, Ammonoidea) (Lower Jurassic). *Paleontol. Contrib. Univ. Kansas*, Pap. 63, 32 pp., 5 pls.
GILLET, S. 1937. Les ammonites du Bajocien d'Alsace et de Lorraine. [The ammonites of the Bajocian of Alsace and Lorraine]. *Mém. Serv. Carte Géol. Alsace-Lorraine*, No. 5, 130 pp, 5 pls., 71 figs. [In French.]
GUERIN-FRANIATTE, S. 1966 *Ammonites du Lias inférieur de France* [Ammonites of the Lower Lias of France]. xviii + 455 pp., 231 pls., 2 vols. (Paris: Centre National des Recherches Scientifiques.) [In French.].
HAHN, W. 1968. Die Oppeliidae Bonarelli und Haploceratidae Zittel des Bathoniums (Brauner Jura ε) im südwestdeutschen Jura [The Oppeliidae Bonarelli and Haploceratidae Zittel of the Bathonian (Brauner Jura ε) in the south-west German Jurassic]. *Jahresh. Geol. Landesamtes Baden-Württemberg*, Vol. 10, pp. 7–72, pls. 1–5. 10 figs. [In German.]
— 1969. Die Perisphinctidae (Ammonoidea) des Bathoniums (Brauner Jura ε) im südwestdeutschen Jura [The Perisphinctidae (Ammonoidea) of the Bathonian (Brauner Jura ε) in the south-west German Jurassic]. *Jahresh. Geol. Landesamtes Baden-Württemberg*, Vol. 11, pp. 29–86, pls. 1–9. 11 figs. [In German.].
— 1970. Die Parkinsoniidae S. Buckman und Morphoceratidae Hyatt (Ammonoidea) des Bathoniums (Brauner Jura ε) im südwestdeutschen Jura [The Parkinsoniidae S. Buckman and Morphoceratidae Hyatt (Ammonoidea) of the Bathonian (Brauner Jura ε) in the south west German Jurassic]. *Jahresh. Geol. Landesamtes Baden-Württemberg*, Vol. 12, pp. 7–62, pls. 1–8., 8 figs. [In German.]
— 1971. Die Tulitidae S. Buckman, Sphaeroceratidae S. Buckman und Clydoniceratidae S. Buckman (Ammonoidea) des Bathoniums (Brauner Jura ε) im südwestdeutschen Jura [The Tulitidae S. Buckman, Sphaeroceratidae S. Buckman and Clydoniceratidae S. Buckman (Ammonoidea) of the Bathonian (Brauner Jura ε) in the south-west German Jurassic]. *Jahresh. Geol. Landesamtes Baden-Württemberg*, Vol. 13, pp. 55–122, 9 pls., 13 figs. [In German.]
HAINS, B. A. and HORTON, A. 1969. (3rd Ed.). British regional geology: the central England district. 3rd Ed. *Mem. Geol. Surv. G.B.*, ix + 141 pp., 11 pls., 17 pls.
HANCOCK, J. M. 1954. New Ampthill Clay fauna from Knapwell, Cambridgeshire. *Geol. Mag.*, Vol. 91, p. 249.
HEMMING, F. (Editor) 1957. Rejection of a proposal for the suppression under the plenary powers of the generic name *Caenisites*, Buckman 1925 (Class Cephalopoda, Order Ammonoidea). *Bull. Zool. Nom.*, Opinion 482, Vol. 17, pp. 15–40.
HIRANO, H. 1971. Biostratigraphic study of the Jurassic Toyora Group. *Mem. Fac. Sci. Kyushu Univ.*, Ser. D, Geology, Vol. 21, No. 1, pp. 93–128, pls. 14–20. 7 figs., 4 tables.
HOFFMANN, K. and MARTIN, G. P. R. 1960. Die Zone des *Dactylioceras tenuicostatum* (Toarcien, Lias) in NW- und SW- Deutschland [The zone of *Dactylioceras tenuicostatum* (Toarcian, Lias) in northwest and southwest Germany]. *Paläontol. Z.*, Vol. 34, pp. 103–149, pls. 9–12, 2 figs. [In German; English summary.]
HOUSE, M. R. 1958. On the Portlandian zones of the Vale of Wardour and the use of *Titanites giganteus* as an Upper Jurassic zone fossil. *Proc. Geol. Assoc.*, Vol. 69, pp. 17–19.
HOWARTH, M. K. 1955. Domerian of the Yorkshire coast. *Proc. Yorkshire Geol. Soc.*, Vol. 30, pp. 147–175, pls. 10–13, 3 figs., 2 tables.
— 1957. The Middle Lias of the Dorset coast. *Q. J. Geol. Soc. London*, Vol. 113, pp. 185–204, pl. 17, 1 fig.
— 1958. A monograph of the ammonite Liassic family Amaltheidae in Britain. *Palaeontogr. Soc. Monogr.*, 53 pp., 10 pls.
— 1962. The Yorkshire type ammonites and nautiloids of Young and Bird, Phillips and Martin Simpson. *Palaeontology*, Vol. 5, pp. 93–136, pls. 13–19.

— 1973. The stratigraphy and ammonite fauna of the Upper Liassic Grey Shales of the Yorkshire coast. *Bull. Br. Mus. (Nat. Hist.) Geol.*, Vol. 24, pp. 235–277., 9 pls.
— 1978. The stratigraphy and ammonite fauna of the Upper Lias of Northamptonshire. *Bull. Br. Mus. (Nat. Hist.) Geol.*, Vol. 29, No. 3, pp. 235–288., 9 pls. 5 figs, 2 tables.
— and DONOVAN, D. T. 1964. Ammonites of the Liassic family Juraphyllitidae in Britain. *Palaeontology*, Vol. 7, pp. 286–305, pls. 48, 49.
HUDLESTON, W. H. 1887. A monograph of the British Jurassic Gasteropoda. Part 1, Gasteropoda of the Inferior Oolite. No. 1, pp. 1–56. *Palaeontogr. Soc. Monogr.*
HUXLEY, T. H. 1864. On the structure of the Belemnitidae; with a description of a more complete specimen of Belemnites than hitherto known, and an account of a new genus of Belemnitidae, *Xiphoteuthis*. *Mem. Geol. Surv. G.B.*, Monogr. 2, 22 pp., 3 pls.
ILOVAYSKIY, D. I. and FLORENSKIY, K. P. 1941. Verkhneyurskie ammonity basseynov rek Urala i Ileka [Upper Jurassic ammonites of the Ural and Ilek basins]. *Mater. k Poznan. Geol. Str. SSSR*, New Ser., No. 1(5), 195 pp, 28 pls., 22 figs. [In Russian; French summary.]
JACKSON, J. F. 1922. Sections of the Junction-Bed and contiguous deposits. *Q. J. Geol. Soc. London*, Vol. 78, pp. 436–448.
JEANNET, A. 1954. Die Macrocephaliten des Callovien von Herznach (Aargau) [The Macrocephalites of the Callovian of Herznach (Aargau)]. *Eclogae Geol. Helv.*, Vol. 47, pp. 223–267, pls. 13–27, 50 figs. [In German.]
JOHNSTONE, M. A. 1927. *The elements of geology*. 285 pp., 118 figs., frontispiece. (London: Nelson).
KELLAWAY, G. A. and WILSON, V. 1941. An outline of the geology of Yeovil, Sherborne and Sparkford Vale. *Proc. Geol. Assoc.*, Vol. 52, pp. 131–174, pls. 8–10.
KENT, P. E. and BARKER, F. T. 1938. Ammonites from the Lincolnshire Limestone. *Trans. Lincolnshire Nat. Union*, Vol. 9, pp. 169–170.
— and CASEY, R. 1963. A Kimmeridge sandstone in North Lincolnshire. *Proc. Geol. Soc. London*, No. 1606, pp. 57–62.
KRYSTYN, L. 1972. Die Oberbajocium- und Bathonium-Ammoniten der Klaus-Schichten des Steinbruches Neumühle bei Wien (Österreich) [The Upper Bajocian and Bathonian ammonites of the Klaus-Schichten of Neumühle quarry near Vienna (Austria)]. *Annln. Naturh. Mus. Wien*, Vol. 76, pp. 195–310., 24 pls. [In German; English summary.]
LAMPLUGH, G. W. and KITCHIN, F. L. 1911. On the Mesozoic rocks in some of the coal explorations in Kent. *Mem. Geol. Surv. G.B.*, 212 pp., 5 pls.
— — and PRINGLE, J. 1923. The concealed Mesozoic rocks in Kent. *Mem. Geol. Surv. G.B.*, 244 pp., 2 pls.
LANG, W. D. 1928. The Belemnite Marls of Charmouth, a series in the Lias of the Dorset coast. *Q. J. Geol. Soc. London*, Vol. 84, pp. 179–257, pls. 13–18.
LEE, G. W. and PRINGLE, J. 1932. A synopsis of the Mesozoic rocks of Scotland. *Trans. Geol. Soc. Glasgow*, Vol. 19, pp. 158–224, pls. 4, 5.
LEHMAN, U. 1971. Jaws, radula and crop of *Arnioceras* (Ammonoidea). *Palaeontology*, Vol. 14, pp. 333–341, pl. 61.
LISSAJOUS, M. 1923. Etude sur la faune du Bathonien des environs de Mâcon [A study of the fauna of the Bathonian of the district around Mâcon]. *Trav. Lab. Géol. Fac. Sci. Lyon*, Mem. 3, 286 pp., 33 pls., 26 figs. [In French.]
LUPPOV, N. P. and DRUSHCHITS, V. V. (Editors) 1958. Osnovy paleontologii. Spravochnik dlya paleontologov i geologov SSSR, Vol. 6 Mollyuski—golovongie 2 [Fundamentals of palaeontology. Manual for the palaeontologists and geologists of the U.S.S.R. Vol. 6 Mollusca—Cephalopoda 2]. 178 pp., 74 pls., 160 figs. (Moscow: Akademia Nauk S.S.S.R.) [In Russian; English translation: HARDIN, H. 1976. (Jerusalem: Keter.)]
LYCETT, J. 1857. *The Cotteswold Hills: handbook introductory to their geology and palaeontology. iii+168 pp., 7 pls.*(London: Piper, Stephenson and Spence.)
— 1860. On the sands intermediate the Inferior Oolite and Lias of the Cotteswold Hills, compared with a similar deposit upon the coast of Yorkshire. *Proc. Cotteswold Nat. Field Club*, Vol. 2, pp. 142–149.
— 1863. Supplementary monograph on the Mollusca from the Stonesfield Slate, Great Oolite, Forest Marble, and Cornbrash. *Palaeontogr. Soc. Monogr.*, 129 pp., pls. 13–45.
— 1865. Notes on the ammonites of the sands intermediate the Upper Lias and Inferior Oolite. *Proc. Cotteswold Nat. Field Club*, Vol. 3, pp. 3–10.
LYELL, C. 1865. *Elements of geology or the ancient changes of the Earth and its inhabitants as illustrated by geological monuments.* 6th edition. 794 pp., 769 figs. (London: John Murray.)
MALINOWSKA, L. 1972a. The Middle Oxfordian Perisphinctidae of Zawodzie near Częstochowa (Poland). *Acta Palaeontol. Pol.*, Vol. 17, No. 2, pp. 167–242, 30 pls. [Polish and Russian summaries.].
— 1972b. Środkowy i gorny Oksford w pólnocno-zachodricej części Jury [Middle and Upper Oxfordian of the north-western Częstochowa Jurassic]. *Biul. Inst. Geol.*, No. 233, Z Badan stratigr.-paleontol. Polsce, Vol. 6, pp. 5–67. 14 pls., 8 figs. [In Polish; English and Russian translations.]
MANGOLD, C. 1970a. Les Perisphinctidae (Ammonitina) du Jura meridional au Bathonien et au Callovien [The Perisphinctidae (Ammonitina) of the southern Jura in the Bathonian and Callovian]. *Doc. Lab. Géol. Fac. Sci. Lyon*, No. 41, Pt. 2. 246 pp., 16 pls., 160 figs. [In French.].
— 1970b. Morphoceratidae (Ammonitina–Perisphinctaceae) Bathonien du Jura méridional, de la Nièvre et du Portugal [Morphoceratidae (Ammonitina-Perisphinctaceae) of the Bathonian of the southern Jura, the Nièvre and Portugal]. *Geobios*, No. 3, Pt. 1, pp. 43–103, pls. 3–7., 38 figs. [In French.]
MAUBEUGE, P. L. 1948. Sur quelques ammonites du Lias de la Belgique, du Luxembourg et de la Lorraine septemtrionale [On some ammonites from the Lias of Belgium, Luxemburg and northern Lorraine]. *Bull. Mus. R. Hist. Nat. Belgique*, Vol. 2, No. 18. pp. 1–8, 2 pls. [In French.]
— 1949. Revision des ammonites du genre Phlyseogrammoceras [Revision of the ammonites of the genus Phylseogrammoceras]. *Bull. Inst. R. Sci. Nat. Belgique*, Vol. 25, No. 36, 17 pp., 2 pls. [In French.]
MELEDINA, S. V. 1977. Ammonity i zonal'naya stratigrafiya Kelloveya Sibiri [Ammonites and zonal stratigraphy of the Callovian of Siberia]. *Tr. Akad. Nauk S.S.S.R.*, Vol. 356, 290 pp., 47 pls., 37 figs., 5 tables. [In Russian.]
MORRIS, J. and LYCETT, J. 1851–1855. A monograph of the Mollusca from the Great Oolite chiefly from Minchinhampton and the coast of Yorkshire. 1851 Part 1, pp. 1–130, pls. 1–15; 1853 Part 2, pp. 1–80; 1855 Part 3, pp. 81–147, pls. 9–15. *Palaeontogr. Soc. Monogr.*
MORTON, N. 1971. Some Bajocian ammonites from western Scotland. *Palaeontology*, Vol. 14, pp. 266–293, pls. 40–51. 4 figs.
— 1972. The Bajocian ammonite *Dorsetensia* in Skye, Scotland. *Palaeontolgy*, Vol. 15, pp. 504–518, pls. 102–105.
— 1975. Bajocian Sonniniidae and other ammonites from western Scotland. *Palaeontology*, Vol. 18, pp. 41–91, pls. 6–17.
MOXON, C. 1841. *Illustrations of the characteristic fossils of British strata.* 46 pp., 34 pls. (London).
MUIR-WOOD, H. M. 1936. Brachiopoda of the British Great Oolite Series. Part 1. *Palaeontogr. Soc. Monogr.*, pp. i-ii, 1–144, pls. 1–5.
NEAVERSON, E. 1925. Ammonites from the Upper Kimmeridge Clay. *Pap. Geol. Dep. Univ. Liverpool*, 46 pp., 4 pls.

NEWTON, E. T. and TEALL, J. J. H. 1897. Notes on a collection of rocks and fossils from Franz Josef Land, made by the Jackson–Harmsworth Expedition during 1894–1896. *Q. J. Geol. Soc. London,* Vol. 53, pp. 477–519, pls. 37–41.

— — 1898. Additional notes on rocks and fossils from Franz Josef Land. *Q. J. Geol. Soc. London,* Vol. 54, pp. 646–651, pl. 29.

NIKITIN, S. 1889. Quelques excursions dans les musées et dans les terrains mésozöiques de l'Europe occidentale et comparaison de leur faune avec celle de la Russie [Some excursions in the museums and in the Mesozoic areas of western Europe and comparison of their fauna with that of Russia]. *Bull. Soc. Belge Geol.,* Vol. 3, Memoirs, pp. 29–58. [In French.]

OPPEL, A. 1857. Die Juraformation Englands, Frankreichs und des südwestlichen Deutschlands [The Jurassic Formation in England, France and south-western Germany]. Vol. 2. *Jahresh. Ver. Vaterl. Naturk. Württemberg,* pp. 439–694. [In German.].

PARSONS, C. F. 1974. The *sauzei* and so-called *sowerbyi* Zones of the Lower Bajocian. *Newsl. Stratigr.,* Vol. 3, pp. 153–180, 4 figs., 2 tables.

— 1976a. Ammonite evidence for dating some Inferior Oolite sections in the north Cotswolds. *Proc. Geol. Assoc.,* Vol. 87, pp. 45–63, 2 pls., 2 figs. 2 tables.

— 1976b. A stratigraphic revision of the humphriesianum/subfurcatum Zone rocks (Bajocian Stage, Middle Jurassic) of southern England. *Newsl. Stratigr.,* Vol. 5, pp. 114–142, 5 figs., 3 tables.

— 1977. Two new Bajocian microconch Otoitid ammonites and their significance. *Palaeontology,* Vol. 20, pp. 101–118, pl. 17, 4 text figs.

PAVIA, G. 1971. Ammoniti del Baiociano superiore di Digne (Francia SE, dip. Basses-Alpes). [Ammonites of the Upper Bajocian of Digne (south-east France, Basses-Alpes département)]. *Boll. Soc. Pal. Ital.,* Vol. 10, No. 2, pp. 75–142, pls. 13–29, 8 figs. [In Italian; French and English summaries.]

PAVLOV, A. P. 1889. Etudes sur les couches Jurassiques et Crétacées de la Russie. 1 Jurassique supérieur de la Russie et de l'Angleterre [Studies on the Jurassic and Cretaceous beds of Russia. 1 Upper Jurassic of Russia and England]. *Bull. Soc. Imp. Nat. Moscou,* New Ser., Vol. 3, pp. 61–127, pls. 2–4. [In French.]

PEACH, B. N. GUNN, W. and NEWTON, E. T. 1901. On a remarkable volcanic vent of Tertiary age in the Island of Arran. *Q. J. Geol. Soc. London,* Vol. 57, pp. 226–243, pl. 9.

PINNA, G. 1966. Ammoniti del Lias Superiore (Toarciano) dell' Alpe Turati (Erba, Como) Famiglia Dactylioceratidae. [Ammonites of the Upper Lias (Toarcian of the Alpe Turati (Erba, Como) Family Dactylioceratidae]. *Mem. Soc. Ital. Sci. Nat. Mus. Civ. Stor. Nat. Milano,* Vol. 14, Pt. 2, pp. 85–136. [In Italian; English and French summaries.].

— and LEVI-SETTI, F. 1971. Dactylioceratidae della provincia mediterranea (Cephalopoda Ammonoidea) [Dactylioceratidae of the Mediterranean province (Cephalopoda Ammonoidea)]. *Mem. Soc. Ital. Sci. Nat. Mus. Civ. Storia Nat. Milano,* Vol. 15, Pt. 2, pp. 49–136, 12 pls., 21 figs. [In Italian.]

PHILLIPS, J. 1865–1870. A monograph of British Belemnitidae. 1865, Part 1, pp. 1–28; 1866, Part 2, pp. 29–52, pls. 1–7; 1867, Part 3, pp. 53–88, pls. 8–20; 1869, Part 4, pp. 87–108, pls. 21–27; 1870, Part 5, pp. 109–128, pls. 28–36. *Palaeontogr. Soc. Monogr.*

PRATT, S. P. 1841. Description of some new species of ammonites found in the Oxford Clay on the line of the Great Western Railway near Christian Malford. *Ann. Mag. Nat. Hist.,* Vol. 3, No. 50, pp. 161–165, pls. 3–6.

PRINGLE, J. 1926. The geology of the country around Oxford. *Mem. Geol. Surv. G.B.,* 2nd Edition, viii+ 191 pp., 4 pls., 12 figs.

— 1936. Ammonites from a transported mass of Jurassic clay at Plaidy, Aberdeenshire, with the description of a new species. *Trans. Edinburgh Geol. Soc.,* Vol. 13, pp. 308–310, pls. 13, 14.

RICHARDSON, L. 1904. *A handbook to the geology of Cheltenham and neighbourhood.* xii + 261 pp., 29 pls., 22 figs. (Cheltenham: Norman, Sawyer.)

— 1910a. On a Fuller's Earth section at Combe Hay, near Bath. *Proc. Geol. Assoc.* Vol. 21, pp. 425–426.

— 1910b. The Inferior Oolite and contiguous deposits of the south Cotteswolds. *Proc. Cotteswold Nat. Field Club,* Vol. 17, pp. 63–136.

— 1911. The Inferior Oolite and contiguous deposits of the Chipping-Norton district Oxfordshire. *Proc. Cotteswold Nat. Field Club,* Vol. 17, pp. 195–231, pl. 26, 2 figs, map.

— 1916. The geology (Lias and superficial deposits) of the Cheltenham—Stratford-on-Avon Railway (G.W.R.) *Trans. Woolhope Nat. Field Club,* for 1914–1917, pp. 137–153, 3 pls.

— 1929. The country around Moreton-in-Marsh. *Mem. Geol. Surv. G.B.,* vi + 162 pp., 6 pls.

RIEBER, H. 1963. Ammoniten und Stratigraphie der Braunjura β der Schwäbischen Alb [Ammonites and Stratigraphy of the Braunjura β of the Swabian Alps]. *Palaeontographica,* Ser. A, Vol. 122, pp. 1–89, pls. 1–8, [In German.]

ROCHÉ, P. 1939. Aalénian et Bajocien du Mâconnais et de quelques régions voisines [Aalenian and Bajocian of the Mâconnais and some neighbouring regions]. *Trav. Lab. Géol. Fac. Sci. Lyon,* Mem. 29, 355 pp., 13 pls. [In French.]

ROMAN, F. 1938. *Les ammonites jurassiques et crétacées* [Jurassic and Cretaceous ammonites]. 554 pp., 53 pls. (Paris: Masson.) [In French.].

SALFELD, H. 1914. Uber einige stratigraphisch wichtige und einige seltene Art der Gattung *Perisphinctes* aus dem oberen Jura Nordwestdeutschlands [On some stratigraphically important and some rare species of the genus *Perisphinctes* from the north-west German Upper Jurassic]. *Jahresber. Niedersächsischen Geol. Ver.,* Vol. 7, pp. 231–251, pls. 11–13, 4 text figs. [In German.]

— 1915. Monographie der Gattung Cardioceras Neumayr et Uhlig [Monograph on the genus *Cardioceras* Neumayr and Uhlig]. *Z. Dtsch. Geol. Ges.,* Vol. 67, pp. 149–204, pls. 16–20, 7 figs. [In German.].

— 1917. Monographie der Gattung Ringsteadia (gen. nov.) [Monograph on the genus *Ringsteadia* (gen. nov.)]. *Palaeontographica,* Vol. 62 (for 1916–1919), pp. 69–84, pls. 8–14, 1 fig. [In German.].

SAPUNOV, I. 1959. Stratigrafski i paleontolozhki proutsvaniya na Toarsa ot okolnostite na gr. Teteven [Stratigraphical and palaeontological studies of the Toarcian in the vicinity of the town of Teteven (Central Balkan Range)]. *Tr. Geol. Bŭlg. Ser. Paleontol.,* Vol. 1, pp. 17–49, 4 pls. [In Bulgarian; Russian and English summaries.].

— 1963a. Toarski amoniti ot cemeychvo Dactylioceratidae ot zapadna Bŭlgariya [Toarcian ammonites of the family Dactylioceratidae from western Bulgaria]. *Tr. Geol. Bŭlg. Ser. Paleontol.,* Vol. 5, pp. 109–147, 6 pls. [In Bulgarian; Russian and English summaries.].

— 1963b. Ammonitite ot Baioskiya rod *Protoecotraustes* Spath (Haploceratidae) [Ammonites of the Bajocian genus *Protoecotraustes* Spath (Haploceratidae)]. *Tr. Geol. Bŭlg. Ser. Paleontol.,* Vol. 5, pp. 149–165, 1 pl. [In Bulgarian; Russian and English summaries.]

— 1973. Ammonites de l'Oxfordien de la partie occidentale des Hauts Plateaux (Algérie) [Ammonites of the Oxfordian of the western part of the Hauts Plateaux (Algeria)]. *Publ. Serv. Géol. Algérie,* New Ser., Bull. 44, pp. 101–137., 7 pls.,2 figs., table. [In French.].

SCHLEGELMILCH, R. 1976. *Die Ammoniten des süddeutschen Lias* [The ammonites of the southern German Lias]. 212 pp., 52 pls. (Stuttgart, New York: Gustav Fischer.) [In German.]

SENIOR, J. R. 1977. The Jurassic ammonite *Bredyia* Buckman. *Paleontology,* Vol. 20, pp. 675–693, pls. 81–84, 7 figs.

— and EARLAND-BENNETT, P. M. 1973. The Bajocian ammonite *Hyperlioceras rudidiscites* S. Buckman in eastern England and its significance. *Proc. Yorkshire Geol. Soc.,* Vol. 39, pp. 319–326, 3 figs.

SIMPSON, M. 1855. *The fossils of the Yorkshire Lias; described from nature.* 1st Ed. 149 pp. (Whitby: Silvester Reed; London: Whittaker.)

— 1884. *The fossils of the Yorkshire Lias; described from nature.* 2nd Ed., 256 pp. (Whitby: Forth; London: John Weldon.)

SOLLY, H. S. and WALKER, J. F. 1891. Note on the fault in the cliff west of Bridport harbour. *Proc. Dorset Nat. Hist. Antiq. Field Club,* Vol. 11, pp. 118–121.

SPATH, L. F. 1919. Notes on ammonites. *Geol. Mag.,* Vol. 56, pp. 27–35, 65–71, 115–122, 170–177.

— 1925. Notes on Yorkshire ammonites. *Naturalist,* pp. 186–211, pl. 18.

— 1927-1933. Revision of the Jurassic cephalopod fauna of Kachh (Cutch). *Mem. Geol. Surv. India Palaeontol. Indica,* New Series, Vol. 9, Mem. 2. 1927, Part 1, pp. 1–71, pls. 1–7, 1928, Part 2, pp. 73–161, pls. 8–19; 1928, Part 3, pp. 163–278, pls. 20–47; 1931, Part 4, pp. 279–550, pls. 48–102; 1931, Part 5, pp. 551–658, pls. 103–124; 1933, Part 6, pp. i-vii, 659–945, pls. 125–130.

— 1928. The ammonites from the Belemnite Marls. *Q. J. Geol. Soc. London,* Vol. 84, pp. 222–232, pls. 16–17.

— 1932. The invertebrate faunas of the Bathonian–Callovian deposits of Jameson Land. *Medd. Grønland,* Vol. 87, No. 7, 158 pp., 26 pls.

— 1935. The Upper Jurassic invertebrate faunas of Cape Leslie, Milne Land. I Oxfordian and Lower Kimmeridgian. *Medd. Grønland,* Vol. 99, No. 2, 82 pp., 15 pls.

— 1936a. The ammonites of the Green Ammonite Beds of Dorset. *Q. J. Geol. Soc. London,* Vol. 92, pp. 438–455, pl. 33.

— 1936b. The Upper Jurassic invertebrate faunas of Cape Leslie, Milne Land II Upper Kimmeridgian and Portlandian. *Medd. Grønland,* Vol. 99, No. 3, 180 pp., 50 pls.

— 1938. *A catalogue of the ammonites of the Liassic family Liparoceratidae in the British Museum (Natural History).* 191pp., 26 pls. (London: British Museum (Natural History)).

— 1939. The ammonite zones of the Upper Oxford Clay of Warboys, Huntingdonshire. *Bull. Geol. Surv. G.B.,* No. 1, pp. 82–96, pls. 6, 7.

— 1943. Problems of ammonite nomenclature VII. On *Ammonites cordatus* and *A. serratus* J. Sowerby. *Geol. Mag.,* Vol. 80, pp. 111–117, 1 fig.

— 1947. Additional observations on the invertebrates (chiefly ammonites) of the Jurassic and Cretaceous of East Greenland. 1 The *Hectoroceras* fauna of south-west Jameson Land. *Medd. Grønland,* Vol. 132, No. 3, pp. 1–69, pls. 1–5.

— 1956. The Liassic ammonite faunas of the Stowell Park borehole. *Bull. Geol. Surv. G.B.,* No. 11, pp. 140–164, pls. 9, 10.

STEFANOV, J. 1961. Batŭt v profila na shoseto gr. Belogradchik-gara Oreshets, ceverozapadna Bŭlgariya [The Bathonian in the section on the Belogradchik-Oreshets station road, north-west Bulgaria]. *Izv. Geol. Inst. Strašimir Dimitrov,* Vol. 9, pp. 337–369, pls. 1–7, 3 figs. [In Bulgarian; Russian and English summaries.].

— 1962. Oksfordski amoniti ot semeistvo Aspidoceratidae v Bŭlgariya [Oxfordian ammonites of the family Aspidoceratidae of Bulgaria]. *Tr. Geol. Bŭlg. Ser. Paleontol.,* Vol. 4, pp. 95–125, 5 pls., 2 figs. [In Bulgarian; Russian and English summaries.]

— 1963. Batski amoniti ot nadsemestvo *Stephanocerataceae* v Bŭlgariya [Bathonian ammonites of the superfamily Stephanocerataceae in Bulgaria]. *Tr. Geol. Bŭlg. Ser. Paleontol.,* Vol. 5, pp. 167–209, 6 pls., 3 figs. [In Bulgarian; Russian and English summaries.]

— 1966. The Middle Jurassic ammonite genus *Oecotraustes* Waagen. *Tr. Geol. Bŭlg. Ser. Paleontol.,* Vol. 8, pp. 29–69, 7 pls., 1 fig. [Bulgarian and Russian summaries.].

— 1972. Monograph on the Bathonian ammonite genus *Siemiradzkia* Hyatt 1900 (nomenclature, taxonomy and phylogeny). *Izv. Geol. Inst. Stravšimir Dimitrov,* Vol. 21, 82 pp., 16 pls.

STRICKLAND, H. E. 1845. On certain calcareo-corneous bodies found in the outer chambers of ammonites. *Q. J. Geol. Soc. London,* Vol. 1, pp. 232–235, 1 fig.

STURANI, C. 1966. Ammonites and stratigraphy of the Bathonian in the Digne–Barreme area (south-eastern France, dept. Basses-Alpes). *Boll. Soc. Paleontol. Ital.,* Vol. 5, No. 1, 57pp., 24 pls. [Italian and French summaries.].

— 1971. Ammonites and stratigraphy of the 'Posidonia alpina' Beds of the Venetian Alps (Middle Jurassic, mainly Bajocian). *Mem. Ist. Geol. Mineral Univ. Padova,* Vol. 28, 190 pp., 16 pls., 46 figs.

SYKES, R. M. and SURLYK, F. 1976. A revised ammonite zonation of the Boreal Oxfordian and its application in northeast Greenland. *Lethaia,* Vol. 9, pp. 421–436, 9 figs.

TATE, R. 1875. On the Lias about Radstock. *Q. J. Geol. Soc. London,* Vol. 31, pp. 493–509.

— and BLAKE, J. F. 1876. The Yorkshire Lias. 475 pp., 19 pls. (London: Van Voorst.)

TINTANT, H. 1963. Les Kosmocératidés du Callovien Inférieur et Moyen d'Europe occidentale. Essai de paléontologie quantitative [The Kosmoceratids of the Lower and Middle Callovian of western Europe. Essay in quantitative palaeontology]. *Publs. Univ. Dijon,* Vol. 29, 500 pp., 58 pls., 92 figs. [In French].

TORRENS, H. S. 1967. The Great Oolite Limestone of the Midlands. *Trans. Leicester Lit. Philos. Soc.,* Vol. 61, pp. 65–90.

— 1968. Some Fuller's Earth sections in the South Cotswolds. *Proc. Bristol Nat. Soc.,* Vol. 31, pp. 429–438.

— 1969. The stratigraphical distribution of Bathonian ammonites in central England. *Geol. Mag.,* Vol. 106, pp. 63–76.

— 1970. New names for two microconch ammonite genera from the Middle Bathonian (Jurassic) of Europe and their macroconch counterparts. *Boll. Soc. Paleontol. Ital.,* Vol. 9, No. 2, pp. 136–148, pl. 36. [Italian summary.]

— 1971. Standard Zones of the Bathonian. Colloque du Jurassique, Luxembourg 1967. *Mém. Bur. Rech. Géol. Min. France,* No. 75, pp. 581–604, 2 tables.

TRUEMAN, A. E. 1918. The evolution of the Liparoceratidae. *Q. J. Geol. Soc. London.* Vol. 74. pp. 247–298, pls. 21–25.

— and WILLIAMS, D. M. 1925. Studies in the ammonites of the family Echioceratidae. *Trans. R. Soc. Edinburgh,* Vol. 53, pp. 699–739, pls. 38–41.

— — 1927. Notes on some Lias ammonites from the Cheltenham district. *Proc. Cotteswold Nat. Field Club,* Vol. 22, pp. 239–253, pls. 27–28.

TURNER, J. A. 1966. The Oxford Clay of Skye, Scalpay and Eigg. *Scott. J. Geol.,* Vol. 2, Pt. 3, pp. 243–252. 3 figs.

— 1970. The ammonites of the Bukowskii Subzone of the Oxfordian of Skye. *Scott. J. Geol.,* Vol. 6, Pt. 4, pp. 371–378, 3 pls.

VERSEY, H. C. 1958. Derived ammonites in basal Cretaceous conglomerate. *Geol. Mag.,* Vol. 95, p. 440.

WALKER, J. F. 1892. On Liassic sections near Bridport, Dorsetshire. *Geol. Mag.,* New Ser., Decade 3, Vol. 9, pp. 437–443.

WEITSCHAT, W. 1973. Stratigraphie und Ammoniten des höheren Untertoarcium (oberer Lias ε) von NW-Deutschland [Stratigraphy and ammonites of the higher Lower Toarcian (Upper Lias ε) of north-west Germany]. *Geol. Jb.*, Ser. A, Vol. 8, pp. 3–81, pls. 1–5. [In German.]

WENDT, J. 1963. Stratigraphisch-paläontologische Untersuchungen im Dogger West-siziliens [Stratigraphical and palaeontological investigations in the Dogger of western Sicily]. *Boll. Soc. Paleontol. Ital.*, Vol. 2, No. 1, pp. 51–145, pls. 6–24, 4 figs. [In German; English and Italian summaries.]

WESTERMANN, G. E. G. 1954. Monographie der Otoitidae [Ammonoidea] [Monograph on the Otoitidae [Ammonoidea]]. *Beih. Geol. Jahrb.*, Vol. 15, 364 pp., 33 pls., 149 figs. [In German.].

— 1956. Phylogenie der Stephanocerataceae und Perisphinctaceae des Dogger [Phylogeny of the Stephanocerataceae and Perisphinctaceae of the Dogger]. *Neues Jahrb. Geol. Paläontol. Abh.*, Vol. 103, pp. 233–279. [In German.]

— 1958. Ammoniten-Fauna und Stratigraphie des Bathonien NW Deutschlands [Ammonite fauna and stratigraphy of north-west Germany]. *Beih. Geol. Jahrb.*, Vol. 32, 103 pp., 49 pls. [In German.]

— 1969. The ammonite fauna of the Kialagvik Formation at Wide Bay, Alaska Peninsula. Part 2: Sonninia sowerbyi Zone (Bajocian). *Bull. Am. Paleontol.*, Vol. 57, No. 255, pp. 1–226, pls. 1–47, 57 figs.

— 1975. Bajocian ammonoid fauna of the Tethyan affinities from the Kambe Limestone Series of Kenya and implication to plate tectonics. *Newsl. Stratigr.*, Vol. 4, pp. 23–48, 2 pls., 6 figs., 1 table.

WETZEL, W. 1937. Studien zur Paläontologie des nordwesteuropaischen Bathonien [Studies on the palaeontology of the north-west European Bathonian], *Palaeontographica*, Ser. A, Vol. 87, pp. 77–157, pls. 10–15 [In German.]

— 1966. Uber einige umstrittene Bath-Ammoniten nebst paläobiologischen Bemerkungen über die Neoammoniten [On some controversial Bathonian ammonites with observations on the Neoammonites]. *Neues Jahrb. Geol. Paläontol. Abh.*, Vol. 124, Pt. 1, pp. 84–102, pls. 12–14, 1 fig. [In German.]

WILSON, V. 1936. The Upper Jurassic rocks of the country between Malton and Castle Howard, East Yorkshire. *Proc. Geol. Assoc.*, Vol. 47, pp. 254–264, pl. 2, fig. 51.

WIMBLEDON, W. A. 1976. The Portland Beds (Upper Jurassic) of Wiltshire. *Wiltshire Nat. Hist. Mag.*, Vol. 71, pp. 3–11, 2 figs.

— and COPE, J. C. W. 1978. The ammonite faunas of the English Portland Beds and the zones of the Portlandian Stage. *J. Geol. Soc. London*, Vol. 138, pp. 183–190, 3 pls., 2 figs.

WOODWARD, H. B. 1893. The Jurassic rocks of Britain. 3: Lias of England and Wales (Yorkshire excepted). *Mem. Geol. Surv. G.B.*, 399 pp.

— 1895. The Jurassic rocks of Britain 5: The Middle and Upper Oolitic rocks of England (Yorkshire excepted). *Mem. Geol. Surv. G.B.*, xiv + 499 pp., 145 pls., map.

WRIGHT, T. 1878–1884. Monograph on the Lias ammonites of the British Islands. 1878, Part 1, pp. 1–49, pls. 1–8; 1879, Part 2, pp. 49–164, pls. 9–18; 1880, Part 3, pp. 165–264, pls. 19–40; 1881, Part 4, pp. 265–328, pls. 22A, B, 41–48; 1882, Part 5, pp. 329–400, pls. 49–52, 52A, 53–69; 1883, Part 6, pp. 401–440, pls. 70–77; 1884, Part 7, pp. 441–480, pls. 78–87. *Palaeontogr. Soc. Monogr.*

ZIEGLER, B. 1962. Die Ammoniten-Gattung *Aulacostephanus* im Oberjura (Taxonomy, Stratigraphie, Biologie) [The ammonite genus *Aulacostephanus* in the Upper Jurassic (taxonomy, stratigraphy, biology)]. *Palaeontographica*, Ser. A, Vol. 119, pp. 1–172, pls. 1–4. [In German.]

INDEX

Plate 1

1 *Proplanulites opimus* S. S. Buckman HOLOTYPE; GSM 26085
2 *Simplicidactylites simplicicosta* S. S. Buckman HOLOTYPE; GSM 38304
3 *Proplanulites oidaleus* S. S. Buckman HOLOTYPE; GSM 26093
4 *Proplanulites lentus* S. S. Buckman HOLOTYPE; GSM 26092
5 *Proplanulites tridens* S. S. Buckman HOLOTYPE; GSM 26090
6 *Proplanulites partitus* S. S. Buckman HOLOTYPE; GSM 26099
7 *Proplanulites latus* S. S. Buckman HOLOTYPE; GSM 26106
8 *Proplanulites occultus* S. S. Buckman HOLOTYPE; GSM 30775
9 *Proplanulites lyprus* S. S. Buckman HOLOTYPE; GSM 26080
10 *Leptodactylites leptum* S. S. Buckman HOLOTYPE; GSM 38018
11 *Proplanulites petrosus* S. S. Buckman HOLOTYPE; GSM 26091

All figures natural size

Plate 2

1 *Proplanulites rudis* S. S. Buckman HOLOTYPE; GSM 30525
2 *Proplanulites capularis* S. S. Buckman HOLOTYPE; GSM 26081
3 *Proplanulites rufus* S. S. Buckman HOLOTYPE; GSM 26104
4 *Proplanulites stiphrus* S. S. Buckman HOLOTYPE; GSM 26088
5 *Proplanulites fulvus* S. S. Buckman HOLOTYPE; GSM 26097
6 *Proplanulites auriculatus* S. S. Buckman HOLOTYPE; GSM 30526
7 *Proplanulites involutus* S. S. Buckman HOLOTYPE; GSM 30531
8 *Proplanulites ferruginosus* S. S. Buckman HOLOTYPE; GSM 26105

All figures natural size

1

2

3

4

5

6

7

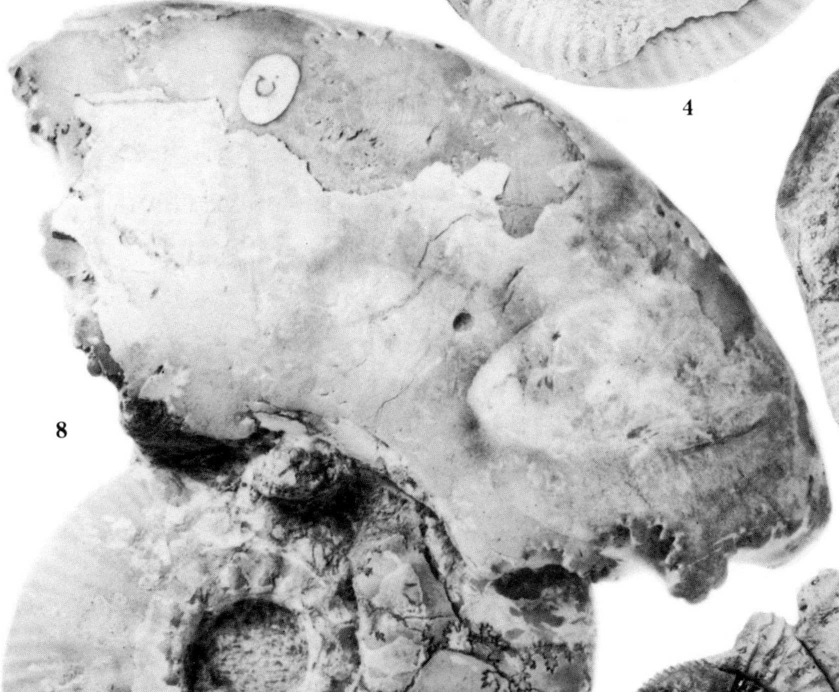

8

9

10

11

1

2

3

4

5

6

8

7

Dd. 699060 K10

Printed in England for Her Majesty's Stationery Office
by Commercial Colour Press, London E7